Fixing English

D1290652

Over the past three hundred years, attempts have been made to prescribe how we should and shouldn't use the English language. The efforts have been institutionalized in places such as usage guides, dictionaries, and school curricula. Such authorities have aspired to "fix" the language, sometimes by keeping English exactly where it is, but also by trying to improve the current state of the language.

Anne Curzan demonstrates the important role prescriptivism plays in the history of the English language, as a sociolinguistic factor in language change and as a vital meta-discourse about language. Starting with a pioneering new definition of prescriptivism as a linguistic phenomenon, she highlights the significant role played by Microsoft's grammar checker, debates about "real words," nonsexist language reform, and efforts to reappropriate stigmatized terms. Essential reading for anyone interested in the regulation of language, the book is a fascinating re-examination of how we tell language history.

ANNE CURZAN is Professor of English in the Department of English Language and Literature at the University of Michigan.

Fixing English

Prescriptivism and Language History

Anne Curzan

CAMBRIDGE
UNIVERSITY PRESS

CAMBRIDGE
UNIVERSITY PRESS

University Printing House, Cambridge CB2 8BS, United Kingdom

Cambridge University Press is part of the University of Cambridge.

It furthers the University's mission by disseminating knowledge in the pursuit of education, learning and research at the highest international levels of excellence.

www.cambridge.org
Information on this title: www.cambridge.org/9781316604885

© Anne Curzan 2014

First published 2014
First paperback edition 2015

A catalogue record for this publication is available from the British Library

Library of Congress Cataloguing in Publication data
Curzan, Anne.
Fixing English : prescriptivism and language history / Anne Curzan.
  pages   cm
ISBN 978-1-107-02075-7 (hardback)
1. English language – Grammar, Historical.   2. English language – Usage – History.   3. English language – History.   4. Historical linguistics.   I. Title.
PE1101.C87   2014
420.9–dc23

                                                          2013037433

ISBN 978-1-107-02075-7 Hardback
ISBN 978-1-316-60488-5 Paperback

In memory of Richard W. Bailey

Contents

Figures

Acknowledgements

The thinking behind this book project, as well as the actual writing of it, have been shaped by more people than I can possibly name here, but I want to acknowledge some of the most important ones. Let me begin by thanking my former adviser, colleague, and dear friend Richard W. Bailey, whose erudite and unwavering mentorship shaped me into a historian of the English language, empowered to ask new questions about how we tell language history. My wonderful colleagues Michael Adams and Robin Queen have continued to shape my thinking in invaluable ways and were kind enough to read and comment on every chapter of this book as I wrote. I would also like to thank the members of my writing group of ten years – Anne Gere, Mary Schleppegrell, and Meg Sweeney – who have helped this book find its shape, its voice, and its audience.

The book and I both benefitted from valuable assistance from several graduate student research assistants, including Staci Shultz, Randall Pinder, Shelly Swearingen, Crystal VanKooten, and Chris Parsons. I appreciated the opportunity to present parts of this work at various conferences, and for all the smart, productively challenging questions I received from audience members, I am most grateful. All of the following University of Michigan colleagues have kindly read and commented on material over the past couple of years: Scotti Parrish, Cathy Sanok, Susan Najita, Andrea Zemgulys, Eileen Pollack, Van Jordan, and Jennifer Wenzel.

I have learned incredible amounts from all the scholars of the history of English and of prescriptivism cited in this book, whose work has shaped my own. I specifically want to thank Deborah Cameron for writing the book *Verbal Hygiene*, which I read in 1995 when it came out and thought, "I wish I had written that book." I hope this book usefully extends her groundbreaking work.

On a more personal note, I want to extend heartfelt thanks to Lisa Damour, whose friendship was key to finishing the project. And I wouldn't be where I am without my family, who have provided me unwavering love and support at every step.

My editor Andrew Winnard has believed in this project from the very beginning, and I am grateful for his support of the book throughout the process. Several anonymous reviewers provided useful feedback at key points, and I thank them for their time and intellectual energy in making the book better. I take full responsibility for any missteps or errors that remain in the book.

Introduction: does prescriptivism fail?

In January 2010, the American Dialect Society voted *fail*, the noun, the Most Useful Word of the Year. I first encountered the word a year and a half earlier, when the students in my Structure of English course taught me the slang phrase "epic fail." An epic fail is not just any fail: it is a fail of monumental proportion, often, my students explained, involving hubris. As *Slate* magazine described it in an article in October of that year: "Not just coming in second in a bike race but doing so because you fell off your bike after prematurely raising your arms in victory" (Beam 2008). The collapse of several major American investment banks in 2008: an epic fail. The University of Michigan football team losing to Appalachian State in 2007: another epic fail.

Fail as a noun is linguistically interesting because it exemplifies language change, whether it represents a clipping from the noun *failure* or a functional shift from the verb *fail* to the noun *fail*. (The noun *fail* existed earlier in English but was listed by the *Oxford English Dictionary* as obsolete, except in the phrase *without fail*, until this innovative meaning of the noun *fail* was added to the *Dictionary* in 2011.) The emergence of the noun *fail* is the kind of linguistic change that linguists enjoy studying, a change that bubbles up "from the people" – in this case, perhaps, from a late 1990s arcade game in which players were told that "you fail it." This phrase became a more widespread exclamation in response to someone's failure at a range of activities, and once shortened to "Fail!" it would easily have enabled a functional shift of *fail* from verb to noun. The noun *fail* simultaneously exemplifies the kind of change that stereotypical prescriptive language pundits – pundits who take it upon themselves to tell English speakers how they should and should not talk and write in order to use "good" or "correct" English – would lament: Why do we need another noun when we already have *failure*? And why do people insist on nouning verbs?

The previous paragraph sets up a traditional binary in modern linguistics: the descriptive linguist standing in opposition to the prescriptive pundit or "grammarian." Descriptive linguists study language change as a natural and inevitable part of any living language. Prescriptive commentators and scholars react to language change, typically with a desire to "fix" the language: both *fix* in the sense of hold stable (i.e., fix in time) and *fix* in the sense of improve.

1

In linguistic scholarship on the history of the English language, the prescriptivism of the modern period is often framed as, in many ways, an epic fail. It represents a concerted effort by a group of elitist, sometimes self-proclaimed language authorities to stop language change that does not recognize that language change cannot be stopped. It qualifies as an epic fail because, first, modern prescriptivism demonstrates hubris. For example, *New York Magazine* theater critic John Simon, a self-proclaimed language prescriptivist, declares outright in the PBS documentary "Do You Speak American?" (2005) that descriptive linguists, with their assertions about the inevitability of language change, are "a curse upon their race, who of course think that what the people say is the law." Lynne Truss, in her runaway best-seller *Eats, Shoots & Leaves: A Zero Tolerance Approach to Punctuation* (2003), scolds that incorrect use of punctuation stems from lazy writers who do not care enough, and she encourages the sticklers of the world to unite in public criticism of these writers' behavior, including taking red pens to badly punctuated grocery store signs.

Second, modern prescriptivism has chalked up a significant number of failures: it has witnessed – or some might say suffered from – several centuries of language change that has flown in the face of prescriptive criticism. For instance, nineteenth-century grammarian George Marsh chimed in as one of many voices railing against the passive progressive, a construction new to that period. In *Lectures on the English Language* (1863, 649), Marsh writes:

The phrase 'the house *is being built*' for 'the house *is building*' is an awkward neologism, which neither convenience, intelligibility, nor syntactical congruity demands, and the use of which ought therefore to be discountenanced, as an attempt at the artificial improvement of the language in a point which needed no amendment.

Almost a century and a half later, this lament seems quaint. Dean Alford, in the *Queen's English* (1875), condemns *desirability* and *reliable* as terrible words – a prescriptive stance that again appears naïve and fruitless, given how standard both words have become. Yet the complaints continue, from declaring the verb *incentivize* a form of "boorish bureaucratic misspeak" (Rothstein 2000) to lambasting *invite* as a noun that "eviscerates the language" (Leslie S. March, quoted in Bradley 2008).

Linguistic scholarship on the history of English has often highlighted the unrealistic goals of prescriptive efforts and has presented examples of ways in which language change defies prescriptive mandates. The scholarship thus sets up an evaluation of prescriptivism and its goals based on its success or lack thereof in stopping language change. In keeping with such an evaluative frame, Samuel Johnson's famous quotation from the Preface to his 1755 *Dictionary of the English Language* is often showcased as the confession of a prescriptivist who has seen the light, who has recognized his own hubris and the epic fail of his original plan for his dictionary:

Those who have been persuaded to think well of my design, require that it should fix our language, and put a stop to those alterations which time and chance have hitherto been suffered to make in it without opposition. With this consequence I will confess that I flattered myself for a while; but now begin to fear that I have indulged expectation which neither reason nor experience can justify. When we see men grow old and die at a certain time one after another, from century to century, we laugh at the elixir that promises to prolong life to a thousand years; and with equal justice may the lexicographer be derided, who being able to produce no example of a nation that has preserved their words and phrases from mutability, shall imagine that his dictionary can embalm his language, and secure it from corruption and decay, that it is in his power to change sublunary nature, or clear the world at once from folly, vanity, and affectation.

Johnson still seems to be describing language change as corruption and decay – a claim that I, as a linguist, would dispute – but he recognizes in this excerpt that language change is inevitable. And while Johnson is right that his dictionary did not, and could not, embalm the language, I argue in this book that histories of English are mistaken if they minimize or marginalize the modern prescriptive project as failed because it has failed *to stop* those alterations which time and chance have made in language. In marginalizing prescriptivism, they can miss important developments in Modern English usage and in meta-discourses about usage, both of which are part of language history.

If the sole goal of language prescriptivism is assumed to be stopping language change, then prescriptivism fails. But I argue here that the goals of prescriptivism are often more complicated than that, and it oversimplifies scholarly inquiry to evaluate prescriptivism only with respect to its "success" versus "failure" in stopping change. To begin, the two meanings of *fix* productively highlight at least two major aims of prescriptive efforts: in some cases to resist language change and preserve an older and/or standard form that is seen as fully adequate if not superior; in other cases to improve upon the language, either by introducing new forms or distinctions or by proposing a return to older, more conservative forms. Second, if scholars reframe their questions about language prescriptivism around how it may or may not influence language change and how it shapes modern meta-discourses about language, there is much better evidence that prescriptivism at least in part "succeeds." It may not succeed in the way that any given prescriptivist hopes it might, but the sheer presence of prescriptive efforts has the power to affect attitudes about usage as well as, in some cases, the development of actual language usage. This is one among many reasons why the concept of success, like that of failure, probably does not serve the purposes of scholarly investigation well. Success and failure take the stated goals of prescriptivism as the endpoint and the basis of measurement. I contend that the stated goals should not be the focus of inquiry. A more interesting set of questions focuses on the power of prescriptivism, regardless of its specific aims and desired outcomes, to shape the English language and the sociolinguistic contexts in which the English language is written and spoken.

An analogy may be useful here. If we imagine a living language as a river, constantly in motion, prescriptivism is often framed as the attempt to construct a dam that will stop the river in its tracks. But, linguists point out, the river is too wide and strong, too creative and ever changing, and it runs over any such dam. However, if we imagine prescriptivism as building not just dams but also embankments or levees along the sides of the river to control water levels and breakwaters that attempt to redirect the flow of the river, it becomes easier to see how prescriptivism may be able to affect how the language changes. The river may flood the embankment or spill over the breakwater, but that motion will be different due to the sheer presence of the barriers. And even if prescriptivism is seen as only the dam, which is then overwhelmed by the power of the river, the sheer presence of the dam affects the flow of the river. In this way, the consciously created structures around or in the river, like prescriptive language efforts, constitute one of many factors that must be accounted for to understand the patterns of the river's movement – or of a language's development over time.

All that said, even helpful analogies between language and physical phenomena are also often problematic. First, they tend to abstract language away from the speakers who are responsible for the existence of any language, making a living language into a kind of life form in and of itself. Historical sociolinguistic scholarship rightly emphasizes the need to focus on the speakers who change a language; and in this book I stress the value of ensuring the focus extends to include the speakers, books, and now computer programs that have prescriptive things to say about the ways in which the language is changing. Language change is often systematic but not mechanistic. The idiosyncrasies, which are as much a part of language change as the larger, more systematic patterns, stem from the idiosyncrasies of human speakers. Second, the English language is not one river. As John McWhorter (1998) describes it, any language is a bundle of dialects, and the English language is no different. Much of this book will focus on modern American English, and that too encompasses many dialects; but the argument about the importance of prescriptivism holds for other world varieties of English and other languages. In addition, as I argue in more detail in Chapter 2, the "English language" and its history should comprise written and spoken English as two different, interrelated, and interacting forms of English (often standard English in the case of the written). Finally, the prescriptive rules here analogized with levees and breakwaters tend to focus on only one small part of the language, separating out a word or a construction for censure or improvement in ways that the water in a river simply cannot be differentiated for attention to only one part of the water.

If the general reframing highlighted by the river analogy holds, though, and prescriptivism can and does influence the history of a language, intriguing and important puzzles remain to be solved by historians of English: What have been and continue to be the effects of prescriptivism on Modern English usage? And how have modern prescriptive efforts shaped the meta-discourses about language that swirl around and interact with actual usage? To think about these two questions from a different perspective, what does a language history miss if it does not account sufficiently for the presence of widespread institutionalized prescriptivism?

I define the term *prescriptivism* in more detail in the next chapter, teasing apart four major strands of prescriptive rules that language authorities have historically imposed on the language and its speakers. For now, it will suffice to restrict the term to those language rules about "good" or "better" "or correct" usage created, perpetuated, and enforced by widely recognized, often institutionalized language authorities, and then subsequently perpetuated at the more individual level, often with reference to these culturally sanctioned language authorities. For English, these language authorities have never been gathered in one academy, despite calls for such an institution by writers such as Jonathan Swift and an attempt at its creation by John Quincy Adams – and despite the model provided by the Académie française. Instead, English speakers have relied on a network of authorities or "language mavens," to adopt a term introduced by William Safire and further popularized by Steven Pinker (1994). These authorities have historically been lent authority through the power of publication: creating grammar books and style guides; editing books and dictionaries; opining on language in newspaper columns. The exception perhaps is English teachers, whose institutional authority allows them to enforce prescriptive rules; typically they rely, however, on published works such as grammar books, style guides, and dictionaries. As discussed in detail in Chapter 3, the Microsoft Word Grammar Checker has also become one of the most powerful prescriptive forces that English writers encounter on a regular basis.

There is a reason I phrased the questions above about the effects of prescriptivism as questions about Modern English usage and the discourses circulating around it. The questions are inherently modern ones, given that the rise of institutionalized prescriptivism is a modern phenomenon, dating back to the eighteenth century or a bit before and becoming a powerful social force in the nineteenth century. The eighteenth century witnessed the early proliferation of grammar books and dictionaries, including Samuel Johnson's famous dictionary – resources designed to record and regulate the language, which had come to be recognized as eloquent, worthy of being used for literature and a range of academic subjects. Up until the middle of the sixteenth century, English was generally seen as unworthy and "rude" compared with Latin and French; with a change in attitudes about English's worth and potential came a massive influx of borrowed terms, sometimes needed in order to enable English to handle technical academic discussions, sometimes added for rhetorical flourish. And as English expanded and became more eloquent, grammarians and rhetoricians also got the sense that it was becoming unruly. In the eighteenth century, Johnson was far from alone in his laments about the corruption and decay of English, and many English language scholars and commentators shared his desire to "fix" the language in the sense of stabilize it.[1]

Fix the language they did not. However, they succeeded in creating several centuries of language anxiety and a firmly entrenched belief system about the correctness of standard varieties of English and the authority of resources such as dictionaries and usage manuals. These outcomes affect the history of Modern English at multiple levels, including: the favoring and disfavoring of specific constructions, particularly in formal contexts; the creation of language resources that have become standard in the education of most English speakers, if not a routine part of their daily lives; and the fostering of meta-discourses that serve to regulate the language of others, from whether or not a construction is "allowed" in formal writing to whether or not a word is "a real word" (as noted above with the word *fail*), all of which can perpetuate class and educational hierarchies based on language use.

These changes in language use and in meta-discourses about language are equally part of the history of English, as I discuss in Chapter 2. The history of English should be viewed as comprising not only the changes that happen in the language despite prescriptivism but also those changes that are in various ways influenced by the language prescriptivism that has characterized the modern period. The fact that the passive progressive (e.g., *the house is being built*) has become standard despite prescriptive criticism constitutes as interesting a development in the history of English as the current overuse of *whom* in formal contexts (e.g., *the person whom is involved*). The latter represents at least in part a response to prescriptive efforts to enforce "correct" use of *who* and *whom*, efforts that have made some speakers anxious that where they might want to use *who*, *whom* is actually "correct." As this example shows, prescriptivism can have unintended, "rogue" consequences, but it has consequences nonetheless. In this case, rather than stopping the replacement of *whom* with *who* wholesale and creating (or returning to) a time when *who* is always used in subject position and *whom* in object position, prescriptivism has created a situation in which some speakers and writers may replace *who* with *whom* in formal contexts. In all likelihood, *who* will replace *whom* in all contexts in the long run, and a

---

[1] There are several excellent recent histories of the rise of Standard English, of language anxiety, and of prescriptive projects, including David Crystal's *Fight for English: How Language Pundits Ate, Shot, and Left* (2006), Jack Lynch's *The Lexicographer's Dilemma* (2009), and Tim Machan's *Language Anxiety* (2009). See also Edward Finegan's comprehensive chapter on "Usage" in Volume VI of the *Cambridge History of the English Language* (2001), as well as his earlier book *Attitudes Toward English Usage: A History of the War of Words* (1980), and Dennis Baron's *Grammar and Good Taste: Reforming the American Language* (1982).

history of the pronouns needs to take prescriptivism into account to understand the progression of the change as it takes what might otherwise be unexpected turns. Remember the levees. If histories of English evaluate the prescriptive project solely in terms of its success or failure to stop language change, they can miss these real-world consequences for speakers, both in how they use the language and how they think about their and others' use of the language.

Linguists do not yet, however, completely understand how prescriptivism can or has shaped the history of Modern English. In response to the widely held idea among non-linguists that language change might be slowing down in the modern era due to rampant prescriptivism and standardization, linguists have often swung perhaps too far in the other direction, arguing that these efforts have no effect, that language change carries on despite prescriptivism, unhindered by it – brushing prescriptivism off like the proverbial fly. The following summary statement by Rosina Lippi-Green, in the first edition of *English with an Accent* (1997), effectively captures the published stance of a significant number in the field: "Language changes whether we like it or not. Attempts to stop spoken language from changing are not unknown in the history of the world, but they are universally without success" (10).[2] Certainly language will change anyway; there is no debate among linguists about that fact – although much of the public has yet to be convinced of, or to become less wary and concerned about, the inevitability of language change. But are all attempts to prescribe or proscribe language in response to change "without success"? In his book *The Fight for English*, David Crystal (2006, ix) describes his focus as: "the story of the fight for English usage – the story of a group of people who tried to shape the language in their own image but, generation after generation, failed." Crystal's statement is completely accurate in asserting that usage pundits have proven unable to mold the language into the (more) ideal language they think it should be; English speakers are too creatively unruly – and too many – to be guided that coherently. But these people who have tried to shape language have not been unsuccessful in shaping language and the sociolinguistic contexts in which it is used, even if the end product does not match their ideal image.

In her groundbreaking book *Verbal Hygiene* (1995), Deborah Cameron productively shifts the question away from whether or not prescription is a good thing or an unnatural imposition. She argues that verbal hygiene, which she defines as the desire to regulate, improve, and clean up the speech of others, is a natural part of all speech communities: it is "observed to occur in all speech

---

[2] In the second edition of *English with an Accent* (2012), Lippi-Green revises the sentence but still condemns prescriptive responses to language change to failure: "And still people will take up the battle cry and declare war on language change. All those attempts – and there have been a lot of them – are doomed to failure, unless they are instituted by means of genocide" (8).

communities to a greater or lesser extent" (5). In other words, as soon as a group of speakers come together, living and/or working together as a community, some speakers will begin telling other speakers how to talk ("better," in ways deemed more appropriate, in ways deemed more cool, etc.). While verbal hygiene may be imposed, particularly if it comes from speakers or institutions with significant social or political power and gatekeeping capacities, it is not unnatural to language use and communities. Cameron asserts that more interesting than the question "should we prescribe?" are questions about "who prescribes for whom, what they prescribe, how, and for what purposes" (11). These questions are centrally important and provide a richer way to consider verbal hygiene as a sociolinguistic phenomenon.

With Cameron's work as one critical starting point, I shift the focus from cause and purpose to effects – and as a result to more historical questions. As a historian of English, I have become increasingly aware of the limited integration of prescriptivism into histories of the language in the modern period; it is typically relegated to the historical context, largely divorced from developments in the language itself. The dynamics of some speakers telling other speakers how they should use the language, and speakers' responses to those prescriptions, are some of the many factors that influence speakers' linguistic behavior. And altering individual linguistic behavior, of course, alters the course of a language more generally. In addition, histories of English have mirrored the prescriptive preoccupation with a fairly narrow set of prescriptive rules about punctuation, grammar, and style, and, as a result, they have often sidelined some of the most powerful prescriptive discourses affecting usage, such as nonsexist language reform.

To think productively about the questions I am posing about the effects of prescriptivism on the history of the language, historians of English need to recognize an array of prescriptive efforts as a natural part of language communities, not an unnatural imposition on naturally occurring language change. As Cameron points out, recognizing the humanness of the prescriptive impulse is not the same as condoning all prescriptive efforts; while language-based power dynamics are a natural part of speech communities, not all exercises of this power are responsible or well founded. They are, however, part of history. From this perspective, then, changes that result from prescriptive forces are also not unnatural changes but part of the puzzle that language historians are seeking to solve about why varieties of the language have changed in particular ways.

I am not the first to make an argument along these lines, but the argument has yet to have a significant enough impact on the canonical historical narrative of the English language (or arguably on studies of language variation and change more generally). Over twenty years ago, James Milroy and Lesley Milroy, in their foundational book *Authority in Language* (1991), challenged sociolinguists to think seriously about prescriptivism's effects:

When we view language as fundamentally a social phenomenon, we cannot then ignore prescription and its consequences. The study of linguistic authoritarianism is an important part of linguistics. (11)

Sharon Millar (1998, 178), in a brief but important article, also questions the "failure" of prescriptivism and proposes that "prescription may have something to teach linguists." Sociolinguistics has demonstrated the importance of phenomena such as language stigma and prestige. Millar crucially extends these findings: "Since prescriptive activities are involved in the propagation of ideas about 'good' and 'bad', 'prestigious' and 'stigmatized', they may be a useful source of information for the sociolinguist seeking to understand how mechanisms of change and maintenance operate" (178).

The past decade has witnessed the publication of several excellent volumes dedicated to the historical development of prescriptivism (e.g., Beal et al. 2008; Tieken-Boon van Ostade 2008d; Percy and Davidson 2012). Handbooks on the history of English have often included a treatment of prescriptivism as part of a chapter on standardization or variation (e.g., Görlach 1999; Crowley 2008) or on usage (e.g., Finegan 2001). Some recent histories of the language that adhere less to the traditional periodization model (i.e., Old English, Middle English, etc.) have successfully integrated language attitudes into the discussion of language history (e.g., Crystal 2004; Mugglestone 2006). And a growing body of scholarship has examined the relationship of prescriptive grammar to usage (Tieken-Boon van Ostade 1982, 2002; Auer and González-Díaz 2005; Yáñez-Bouza 2006, 2008; Anderwald 2012). However, institutionalized prescriptivism as a sociolinguistic phenomenon has yet to be effectively integrated as a factor into the broader study of "language change" in the history of English. As Anderwald (2012) points out, current scholarship takes contradictory stances on prescriptivism, from accepting its influence (perhaps too uncritically) to dismissing it as having no "real" effect.

There are signs of progress in terms of the integration of prescriptivism into the telling of the language's history, but currently it seems to be largely confined to books that address historical developments in language attitudes rather than technical, structural developments in the language (I address some of the disciplinary issues involved in history of English scholarship in Chapter 2).[3] For example, Tim Machan (2009, 8), in his book *Language Anxiety*, describes the "social desire to stigmatize or ameliorate a particular word" as one of several social factors influencing language change. Jack Lynch (2009, 6) in *The Lexicographer's Dilemma* writes of language commentators: "In a sense, they've all been failures: despite their combined efforts, the language is every

---

[3] Leech et al. (2009) is a notable exception. These studies of change in twentieth-century American and British English consistently consider prescriptive influences as a possible factor in the patterns of change observed with, for example, relative pronouns and the subjunctive.

bit as messy and irrational as it was three hundred years ago. But all have shaped and influenced the language we speak today. To understand our language, we have to understand them." But in books focused primarily on structural developments in the language, prescriptivism has more often been framed as a factor that gets in the way of change. For example, in her textbook on the history of English, Elly van Gelderen (2006, 8) describes prescriptive rules as factors that "inhibit internal change," and does not explicitly include them as factors that might cause "external change" in the same way that contact with other languages does, a point I return to in Chapter 2. We should beware of wording that could be read to suggest that changes in the language caused by prescriptive impulses are not somehow "real" language change, internal or external: it falls into the binary of suggesting that some changes are "natural" to language and others are unnaturally imposed. The natural–unnatural binary can prove unhelpful in thinking about the relationship of prescriptivism and language history.

This book offers a new perspective on the role and importance of prescriptive efforts in the history of English in the modern period. It includes four case studies that highlight significant prescriptive discourses in the modern period that have not received adequate attention to date – discourses that entrench, exploit, and challenge ideologies of correctness and legitimacy in language, and discourses that have in several cases demonstrably affected modern English usage. The first of seven chapters develops an extended, more nuanced definition of prescriptivism than has previously been available in linguistic scholarship. The second chapter discusses some of the repercussions for history of English scholarship of taking prescriptivism into account, proposing three guiding principles for scholarship in the field. Chapter 3 surveys research on the effects of grammatical prescriptivism on written usage as context for a detailed case study of Microsoft Word Grammar Checker, which has become a pervasive force on writers' awareness of specific usage rules and potentially on the prose that they produce. Chapter 4, in focusing on the rise of the English dictionary, examines the idea that there are "real" and "not real" or illegitimate words in English – and the effects of that idea on notions about acceptable public language. The surprisingly successful effects of nonsexist language reform efforts, which have sometimes challenged tenants of institutionalized prescriptivism, are the subject of Chapter 5. And Chapter 6 explores the consequences of efforts to reappropriate words such *gay*, *queer*, *dyke*, and "the N-word," which both challenge and change institutionalized prescriptivism. The final chapter addresses the challenge prescriptivism presents to linguists trying to disseminate alternative views of language variation and change as part of the public conversation about language.

The extended examples of prescriptive language efforts included in this book present only a snapshot of prescriptivism's importance in and effect on the history of English. The examples are limited primarily to the United States and in some cases the United Kingdom, which obviously tells only part of the story of the history of English. Nonetheless, they constitute one further step in response to the intellectual challenge that James Milroy and Lesley Milroy posed more than twenty years ago. So this book is not about whether prescriptivism is or is not an epic fail in stopping language change. That question simply is not complicated enough. Instead, this book seeks to capture the complexity of efforts to fix English and at least some of the complexity of those efforts' effects. It is my hope that this work will support the valuable research by other scholars investigating specific ways prescriptivism has shaped the English language and its speakers – as well as other languages and their speakers. More broadly, I hope the book will promote the ongoing shift away from viewing prescriptivism as an "unnatural" imposition on or hindrance to language change, framing it instead as an integral part of telling language history.

1   Prescriptivism's umbrella: standards, style, restoration, and political intervention

In linguistics, prescriptivism often serves as a foil: the linguistic "bad guy," so to speak, or the "threatening Other," to quote Deborah Cameron (1995, 5). In a frequent scholarly move (which I myself have made in other publications), prescriptivism is contrasted with descriptivism, typically as a way to distinguish the goals of linguistic inquiry from the goals of most usage guides. The assumption often is that readers will be more familiar with the approach of usage guides, thinking of this approach as "grammar" or "the study of grammar"; the contrast, therefore, can open up for readers a different way of studying grammar or language more generally. And the message is, not just different, but better.

The typically sharp dichotomy between descriptivism and prescriptivism helps not only to put distance between the academic discipline of linguistics and the more familiar prescriptive pronouncements about usage based more on opinion than empirical research, but it also assigns more value to the academic discipline. It promotes the examination of language in terms of cognition and biology, not just culture. The now canonical prescriptive–descriptive binary in linguistics can be traced back at least to Otto Jespersen, who wrote in *Essentials of English Grammar* (1933, 19): "Of greater value, however, than this *prescriptive* grammar is a purely *descriptive* grammar."[1] Descriptivism is the "good guy" in the study of language. As a result, prescriptivism has rarely received an extended definition in its own right, the challenge I take up in this chapter. I am attempting a descriptive account of prescriptivism, given its importance as a sociolinguistic phenomenon.

About a year ago, I was describing this book to a colleague and explained that much work remained to be done in untangling the strands that make up the complex phenomenon of prescriptivism. He responded, with the bluntness you have to appreciate in a colleague and the dismissiveness of prescriptivism expressed by many language scholars, "Why would that be a worthwhile project?"

---

[1] Jane Hodson (2006, 60) traces the division back to Ferdinand de Saussure's *Course on General Linguistics*, an important revision of the traditional history picked up in Beal and Sturiale (2008, 9).

There are several reasons why linguists stand to benefit from a more nuanced definition of prescriptivism. First, in order to understand the stakes of prescriptivism for speakers and writers and the reasons for its influence or lack thereof, we need to understand the different kinds of prescriptive rules people encounter – and the different degrees to which these rules are naturalized. Prescriptive advice sets up some kinds of "good English" or "correct English" as more naturally right than other kinds of "good English," and these gradations of correctness and their relationship to standardness highlight the different consequences for speakers and writers in adhering to usage prescriptions.

Second, and closely tied to the first reason, this kind of differentiation can help linguists think more systematically about the potential and real effects of prescriptivism on language change; different kinds of prescriptive rules, depending on what kind of language they target and with what aim, hold the power to shape attitudes and usage at varying levels, including the extent to which they affect written usage (the easiest to shape consciously), spoken usage, or both. As we disentangle the strands of prescriptivism, we find that while standardization is a central purpose, it is not the sole purpose of prescriptivism, especially as standardization becomes entrenched. In this reframing, prescriptivism stops being a static phenomenon and is allowed to evolve along with the process of standardization.

Reframing prescriptivism as an evolving sociolinguistic phenomenon helps to integrate it into the living language system, which is characterized by variation and change. Standard varieties of living languages are not immune to evolution; as Raymond Hickey (2012, 15) notes, "It is a truism to say that standard forms of language continually change." Prescriptive impulses respond to the variation and changes in language, including in the standard varieties. Prescriptions also can come to function differently, or become irrelevant, as speakers' patterns of usage and attitudes about usage shift over time. The sociolinguistic system is a dynamic one, and prescriptivism presents no exception.

Lastly, for linguists to address prescriptivism effectively in public venues – as many linguists are committed to doing – it will help to understand better the phenomenon (or phenomena) we're addressing. For example, some prescriptive rules and beliefs are more entrenched, with stronger ideologies to back them, than others. As I will show, the examples linguists choose do not always align with the larger arguments about prescriptivism. And too often, when linguists are critically assessing prescriptivism, both in public discussions and academic ones, we are doing so on prescriptivists' terms. If linguists can provide a working model of prescriptivism and its various strands that makes sense to those inside and outside the academy, it will lay the groundwork for a more productive public conversation about language standards and "correctness" and their relationship to linguistic diversity and change.

The descriptive–prescriptive binary

The *Oxford Companion to the English Language* (1992, 286) provides a typical contrastive explanation of the two terms in its entry DESCRIPTIVISM AND PRE-SCRIPTIVISM (note that neither term receives a separate, individual entry):

> *Descriptivism* is an approach that proposes the objective and systematic description of language, in which investigators confine themselves to facts as they can be observed: particularly, the approach favoured by mid-20c US linguists known as *descriptivists*. *Prescriptivism* is an approach, especially to grammar, that sets out rules for what is regarded as correct in language.

Descriptivism focuses on what speakers do with language, based on empirical evidence; prescriptivism lays down rules for what speakers should do with language. This entry defines prescriptivism as a phenomenon more encompassing than grammar, but in the phrase "especially to grammar," the entry hints at the frequent conflation of prescriptivism and prescriptive grammar, a phenomenon to which I will return.

It's not that nuances of prescriptivism are entirely absent from available definitions of the term/concept, but they are rarely if ever focal. This allows prescriptivism to function as a broad umbrella for quite different prescriptive phenomena, too often left undistinguished. An earlier entry in the *Oxford Companion*, on descriptive and prescriptive grammar, serves as an instructive example of the span of the umbrella. The entry defines both terms and with prescriptivism hints at a fundamental tripartite distinction among the kinds of rules prescriptive approaches offer, but it does not explicitly address the distinction as such and the examples muddy the waters:

> A *descriptive grammar* is an account of a language that seeks to describe how it is used objectively, accurately, systematically, and comprehensively. A *prescriptive grammar* is an account of a language that sets out rules (*prescriptions*) for how it should be used and for what should not be used (*proscriptions*), based on norms derived from a particular model of grammar. For English, such a grammar may prescribe *I* as in *It is I* and proscribe *me* as in *It's me*. It may proscribe *like* used as a conjunction, as in *He behaved like he was in charge*, prescribing instead *He behaved as if he were in charge*. Prescriptive grammars have been criticized for not taking account of language change and stylistic variation, and for imposing the norms of some groups on all users of a language. (286)

The two examples provide a fairly narrow picture of prescriptivism. Both of the examples, *I* vs. *me* in *It is I* and *like* as a conjunction, are fundamentally about style or formality of discourse. They are not about policing the boundaries of standard English. Both standard and nonstandard varieties of English use *me* in *It's me* in colloquial usage and employ *like* as a conjunction. The two rules are also not focused on preserving older forms of English – i.e., "stopping language change" – as both *It's me* and *like* as a conjunction have long histories in English. These two examples capture the prescriptive focus on finer points of usage that can distinguish those who have been educated in formal style from those who have not. The final sentence about critiques of prescriptive grammar, however, widens the focus and captures the breadth of the prescriptive umbrella: it explains that prescriptive grammar does not always account for stylistic variation (as the two examples demonstrate), for language change, or for the legitimacy of nonstandard varieties of English. The distinction between style and standards, and the place of preservation or restoration in this version of prescriptivism's umbrella, will be central to this chapter.

As noted above, the contrast in linguistics between descriptive and prescriptive approaches promotes descriptivism as the legitimate method of linguistic inquiry. As well it should. Modern linguistics has devoted itself to explaining how language works – not how it should work according to some view of "should," but how it does work (socially, cognitively, historically, etc.). But the contrast has also led to the dismissal of prescriptivism as an unnatural imposition on the language, not the kind of thing that linguists should or do concern themselves with (discussed in the Introduction). It is one thing to assert that linguists should follow descriptive rather than prescriptive methods in collecting and analyzing language data and formulating linguistic theories. It is different – but has not always been seen as such – to assert that linguists should not take prescriptivism seriously as an integral part of language use. In the process of justifiably excluding prescriptivism as a scholarly approach, scholars have often unjustifiably excluded prescriptivism as a sociolinguistic factor and as a legitimate object of scholarly inquiry.

Key groundwork for the study of prescriptivism as a factor in language change was laid by Deborah Cameron in her book *Verbal Hygiene* (1995). She attempts to debunk the pervasive assumption in linguistics that prescriptivism is an unnatural imposition on the language. As she argues, it seems to be natural to speech communities that some speakers will impose their beliefs about good and bad, appropriate and inappropriate usage on other speakers, be that at the individual level of a speaker making fun of another speaker's way of talking or at a more institutional level through, for example, the publication of usage guides, in a community that has undergone language standardization. The term *verbal hygiene*, which Cameron coined, captures the range of ways that speakers seek to regulate the language of other speakers. And, as a natural part of human speech communities, verbal hygiene or prescriptivism (I return to the distinction below) merits the systematic attention of linguists.

Some of the most incisive critical work on prescriptivism has occurred in linguists' critiques of the phenomenon. In analyzing the problems with the reasoning behind many prescriptive rules, scholars such as Rodney Huddleston and Geoffrey Pullum (2002, 5–11), in their stunningly comprehensive descriptive grammar, gesture toward the aims of prescriptivism (e.g., trying to enforce one formal style as "grammatically correct"). This chapter turns the tables from critique to definition, to marshal this kind of critical analysis of prescriptive rules into a detailed description of prescriptivism, teasing apart four central strands of this sociolinguistic phenomenon. In order to achieve this, I have delimited the territory encompassed by the word *prescriptivism*, limiting it to institutional prescriptive efforts.

Individual versus institutional prescriptivism

This book focuses primarily on institutionalized prescriptivism: prescriptivism that has been institutionally "endorsed" through publication, adoption in schools, use as a standard for newspaper editing, etc. In other words, prescriptivism with the cultural and social power that comes with institutionalized authority. I use the term *prescriptivism* rather than *verbal hygiene* to capture this specific attention to institutionalized efforts that take as their explicit goal the systematic regulation of English usage. These institutionalized efforts, of course, manifest themselves at the level of the individual, be that a usage guide writer, an English teacher, a newspaper columnist, or a publishing house editor. But, in each case, the individual relies on the authority of the institution that has endorsed the prescriptive rules they are advancing. The individual, in some cases, may not even know the exact source of the authority; more than one English teacher has said "they say you shouldn't end a sentence with a preposition" without being quite sure who "they" are. But the standard language ideologies that support prescriptive rules encourage both the individual enforcers and their audiences to accept this authority. These institutionalized efforts can have real effects on individual speakers' lives and speech patterns, on how speakers think about and use language, and on what speakers feel licensed to say about others' and their own language use.

There are many other verbal hygiene efforts at play every day, on a more individual level, as speakers tell other speakers how they should and should not talk. These efforts often rely on community norms or personal authority. These efforts also have effects on usage, although harder to track in any broader way as they are less systematic, less often recorded in written form, and typically less widespread. However, in Chapter 6, I examine what began as more grassroots verbal hygiene efforts to change usage, specifically about identity terms, which challenged and then in some cases changed institutionalized prescriptivism. And, in that process, these efforts have had significant impact on actual usage, on the history of the English language.

The terms *verbal hygiene* and *prescriptivism* can usefully distinguish between, respectively, all forms of linguistic regulation and institutionalized ones. Cameron (1995, 9) explains her choice of *verbal hygiene*, rather than *prescriptivism*, for "the more general impulse to regulate language, control it, and make it better" by noting that *prescriptivism* "is strongly associated with those forms [of language regulation] that are most conservative, elitist and authoritarian." Millar (1998) takes a different approach in an effort to disentangle prescriptivism from standardization; she defines the term *prescriptivism* to encompass all conscious and explicit regulation: "the conscious attempt by language users to control or regulate the language use of others for the purpose of enforcing perceived norms or of promoting innovations" (187). This definition establishes two important characteristics of prescriptivism. First, it distinguishes prescriptive activity (the conscious and explicit regulation of others) from normative activity (the regulation of self to conform to norms).[2] Second, the definition allows prescriptivism to promote innovation, as opposed to being a consistently conservative force. That said, there remains a value in restricting the term *prescriptivism* to refer to the conscious and explicit efforts to regulate the language of others that carry institutional authority – typically the authority that comes with publication and adoption in the educational system – as I will do here. It circumscribes an important and powerful sociolinguistic phenomenon, often associated with standardization but not always.

I have also chosen to use the term *prescriptivism* in this book for a very pragmatic reason. The term's currency in linguistics and outside it in public discourse argues for offering a more nuanced definition of it, rather than seeking to replace it with another term, potentially leaving the current definition of *prescriptivism* undisturbed. Linguists need to shift the ground on which we are having public debates about prescriptivism, but there are good reasons to keep the term itself.

As I detail in the remainder of this chapter, both linguists and non-linguists stand to benefit from teasing apart carefully prescriptivism and prescriptive grammar as well as several threads of prescriptivism. To begin, linguists can help explain and maintain the useful distinction already available in the field between prescriptivism more generally and prescriptive grammar specifically; the conflation of the two muddies the waters in public discussions of language diversity, education, and the language norms or standards of the various contexts in which English is spoken and written. Then I propose in this chapter a new working model of institutionalized prescriptivism that distinguishes four distinct but overlapping strands of prescriptivism with different aims: promoting standardization, differentiating style, restoring older usage, and reforming language in politically or socially responsive ways. The four different types of prescriptivism foster a range in the severity of judgments against those who "break the rules" and potentially have different effects on spoken and/or written usage. My hope is that this model, with some adaptation to the contextual

[2] James Milroy and Lesley Milroy (1991) usefully distinguish between norms, which can function locally and often have not undergone standardization, and supra-local standards. As many scholars have pointed out, language and language communities are inherently normative.

circumstances, can be implemented across time periods and languages to create more shared and sustained dialogue about prescriptivism and its role in language history.

Before turning to the primary challenge of defining prescriptivism along these lines, I first provide a brief discussion of descriptivism – a reversal of the typical order in which prescriptivism is described first, as the foil for a more extended discussion of descriptivism.

Defining descriptivism

Descriptive approaches to language, which are typically set up in contrast to prescriptive ones, attempt to capture the range of ways that speakers of a language communicate with each other using systematically constructed, meaningful utterances. Linguists describe these utterances as "well-formed" because they follow the systematic patterns of the grammar of that variety of the language and speakers accept them as possible utterances, not because they necessarily correspond to the standard variety of that language. Descriptivism works from the assumption that all speakers of a language are speakers of a specific variety or dialect of the language (Wolfram 1991, 2); or, put differently, a "language," which sounds unitary and uniform, is in reality a set of dialects collected together under this label (McWhorter 1998, 3). Descriptive approaches to language describe the patterns that surface in the structure of a language's words, sentences, and utterances, including all the variations in different dialects and registers. Descriptive "rules" describe regularities in a language variety's structure that are developed through analysis of what speakers do; they are sometimes invariant but not always.

To provide an example, one invariant rule of modern English grammar – of all varieties of English, as far as I know – is that modal auxiliaries appear before the main verb in declaratives. We say and write *may say* but not **say may*. Another rule allows but does not require the contraction of forms of 'to be' (both as a main and auxiliary verb) with the subject: we can say or write *I am tall* or *I'm tall, my friend is going* or *my friend's going*. But there is a systematic exception to this rule: no form of 'to be' can be contracted in clause-final position. So we cannot say **They're not going, but I'm*; it is acceptable to say *They're going, but I'm not*, because the contraction is no longer in sentence- (or clause) final position. These descriptive rules capture well-formedness – what native speakers would consider grammatically allowable in the sense of well-formed according to their intuitive sense of what is possible in the language.

The descriptive rule for optional contraction of 'to be' also captures variation in how speakers use the language, some of it linked to formality and some to personal preference. Both contracted and uncontracted forms of 'to be' are well formed, and speakers may choose one over the other based on the formality of the utterance and/or medium (e.g., written vs. spoken) or based on personal stylistic preference. In informal speech, speakers use contractions the majority of the time, perhaps as high as over 70 percent of the time (Biber et al. 1999, 241). But, because as part of education in writing, many English speakers have been told not to use contractions in formal writing, they tend to avoid the constructions in this context. This example shows the ways in which prescriptivism about formal writing affects the practice of language users.[3]

Another variable descriptive rule dependent, at least sometimes, for some speakers, on formality is the pronunciation of *often*. Some speakers use just one pronunciation or the other; some percentage of English speakers have two pronunciations of this word, one with /t/ and one without. And, while variation between the two pronunciations may not be entirely predictable for all of these speakers, some speakers describe a tendency to use the /t/-full pronunciation in more formal contexts, on the assumption that the pronunciation that corresponds more closely to the spelling is more "correct" and, therefore, more appropriate in formal contexts.

Other descriptive rules capture language change. For example, many speakers of present-day English use the subject form *who*, rather than the object form *whom*, in object position: that is, *Who did you see?* rather than *Whom did you see?* This observation about usage is a descriptive rule, as it depicts a pattern of usage across speakers. Why are speakers showing this kind of variation with *who* and *whom*? The forms *who* and *whom* originate in a case system in English, a system that distinguished subject, object (direct and indirect), and possessive forms by word endings. These case endings on nouns had largely disappeared by the time of Chaucer, except for some remnant -*e*'s, the plural -*s*, and the possessive -*s*, which many present-day varieties of English maintain to this day. So a rose (the noun) is a rose is a rose, no matter whether it is the subject or the object of a clause, whether it is the object of a preposition or not. Only English pronouns, personal and interrogative, continue to mark the subject–object distinction: for example, *I* is the subject form and *me* the object form, *we* and *us*, *he* and *him*, *she* and *her*, *they* and *them*, *who* and *whom*. (The pronoun *it* historically had the same subject and direct object form, and the pronoun *you* stopped making a distinction between subject and object consistently by the Renaissance.)

The loss of case is an ongoing process in the history of English, one slowly working its way into – or through – the pronoun system. *Whom* is especially vulnerable to the change, given the way that most varieties of English make *wh*-questions. In a *wh*-question, the *wh*-word, in this case *who* or *whom*, is

---

[3] Sometimes descriptivism privileges spoken language at the expense of written language, but as I discuss in Chapter 2, the written language should be treated as a legitimate part of speakers' linguistic competence and of the history of English.

typically fronted in a clause: for example, *who(m) did you see*? The pronoun in this question is the object of *see*, and the question could be reworded as *you saw who(m)?* In this second version, the pronoun's role as an object is clearer. However, when *who(m)* is fronted in *who(m) did you see?*, which is the typical form of the question, the pronoun appears to be in subject position – it is, after all, at the very beginning of the sentence/question – and so speakers often opt for *who*. Speakers and writers are more likely to use *whom* directly after a preposition (e.g., *for whom?*), but even that trigger seems to be weakening. In other words, the patterns of the distribution of *who* and *whom* are changing in English, and have been changing for centuries in fact,[4] such that *who* is displacing *whom* in many grammatical contexts. Descriptive grammatical rules try to capture current usage rather than judge the innovative use – in this case using *who* for *whom* – as better or worse than the earlier ones.

Some descriptive grammatical rules reveal dialect differences. For instance, many modern dialects of English have compensated for the loss of the historical distinction between singular and plural second-person pronouns – *thou/thee* vs. *ye/you* – through the introduction of new plural second-person pronouns, which vary by dialect region: to name just a few, *yous, yinz, y'all, you guys*. That standard varieties of English collapse the singular and plural into the one pronoun *you* does not, descriptively, make these varieties any better or worse than nonstandard varieties that have a distinct second-person plural pronoun.

None of the above summary of descriptivism should be taken to suggest that descriptive approaches to language are in no way prescriptive, but it's a very different kind of prescriptive move from adjudicating what is "right" and "wrong" in usage. As Cameron (1995) importantly reminds us, the message of descriptive linguistics is fundamentally prescriptive: that descriptive approaches to language/grammar are a better way to consider language and its structure and use than prescriptive approaches. Echoing Jespersen's use of the phrase "of greater value" to describe descriptive grammar, the field of linguistics has a long tradition of dismissing prescriptive approaches to language as misguided and demonstrating how descriptive approaches are more intellectually sound. The defense is a persuasive one and rests on rigorous academic study, empirical evidence, and disciplinary authority. It also advocates a particular way of thinking about language (which is not inherently a bad thing). In addition, unless linguists are extremely careful, descriptive rules of "English" can unintentionally privilege some varieties – typically standard varieties – over others in defining

---

[4] Leech et al. (2009, 2–4) highlight historical evidence that suggests *who* has been used as an object form in informal English (as both an interrogative and relative pronoun) since about the fifteenth century. They suggest that what might be changing is stylistic conventions in more formal registers, which could have the effect of making it look like *whom* is in decline in the twentieth century as opposed to earlier.

what is and isn't well formed in "English," which blurs any line in terms of what it means to describe versus prescribe a standard variety.

So, in sum, descriptive rules encompass rules that describe well-formedness in varieties of English as well as rules that describe patterned (or sometimes free) variation across individual speakers, across registers (e.g., more and less formal uses of language), across time, and across dialects. I now turn to defining prescriptivism, which involves first distinguishing prescriptivism from prescriptive grammar and then teasing apart the threads of prescriptivism in terms of the aims of different kinds of prescriptive rules.

Prescriptivism, prescriptive grammar, and usage

In surveying the fairly expansive collection of prescriptive language guides I have acquired over the years, I am struck by the wide range of territory that prescriptive language authorities call their own. In reading through the discussions of prescriptive grammar in my even more extensive collection of linguistics books, I am aware of how many definitions of "prescriptive grammar" gloss over the diversity of advice in these guides. To provide a concrete example of the diversity, I will turn to one of the first prescriptive guides that I bought in graduate school (to add to books like Strunk and White's *Elements of Style*, which I still had from college): *The Grammatically Correct Handbook: A Lively and Unorthodox Review of Common English, for the Linguistically Challenged*, by Ellie Grossman.

I became aware of this book when I heard Grossman interviewed on the Derek McGinty show on National Public Radio, shortly after the publication of her book in 1997. I was struck by how caller after caller expressed their anxiety that their English was not correct and asked earnestly for guidance about what was right and wrong – guidance Grossman was very willing to provide. Her advice included using one's shower time to recite the correct pronunciation of *often* (no "t"), *connoisseur* (last syllable as "sir"), and *dour* ("do-er"), and taping to one's bathroom mirror a list of proper pronoun use to study while brushing one's teeth ("between him and me, between us and them, between you and her ... "). Ellie Grossman, like Lynne Truss, does not claim linguistic training but rather proffers as her main credentials genuine care and concern about the state of the English language, years of work as a professional writer, and a "good" early English education: "I was taught English by Miss Thomas, Mrs. Pringle, Mrs. Marmur, et al., in the days when English teachers knew what they were talking about. Good grammar, correct usage, and proper pronunciation all became part of me" (2). And, while that last sentence seems to make a distinction among grammar, usage, and pronunciation, the book itself makes no such distinctions (and I am not sure what they would be, as most definitions of usage would encompass pronunciation and much of what Grossman probably means by "good grammar").

If we take Grossman's book as an example of what counts as "grammar" in public discourse and in many published guides (the book is called *The Grammatically Correct Handbook*, after all), it covers among other things:

- Pronunciation issues (e.g., the placement of stress in *applicable* and *affluent*, the /t/ in *often*, the final syllable in *connoisseur*).
- Spelling issues as they relate to pronunciation (*loath* vs. *loathe*, *corps* vs. *corpse*).
- Punctuation issues such as the placement of the apostrophe in possessives and contractions.
- Lexical issues, including confusion between two words (*prostate* and *prostrate*), semantic change that has made two terms fairly synonymous (*anxious* and *eager*), and regional variation (*bring* vs. *take*).
- Morphological issues such as Latin plurals (e.g., *phenomena*, *data*), formation of past participles (e.g., *have seen* vs. *have saw*), and flat adverbs (e.g., *play aggressive*).
- Syntactic issues such as agreement (*there is* vs. *there are*, *none* and *no one* as singular pronouns), use of the subjunctive, and the placement of prepositions.
- Stylistic issues such as whether *refer back to* is redundant (and arguably the placement of prepositions).

This range is typical of many usage guides, which often talk about all of these issues as "grammar" and "usage" interchangeably. But the distinction between the two is a useful one.

In public discourse, "grammar" is often used to refer to prescriptive approaches to usage, with "usage" encompassing spelling, pronunciation, punctuation, word meaning, and stylistic choice, in addition to morphology and syntax. In linguistics, however, *grammar* is usually understood to refer to the system speakers employ to create meaningful phrases and clauses out of words (also referred to as syntax) and the system for creating words (e.g., the patterns that govern prefixes and suffixes), referred to as morphology. Some definitions of *grammar* in linguistics also encompass phonology – the system of sounds used in a language to create meaningful words. Put another way, grammar, in linguistics, describes the rules or patterns that speakers follow to create meaningful utterances; it describes what it means to "know a language" in the sense of being able to use it to speak purposefully and meaningfully with other speakers. I use *speak* not *communicate* deliberately in the previous sentence, because for linguists the primary focus is the spoken language and the linguistic sign,[5] not

---

[5] Ferdinand de Saussure's definition of the linguistic sign remains foundational to this day. The linguistic sign comprises the signifier (the linguistic form – e.g., the string of sounds in a word) and the signified (the concept to which the signifier refers), and the conventional relationship between the two.

the written form developed to capture the language and the linguistic sign on the page (or velum or stone or other material).

The prescriptive preoccupation with word choice (e.g., whether *anxious* should be used to mean 'eager'), punctuation (e.g., whether or not to use a comma after an introductory prepositional phrase), and pronunciation (e.g., whether the last syllable of *connoisseur* is pronounced as 'sir' or 'sewer'), in addition to issues of sentence structure (e.g., whether a preposition can be stranded at the end of a sentence), demonstrates how far beyond grammar prescriptivism reaches, into all areas of usage, including style. Prescriptivists may refer to it all as grammar, but it extends beyond what any basic linguistics textbook would call grammar.

Yet when linguists refer to "prescriptive grammar," they sometimes slip into doing so on the terms of prescriptivists themselves. The following passage from Tim Machan's excellent book *Language Anxiety* (2009, 35) illustrates this phenomenon:

Prescriptive grammar, generally, refers to what the word *grammar* invokes in the minds of most educated people: rote drills about *i* before *e* in spelling or never ending a sentence with a preposition that often seem to run contrary to what people naturally wish to do with English and that were learned partially and sometimes painfully in schoolrooms and through exercises. Locatable in dictionaries as well as grammar books, this kind of grammar has standards of absolute right and wrong that provide, in the form of explicit rules, a way to measure grammatical competence.

Machan's primary focus in the discussion from which this passage is taken is on competing definitions of "rules," descriptive versus prescriptive. Machan states carefully in the first sentence of this excerpt that he is defining prescriptive grammar on "educated people's" terms – on what the word *grammar* invokes for them. But he does not then explicitly challenge this definition. In the second sentence, the phrase "this kind of grammar" becomes a bit slippery: it does not sharply distinguish between common beliefs about grammar and linguistic definitions of grammar. The passage does, however, effectively target the pre-occupation in public discourse with rules about correct usage. And I use the term *usage* here very strategically, as Machan's examples, which include spelling rules, are not exclusively about grammar as linguists typically define it.

The term *usage* is complicated in much the same way that the term *grammar* is: it means different things to different people. The most basic definition of *usage* is the way in which words or phrases are actually or customarily used – spoken or written – in a speech community. American English usage, in other words, is how speakers of American English, all of them, habitually use the language when they speak and write. However, people often use the word *usage* as a shorthand to talk about "standard usage" or "good usage." When they buy a usage guide, they are hoping to find guidance about what forms of English are regarded as standard or good – not just all the forms of English that are used.

Usage rules, then, become a guide not to how we do speak every day, but how we should speak if we want to adhere to particular set standards.

That said, the word *usage* carries less connotational baggage for many speakers than grammar, and its standard definition continues to be more encompassing than that of *grammar*. Usage covers both spoken and written language, including the spoken feature of pronunciation and the written features of spelling and punctuation, as well as broader topics shared by both such as morphology, syntax, word choice, and style. In this way, the term *usage* has the potential to assist in distinguishing prescriptivism (which covers all areas of usage) from prescriptive grammar. To talk about usage rather than grammar usefully reminds us how big the prescriptive umbrella is and requires us to distinguish the kinds of usage questions in play, from whether they target spoken or written language to whether they attempt to legislate on grammatical or stylistic issues.

Defining prescriptivism

It is a commonplace in linguistics to state that prescriptive approaches to language set up and aim to enforce what speakers should say or write according to established notions of "good"/ "correct" and "bad"/ "incorrect" language use (often in opposition to innovative developments in usage). As Rodney Huddleston and Geoffrey Pullum put it in *A Student's Introduction to English Grammar* (2005, 4): "Prescriptive books aim to tell people how they should speak and write – to give advice on how to use the language." The issue gets fuzzier from there, in terms of exactly what form of the language is being set up as good or correct, in relation to which other uses of language can be deemed bad or incorrect. Is it standard usage? Formal usage? "Educated" usage? Older usage? Socially acceptable usage? The answer is yes. It is all of these, depending on which strand of prescriptivism is in play.

I argue that within the general definition of prescriptivism there exist four distinct yet interrelated strands:
- Standardizing prescriptivism: rules/judgments that aim to promote and enforce standardization and "standard" usage.
- Stylistic prescriptivism: rules/judgments that aim to differentiate among (often fine) points of style within standard usage.
- Restorative prescriptivism: rules/judgments that aim to restore earlier, but now relatively obsolete, usage and/or turn to older forms to purify usage.
- Politically responsive prescriptivism: rules/judgments that aim to promote inclusive, nondiscriminatory, politically correct, and/or politically expedient usage.

This four-part distinction relies on the aims of the prescriptive rules, not the level of usage they target. A pronunciation rule, for instance, may be about standardization or stylistic differentiation; a prescription on word meaning may aim at restoration or standardization. Rules may move from one category to another as the language changes, and the focus of prescriptive efforts may shift over time. For example, as standardization has become firmly rooted in the literate cultures of much of the native English-speaking world, the focus of prescriptive usage guides has become largely stylistic; the boundaries of the standard variety of English of the nation are naturalized enough that there is less need to prescribe standard forms in usage guides.

This model is not the first to be proposed for prescriptive language phenomena. In their book *Language and Authority* (1991, 37–44), James Milroy and Lesley Milroy propose a two-part distinction in the "complaint tradition," which is one manifestation of prescriptive advice or rule-propagation. As the Milroys describe them, Type 1 complaints are implicitly legalistic, concerned with correctness and misuse, dedicated to the maintenance of the norms of Standard English, and in opposition to the tendency of language to change. Familiar complaints about incorrect apostrophe use, nonstandard past tenses (e.g., *seen* for *saw*), and nonstandard concord (e.g., *you was* for *you were*) would all fall into this category. Type 2 complaints are moralistic, concerned with clarity and effectiveness in the public use of Standard English, and in opposition to abuses of language that mislead. In this category are critiques of malapropisms (e.g., *flaunt* for *flout*), semantic shifts that might create ambiguity (e.g., *crescendo* to mean 'a loud noise'), and manipulative language (in the Orwellian tradition). According to this framework, Type 2 complaints "do not devote themselves to stigmatizing specific errors in grammar, phonology, and so on" (38).

There are many useful things about this model, including the groundbreaking effort to categorize kinds of prescriptive phenomena. The model has not, however, been consistently taken up in scholarly literature about prescriptivism as a theoretical or classificatory framework, which suggests it has proven difficult to apply. I see at least two issues, and these are places where the four-part model I am proposing diverges from the Milroys' model.

The distinction between Type 1 and Type 2 complaints drives at the difference between standards and style respectively. However, by putting all complaints or rules focused on specific errors in grammar, phonology, and the like under Type 1, some rules that focus on specific stylistic issues (e.g., stranded prepositions) rather than on standard usage land in Type 1 – and the line between standardization and style immediately gets blurred. Second, issues of morality pervade complaints and prescriptions about standards and style. In the process of trying to define prescriptivism, I also realized that there is a type of prescriptive advice, sometimes related to purism, that aims to resurrect old or archaic usage, which is not captured under standards or style.

The first three strands of my typology appear in current treatments of prescriptivism, but they are not consistently all present in any one definition, and they are rarely if ever discussed as distinguishable categories of prescriptivism.

Sometimes one strand is privileged at the expense of others; other times, the strands become twisted. The fourth strand is rarely discussed as institutionalized prescriptivism at all (with a couple of notable exceptions, to which I will return), but it should be. Before explicating each strand in some detail, I provide a few examples of current treatments of prescriptivism to show what is at stake in disentangling the strands.

According to many definitions of prescriptivism, the correctness of an utterance is judged in relation to a (formal) norm, typically a standard variety of the language and often the edited written standard variety. For example, David Crystal provides this general definition in *The Cambridge Encyclopedia of Language* (1997, 2):

In its most general sense, prescriptivism is the view that one variety of language has an inherently higher value than others, and that this ought to be imposed on the whole of the speech community. The view is propounded especially in relation to grammar and vocabulary, and frequently with reference to pronunciation. The variety which is favoured, in this account, is usually a version of the 'standard' written language, especially as encountered in literature, or in the formal spoken language which most closely reflects this style. Adherents to this variety are said to speak or write 'correctly'; deviations from it are said to be 'incorrect'.

Formality, or a kind of style, and standardness take center stage in this description, with education implied, arguably, in the reference to literature. In fact, there is no clear distinction between formality and standardness, as it appears that the standard written language being referred to here is relatively formal. Crystal lists grammar, vocabulary, and pronunciation as the focal issues of prescriptivism, perhaps because these three cross the spoken–written divide; I would add the issues of punctuation, spelling, and style. Crystal's sense that the standard version of the language is central to prescriptivism is echoed in other definitions of prescriptivism.

Standardness without reference to style or formality also characterizes some descriptions of prescriptivism's aims. For example, Mark Honegger, in *English Grammar for Writing* (2005, 234), privileges the role of prescriptive grammar in elevating the standard:

Prescriptive judgments are the judgments of those who want language users to conform to a standard. For example, we all grow up learning in school that the word *ain't* is not "proper" English. What is the basis for this judgment? The word *ain't* is used in certain dialects of English, where it exists primarily as a spoken, not written, form. However, it is not part of the dialect that formed the basis for standard English and is considered substandard.

It is certainly true that prescriptive rules play an important role in the standardization process, as discussed below. They tend to elevate the standard above other varieties as "correct" English, rather than merely "standard" English. The word *ain't* serves as a prototypical example of this kind of standardization.[6] This description fails to capture, however, that prescriptive rules also legislate on fine points of usage, where both the prescribed and proscribed options arguably fall within standard usage, although only one within formal or edited standard usage. Furthermore, prescriptive rules sometimes aim to preserve or restore older words or constructions mainly for the sake of honoring older forms of the language.

The field has witnessed important moves in the direction of disentangling the strands of prescriptivism, but again more often in the process of critique than definition. Huddleston and Pullum (2005, 4) directly address the conflation of standardness and formality, primarily to expose a failing of prescriptive grammar:

Perhaps the most important failing of the bad usage books is that they frequently do not make the distinction we just made between STANDARD VS NON-STANDARD DIALECTS on the one hand and FORMAL VS INFORMAL style on the other. They apply the term 'incorrect' not only to non-standard usage . . . but also to informal constructions . . . But it isn't sensible to call a construction grammatically incorrect when people whose status as fully competent speakers of the standard language is unassailable use it nearly all the time. Yet that's what (in effect) many prescriptive manuals do.

Left unstated, but certainly implied for linguists, is that it is also not justifiable to call nonstandard usage that speakers use nearly all the time grammatically incorrect. Huddleston and Pullum go on to state, after providing the example of *It is I* versus *It is me*:

Grammar rules must ultimately be based on facts about how people speak and write. If they don't have that basis, they have no basis at all. The rules are supposed to reflect the language the way it is, and the people who know it and use it are the final authority on that. And where the people who speak the language distinguish between formal and informal ways of saying the same thing, the rules must describe that variation. (5)

Given the previous discussion of standard English speakers' use of informal constructions, it is not completely clear if "the people" in this description are standard English speakers or all English speakers. It is absolutely true that prescriptive guides would benefit from distinguishing formal from informal usage. And the people who are the final authority are standard and nonstandard English speakers, whose usage, both formal and informal, should be recognized as being as fully systematic and worthy of description.

In the face of usage guides that often do not distinguish among the kinds of rules they offer, linguists should provide a clear lead in differentiating the strands of prescriptivism. The four categories described in this chapter provide

---

[6] The word *ain't* is slippery in its relationship to formality. While it is typically labeled nonstandard, it appears regularly in edited standard English as a marker of informality or a rhetorical device for emphasis.

one possible foundation, both for distinguishing the aims of different kinds of prescriptive rules and for differentiating the stakes for speakers in adhering to, or not adhering to, these rules.

The various analogies proffered for prescriptivism can help introduce the different stakes involved. First, prescriptive rules are compared with traffic laws, an analogy that usefully highlights the ways in which these kinds of usage rules can function to create a governing standard. As Tim Machan writes, prescriptive rules are "akin to the driving rules of the road, whose violation results in accidents and citations" (2009, 35). So, under this analogy, we follow prescriptive language rules in order to participate in the same system as everyone else, facilitating orderly communication. Second, prescriptive rules are often compared with etiquette rules such as table manners – the imposed social conventions that govern polite behavior. So, under this analogy, we learn prescriptive rules in order to speak correctly in the sense of politely or with refinement. Third, prescriptive rules aren't usually, but could be, compared with conservative parenting rules, which rely on parents' sense that how things were done when they were growing up serve as the model for correctness of how things should be done now. So we learn prescriptive rules in order to speak correctly in the sense of preserving an earlier state of the language.

The differences among these three analogies are instructive about the stakes involved in breaking prescriptive language rules, due to the naturalization of a subset of them. With the more traffic law-like rules, "correct" may be seen as synonymous with "the only right way to do things," and "incorrect" may be seen as broken or "bad English." These rules are about standardization, be that of transit or of language. With the more etiquette-like rules, it is more clearly about style – and while a stylistic preference may still be labeled "correct" as easily as "good," the "incorrect" is often not as stigmatized – it is not "broken." Much politically responsive prescriptivism also aligns with this analogy. With the more nostalgic rules, the prescribed form may be accepted at some level as "correct" but simultaneously quaint and/or potentially not standard, and a competing form may carry equal status, not stigmatized much if at all. I explain the critical distinctions among standardization, style, restoration, and political responsiveness in more detail below.

Standardizing prescriptivism

The first key strand of prescriptivism stems from the role of prescriptivism in the process of language standardization. Prescriptivism constitutes an essential mechanism for maintaining a standard language, effectively captured in the model of standardization proposed by James and Lesley Milroy (1991). The Milroys insist on a focus on standardization as a process rather than on standard languages as a product (standard English is notoriously difficult to pin down in all its details).[7] They point out that standardizing language, like standardizing money, has a functional component but then can create hierarchies unlike anything in the monetary system:

[Standardization] aims to ensure fixed values for the counters in a system. In language, this means preventing variability in spelling and pronunciation by selecting fixed conventions uniquely regarded as 'correct', establishing 'correct' meanings of words ... uniquely acceptable word-forms ... and fixed conventions of sentence structure. The whole notion of standardisation is bound up with the aim of functional efficiency of the language. (1991, 23)

In the history of English, standardization has been most successful in stabilizing spelling, which means that spelling requires less prescriptive attention in usage guides; learning standard spelling is inextricably intertwined at this point with learning to read and write. As a result, most overt prescriptive efforts from the eighteenth century onwards have focused on "correct" word meanings, grammatical elements of word and sentence formation, and punctuation – and in some cases pronunciation, although speakers seem to allow a good deal of variation in pronunciation within "unstigmatized" language use.[8]

The Milroys build on the four basic stages of standardization originally proposed by Einar Haugen in the 1960s, showing the place of prescriptivism in the perpetuation of standardized languages. First, one variety of a language is selected as a standard. For English, this first happened for the written language in the early fifteenth century (Fisher 1996); the relationship of the developing written standard and the rise of a spoken standard in the London area remains a vexed area of scholarship (Trudgill 1999; Hickey 2012). Second, this variety is accepted by influential people and institutions; it is subsequently diffused geographically and socially by various means (e.g., official papers, education). As a third stage, the standard variety must be maintained, and this happens in part through the elaboration of function: in other words, the standard comes to be used for a wide range of written registers and spoken purposes, thereby developing the required vocabulary and stylistic devices. In this way, the standard comes to be perceived as increasingly socially valuable, for prestige and social mobility. The establishment of widespread literacy similarly helps to maintain the standard, as the written form of the language is held up as the model of

---

[7] For insightful discussions of the definitional problems, see Wolfram and Schilling Estes (2006, 9–13), Cheshire (1999), Trudgill (1999), and Crystal (2004).

[8] Regional differences in the pronunciation of vowels, for example, sometimes escape prescriptive attention. For instance, some speakers in the United States merge *cot* and *caught* while others do not, without one set of speakers' pronunciation being stigmatized. The merger of *pin* and *pen* is an established shibboleth, distinguishing Southern speakers, but it may be perceived as a "Southern accent" used by an otherwise standard English-speaking speaker. In other words, some phonological differences may not alone be enough to categorize a speaker as nonstandard. However, there are some pronunciations that are categorized as nonstandard, including "aks" for *ask*.

correctness. Once the standard variety has been established as prestigious and valuable for a range of functions, it undergoes codification: the attempt to stabilize its form through dictionaries, style guides, grammar books, and other, often prescriptive, resources. In the history of English, codification was well underway by the eighteenth century and can be traced back at least a century earlier (Tieken-Boon van Ostade 2012). Then, as a fully codified standard becomes accepted as a natural part of the language community, prescriptivism that enforces that standard often becomes more intense. The eighteenth century witnessed a rapid rise in prescriptive texts, to be followed shortly thereafter by a similar flourishing of prescriptivism in the Americas. The Milroys describe the cumulative result of this process in English as follows:

The effect of codification and prescription has been to legitimise the norms of formal registers of standard English rather than the norms of everyday spoken English. Codifiers have legislated and prescribers have tried to put the legislation into effect. One result of this is that there is a general belief that there is only one form of correct, i.e. legitimate, English, and a feeling that colloquial and non-standard forms are perverse and deliberate deviations from what is approved by 'law' i.e. they are 'illegitimate'. (1991, 37)

The reference to "law" here is telling and might bring to mind the analogy of these kinds of prescriptive rules with traffic laws. Standardization aims to minimize variation in the standard variety, to encourage (perhaps a euphemistic verb in some cases) speakers and writers all to use one form – and it is easy to see how this form comes to be seen as the only legitimate form, at the expense of others. It is not just standard: it is "English."

This statement highlights the way in which this set of prescriptive rules, the rules that promote standard English, can become naturalized such that many speakers think of them as "correct English" or simply "English" in all circumstances. They are more "laws" than "etiquette rules"; in other words, they get framed as "how English works" (where "English" implicitly refers to the standard variety), not as a matter of stylistic preference or a marker of educational attainment. In this way, these prescriptive rules typically help to enforce the boundaries around what is considered "standard," and through the naturalization of these rules encourage the conflation of standard English and "English." The term *standard language ideology* is often used to describe the pervasive belief systems that allow this privileging of the standard variety to seem like common sense and, thereby, allow discrimination against nonstandard varieties to seem justified (Lippi-Green 2012). The common sense-ness of these beliefs, and the subsequent naturalization of the prescriptive rules supported by them, lend them their power, as they seem exempt from critical questioning. They are seen, as noted above, as how English works – or how it should work if everyone would use the language "right."

Examples of standard-enforcing prescriptive rules will help here.

The idea that *ain't* is bad English or even "not a real word" captures the power of prescriptive criticism to create commonsense ideas about right and wrong in language. Criticism of *ain't* has been so pervasive and effective that despite the word's widespread use in many nonstandard varieties of American English, as well as in the colloquial speech of many standard American English speakers, many speakers of American English (nonstandard and standard) see the word as improper and the speakers who use it as violating fundamental principles or laws of English. For many speakers of nonstandard varieties of American English, *ain't* serves as the regular contracted form of *am/is/are* + *not* (e.g., *I ain't going, she ain't there*) and *has/have* + *not* (e.g., *he ain't gone yet*). For some speakers of African American English, *ain't* can also serve as a contracted form of *do/does* + *not*. The contraction *ain't* first came to be condemned in the eighteenth century, along with a slew of other contractions such as *won't* and *shouldn't*, and, while other contractions have been elevated to the level of the informal rather than the wrong, *ain't* has remained stigmatized as wrong. People quote the widely circulated myth that "*ain't* ain't in the dictionary," even though it has been in dictionaries for decades. A dictionary such as *Webster's Third New International Dictionary* (1961), which dared to include *ain't* without a usage label such as "nonstandard," is publicly castigated for not fulfilling its responsibilities of policing the standard (Morton 1994; Landau 2001, 254–261; Skinner 2012). Speakers of standard American English who use *ain't* for stylistic purposes, to create an especially emphatic negative or to sound colloquial, are exploiting its accepted nonstandardness. They know *ain't* will be noticed and, in an otherwise standard context, will be assumed to be a rhetorical choice. Its rhetorical power in this context rests on the naturalized premise of its nonstandardness.

The stigmatization of the form *aks* rather than *ask* also serves to police the boundaries of standard (spoken) English. Again, speakers typically do not see "aks" as an issue of stylistic preference – it is, simply, wrong. The only legitimate pronunciation in this case is "ask." It isn't that standard English allows no variation in pronunciation, though. As mentioned earlier, at this point speakers of standard English are using "often" (with a /t/) and "offen" for *often*. And so far the pronunciation "heighth" for *height*, which could easily enough be stigmatized as nonstandard, has escaped prescriptive attention.

The sometimes idiosyncratic nature of prescriptive judgments about standard English is captured nicely in differing judgments about the use of *me* and *I* in conjoined constructions. There are two ways that English speakers violate prescriptive rules when they use personal pronouns in conjoined phrases. First, some speakers use an object form in subject position, in a sentence like *Me and my mom drove over to Chicago*. This use is categorized as nonstandard in American English and naturalized for some as a "lower" or "less educated" construction. Other speakers use the subject form in object position, in a sentence like *This is a wonderful occasion for Michelle and I*. This use is often seen as the result of hypercorrection or an attempt to increase the formality of the utterance by using *I* rather than *me*. While this use is criticized – and President Obama was criticized in print for uttering the example sentence above – it is usually not labeled as nonstandard. It is, at least in some cases, probably an aspirational error, the result of hyper-formality. That said, both constructions have a fairly long history. For example, Shakespeare's *Merchant of Venice* includes an example of pronoun "confusion" that looks very modern: "All debts are cleared between you and I." Both constructions could be stigmatized as nonstandard; or both could be seen as issues of etiquette or formality. But instead, in American English, the severe judgments against subject–position "Me and x" constructions serve to police the standard (in American English and some other varieties), while the less severe objections to object–position "x and I" constructions differentiate more and less refined formal standard English – "improper usage" as opposed to "bad grammar" (the stronger stigma many speakers attach to the "Me and x" construction).

Prescriptivism of this sort has elevated the standard varieties of English to the status of correct English as a matter of common sense or natural law, which has left nonstandard varieties in the complementary set: incorrect English. The naturalization of this view of nonstandard varieties is akin to the naturalization of driving on only one side of the road (be that right or left). In theory, cars could follow other orderly patterns on a road, but the imposed standard of driving on one side has become conventionalized to the point of seeming natural to driving. And it is, in fact, against the law to drive otherwise. So while we may recognize that traffic laws, like table manners, are socially constructed and contingent, the stakes involved in breaking them are different. Obviously, this is a place where the analogy breaks down: speakers and writers are not ticketed for violations of standard English. But they may be judged severely. Using *ain't* or "aks" or *Me and my mom went* can result in a speaker being labeled as ignorant, their English as "broken." In theory, nonstandard varieties are as viable for formal spoken and written English contexts as standard varieties – and, in fact, they are used in some formal spoken contexts (e.g., African American English is regularly employed in sermons in African American churches) – but the elevation of standard varieties has made it seem natural to many speakers that everyone should use this variety as the means of wider communication. And some cannot even imagine that another variety could perform this function, its status as "broken" and incorrect is so naturalized (try to imagine driving in a way that does not involve staying only on one side of the road). Some of these prescriptions about standard English are naturalized to the point that they do not even appear in specialized popular usage guides, which may take it for granted that speakers know, for example, not to use *ain't* if they want to use standard English.

Stylistic prescriptivism

Another set of prescriptive rules focuses on finer points of formal written (and to some extent spoken) usage, the equivalent of etiquette rules for how to use the language properly. This fact does not mean that people necessarily feel less strongly about the rules and their correctness, but the imposition of that correctness may be restricted to more formal, written contexts. There is an understanding that this is a nicety of usage, a nicety that distinguishes those who "know better" from those who don't, but it does not distinguish standard English speakers from nonstandard English speakers. These rules are about style, or skill at creating effective, aesthetically pleasing, appropriate to context (in this case formal contexts) usage. The line between standards and style is a blurry and porous one, and there are specific points of usage that could be argued to be on either side of the line; but the core of the categories, the prototypical prescriptive rules in each, can be productively distinguished.

Justifications for rules about "good style" rely on criteria such as logic (often the application of logic systems that arguably do not characterize human language), avoidance of ambiguity (unambiguous forms are preferred), necessity (words deemed "unnecessary" – by whatever criteria – are dispreferred), concision or simplicity (in this era of plain style), and aesthetics (typically personal, and aesthetics may run counter to criteria such as simplicity). Another fundamental principle is to follow the usage of "educated speakers and writers." The definition of "educated" is typically left unspecified, as is the context in which these educated speakers and writers might be using the language.

The *American Heritage Dictionary* puts this last principle into practice by relying on a Usage Panel for judgments in its usage notes about contested points of usage. This panel, which is made up of professional writers, academics, judges, journalists, and others, is asked to rate the "acceptability" of constructions, to provide guidance to readers about what they deem to be "allowable" in "good" language (although different panelists will think about "allowable" and "good" in different ways).[9] Many of the constructions with usage notes, about which the Panel is consulted, are not about standardness, but about style: standardness is not usually as contested as these finer points of style.

The sentence adverb *hopefully* provides a good example of a contested point of usage that generated a prescriptive rule about "good" style. As a sentence

---

[9] For full disclosure, I am a member of this Usage Panel, and I see my role as endorsing as "acceptable" any usage that is reasonably common according to data from actual usage (and not just written usage of "educated" speakers but American English usage more generally). These stylistic rules are gatekeeping mechanisms, designed to differentiate speakers and writers based on knowledge that is typically acquired in fairly restricted social and educational contexts. The only way to change the rules to be more flexible and accepting of more aspects of variation and change in the language is for some of us on the Usage Panel to be willing to open the gates to actual usage by a range of speakers.

adverb (an adverb modifying the full clause, in some cases describing the stance of the speaker/writer), *hopefully* is "wrong" according to many current language pundits because it is more ambiguous (i.e., who is hoping?) than other sentence adverbs such as *mercifully*, and simply because they find it unpleasing. As Roy Blount explains in his smart, entertaining, and often prescriptive book *Alphabet Juice* (2008, 140–141):

On the analogy of *generally speaking* or *conservatively speaking*, you can say that *hopefully* is short for *hopefully speaking*. Grammatically speaking, that may pass muster, but semantically, isn't there something cheesy about, say, "Hopefully speaking, we will be able to move on from hopefully soon"? "Generally speaking, people need people" is a nod to inevitable exceptions. "Conservatively speaking, the bake sale will pay for itself" is a lowball estimate. Begin a sentence with "Hopefully speaking," and whatever follows sounds like hot air.

This is informed opinion and persuasively presented opinion, but it is still simply one pundit's opinion about what is and is not tolerable ambiguity and what sounds like "hot air." Ben Yagoda, in *If You Catch an Adjective, Kill It* (2007), offers a different, and equally personal, reason for why *hopefully* should not be used to mean 'I hope' or 'it is hoped':

I dislike *hopefully* not because it's wrong – check out Chapter II for an explanation of its kosherness – but because people who use it in writing tend to be imprecise, muddy, solipsistic, and dull. (13)

The accumulation of these kinds of opinions in published work all highlighting the same "problem" in English usage creates the widespread sense that there is a problem and a need for prescriptive guidance. *Hopefully* employed to mean 'I hope' or 'it is hoped' was not identified as a stylistic misstep until the 1960s and prescriptivism on this point has been getting stricter since (see Chapter 2 for more details) – although the tide may shift with the announcement in the spring of 2012 that the *Associated Press Stylebook* changed its treatment of this word and started to allow *hopefully* with the meaning 'it is hoped'.

Many of these prescriptive rules are about style, about using, within a range of options that are all standard, a construction that is considered particularly effective, refined, and/or proper. And some constructions are arguably more effective than others: they may be less ambiguous or preferable for rhetorical or aesthetic reasons (e.g., the construction reinforces a cause–effect relationship or pleasingly maintains the rhythm of the sentence). This category of prescriptive rules can usefully point writers toward some of these more effective constructions. But it is critical to remember that much of what distinguishes one construction as more effective than another is subjective, an imposed aesthetic by one group of writers onto another.

The sentence-final preposition provides another instructive case study. Since the eighteenth century there has been a grammatical tradition of recommending that prepositions not be left stranded at the end of a sentence (the criticism goes back at least to John Dryden in the seventeenth century). So we should say or write (although the advice is especially targeted at the written language, given the complexity of the construction) *that is a rule to which I do not adhere*, rather than *that is a rule that I do not adhere to*. While the rule is widely known, it is actually quite specialized in terms of applicability: it becomes relevant only in two constructions in which one element of the sentence is moved, which can leave the preposition stranded. The first construction is a *wh*-question in which the *wh*-word (*whom, what*, etc.) is the object of a preposition. So the following question has three possible realizations, the first of which (where the *wh*-word is not moved to the front of the question) is possible only through a change in intonation:

(a) You gave the book *to whom?*

(b) *To whom* did you give the book? ("correct" according to the prescriptive rule)

(c) *Who/whom* did you give the book *to?* (with a stranded final preposition)

The second construction is a sentence with a relative clause that contains a relative pronoun functioning as the object of the preposition. If we return to the earlier example, it contains the relative clause *I do not adhere to (that)*. The relative pronoun *that* is fronted to the beginning of the relative clause, and the preposition can optionally be fronted with it (in linguistics, this process is, wonderfully, called "pied-piping," to describe the preposition following the relative pronoun to the beginning of the relative clause). So we can say/write *to which I do not adhere* (the preposition is also fronted) or *that I do not adhere to* (the preposition remains stranded).[10]

As both of these examples suggest, this rule is about formality – or looked at from a different angle, about colloquiality. All of the constructions described above are standard, but they differ in terms of how formal they sound. So if I do not want to sound like an English professor in an email correspondence, I will most certainly write "Who should I send it to?" – a question in which the stranded preposition and the use of *who* for *whom* make the tone more colloquial. To write "To whom should I send it?" would signal a high level of formality – or potentially pretentiousness. I am navigating the niceties of language etiquette in this decision, determining how much knowledge about, and adherence to, the prescriptive grammar that I know I will demonstrate in this email.

The question "Where's it at?" is sometimes brought up as an example of a sentence-final preposition, and it is a question that at least some speakers would categorize as nonstandard. For these speakers, it is not an issue of etiquette – this

---

[10] It is an oddity of English syntax that when the preposition is also fronted, the relative pronoun must be *which*. We cannot say/write **That is a rule to that I do not adhere*.

construction is, instead, somehow wrong. Some critics of this construction lay the incorrectness at the feet of redundancy, arguing that the preposition repeats information already conveyed by *where*. But I don't think preposition stranding or redundancy explain the stigmatization of this question. A very similar question, such as *Which restaurant do you want to meet at?*, would not in all likelihood receive the same level of censure, although it ends with the same preposition. And the sentence *We will return back to Lake Tahoe next year* will strike some as stylistically undesirable, given the redundancy of *return back*, but not as nonstandard. As these examples show, the line between standardization and stylistic discrimination can be a fine one, and very similar constructions can land on different sides of the line.

Returning to the analogies about prescriptivism may help clarify the fine line. These prescriptive rules about stylistic niceties, which have been compared with table manners, could equally well be compared with etiquette rules of driving. We understand, for example, that we should give the driver stopped ahead of us a few seconds to see a green light before we lightly tap the horn. This is good driving etiquette. If we sit on the horn the moment the light turns green, the driver ahead of us may think we are a bit uncouth, but they will not assume we don't know how to drive – as they would if we were not obeying traffic laws by driving on the wrong side of the road. Similarly, violating a prescriptive rule about style may flag our language as not preferred in some way, but not as flat-out wrong, broken, or "not real English."

The discriminations in style perpetuated by this set of prescriptive rules occur within the realm of the standard language, allowing speakers to identify language as formal, colloquial, "educated," erudite, careful, perhaps pretentious, etc. Sometimes these prescriptive rules encourage the retention of older meanings (e.g., *hopefully* meaning 'full of hope') and sometimes they try to enforce a practice that the language never seems to have adhered to (e.g., not ending a sentence with a preposition). The rules typically rely on stylistic reasoning, such as the reduction of ambiguity, aesthetic appeal, or similar criteria.

Restorative prescriptivism

The third category of restorative prescriptivism represents a fairly small class of rules: they encourage the restoration of older meanings purely for the sake of honoring past usage, and they may have little effect on actual usage. Yet the presence and motivations of this subset of prescriptive rules are important for understanding the phenomenon of prescriptivism more generally. Nostalgia characterizes all kinds of human behavior, so it is unsurprising that it motivates some language prescriptivism. Prescriptivism relies to some extent on the idea that the language is on the brink of decline if not already declining, due to poor education, carelessness, declining moral values,[11] or other deplorable human tendencies. A natural corollary of the proposition that language is in decline is the assumption that the language was in a better state at some earlier moment. One model for "correct" language use can logically, then, be found in past usage and invoked when expedient.

This category of prescriptive rules shows significant overlap with both rules to enforce standardization and rules to discriminate among styles, as they too sometimes hold up earlier usage as the norm or as the preferred option. However, we need this third category because some prescriptive rules that aim to restore older forms or meanings seem not to enforce standards or privilege stylistically preferred options. They advocate older forms that are neither standard nor preferred. For this reason, I have opted to use the term *restoration* to describe these efforts, as it suggests the resurrection of a form no longer standard or even preferred.

A good example is the prescriptive effort to remind speakers that *nauseous* "should" mean 'causing nausea', and that if we want to say that we are not feeling well and think we might vomit, we should say that we are nauseated. A search of the Corpus of Contemporary American English, with over 400 million words of American English (spoken and written) from 1990 to the present, shows that only one of the first one hundred hits for *nauseous* means 'causing nausea' (from a work of fiction); the rest, in both spoken and written language (some of it very formal), mean 'feeling ill'. It is difficult to argue that *nauseous* meaning 'causing nausea' is standard at this point – it is not the norm even of formal, standard usage. It may be equally difficult to argue that using *nauseous* with this older meaning signals any distinction among styles or registers for speakers/writers or their audiences. The rule occurs in some usage guides, but it lacks enforcement and support even in the most formal of styles. It lives in isolation in usage guides, with little to no life outside them.

In some cases, the usage being "restored" may never have existed. The prescriptive rule about *shall* and *will* may now fall into this category. While the language itself has never followed this distinction, as far as linguists can tell, prescriptive grammarians going back at least to H. W. Fowler in the early twentieth century concocted a rule now seen as "traditional," that there was a clear-cut distinction between the two in terms of expressing simple future vs. intention. The rule goes as follows: to express simple future, use *shall* in the first person (e.g., *I shall*) and *will* in the second and third person (e.g., *you will*, *she will*); to express intention, use *will* in the first person (*I will*) and *shall* in the

---

[11] There is fascinating scholarship on links between grammar and morality – see, for example, Cameron (1995), and Finegan (1992, 2001). Conversations about language are usually about much more than language, and complaints about "bad language" often get tied to judgments about the character and morality of the speakers of the language.

second and third person (*you shall, she shall*). Some readers may recall having been trained to follow this rule, but it now rarely appears in grammar textbooks or usage guides. In the guide books in which it does appear, it is now isolated from any norms of usage, including the most formal prose. In fact, as *shall* slowly dies from the language (Leech et al. 2009), the rule becomes ever more obsolete.

Concerted efforts to purify language using older forms could also be categorized as restorative prescriptivism. The inkhorn debates of the Renaissance provide a classic example (discussed in detail in Chapter 4), when critics of hifalutin Latinate borrowings advocated the use of Anglo-Saxon compounds, such as *flesh-strings* for *muscles* and *out-born* for *foreign*.

Prescriptive rules for standardization and for style that hold up older forms as correct or preferred may move into this category as they become obsolete – at which point the rule is advocating preservation for its own sake. Like parents setting up rules because that is how it was done in their day, the rules may not be standard or preferable by any identifiable criteria beyond nostalgia for a moment in the past. The stakes for breaking these kinds of prescriptive rules seem much lower, if present at all. In fact, judgments may be more severe for adhering to the rules, for using *she shall* or *the nauseous rollercoaster*, as the prescribed forms violate both standard and preferred usage.

Politically responsive prescriptivism

The fourth strand of prescriptivism – those rules or judgments that aim to promote inclusive, nondiscriminatory, and/or politically correct or expedient usage – does not typically appear in traditional, textbook definitions of prescriptivism in linguistics. As Edward Finegan (2001) points out, one reason for this may be that linguists agree with and endorse many of these language prescriptions. In fact, the Linguistic Society of America passed an official resolution in support of nonsexist language use. Many such prescriptions are seen as progressive and inclusive, as opposed to the other three strands (the more traditional ones), which are often perceived to be conservative and discriminatory. That binary between progressive and conservative oversimplifies the nature of prescriptive efforts on both sides; as a shorthand for common perceptions, however, it may help explain why politically responsive prescriptivism is more typically called "language reform" than "prescriptivism."

But a kind of prescriptivism it is. Usage rules designed to guide writers and speakers toward, for example, nondiscriminatory language are telling people how they should and shouldn't use language in order to use it "right" or at least in an institutionally preferred way. While some of these efforts to control others' language have started outside institutions of power, for instance in movements for civil and political rights, they have resulted in politically responsive rules of usage that are now institutionalized in style guides and elsewhere. In an interesting twist, some of these efforts have directly challenged institutionalized usage rules and in overturning those rules have become institutionalized as prescriptions themselves.

The case of singular generic pronoun usage provides a helpful example. The explicit instruction to use generic *he*, rather than singular generic *they* or any other option, by grammarian Lindley Murray and others beginning in the eighteenth century has been, in linguistics, a textbook example of prescriptivism at work. One stylistic option was imposed on English speakers and writers as correct usage – and a questionable option at that, given that the pronoun 'he' may never have functioned well as a generic pronoun. This prescription was not seriously challenged until the 1970s and the efforts of second-wave feminism to weed out sexist usage. By the 1990s, most style guides had changed their prescription, from advising the use of generic *he* to advising the use of generic *he or she* or revision of the sentence to avoid the issue. I will return to the history of this shift in prescription in Chapter 5. The point here is that it is a shift in prescription, not a shift away from prescription.

In other cases, such as the preferred terms for minority groups in the United States, politically responsive prescriptivism provides rules for usage in areas of the grammar and lexicon where there has been little to no prescription previously. And it is certainly plausible that today's politically responsive prescriptivism will at some point become stylistic prescriptivism, when the social and political context that served as the impetus becomes irretrievable for speakers. As noted earlier, prescriptivism should be seen as a dynamic phenomenon.

Challenges of disentangling prescriptivism

One of the many challenges of defining prescriptivism is that the different strands are entangled and the institutionalized rules themselves tend to use the same terminology of correctness, whether the goal is standardization, style, restoration, or political sensitivity. Bryan Garner's *A Dictionary of Modern American Usage* (1998) provides an instructive example because he makes the unusual move in the Preface of listing the ten principles that guide his approach to providing self-admittedly prescriptive advice on usage. He writes, "As you might already suspect, I don't shy away from making judgments. I can't imagine that most readers would want me to" (xiii). Garner describes the purpose of the dictionary as helping writers, speakers, and editors to sound "grammatical but relaxed, refined but natural, correct but unpedantic" (x). Standardness is implicit in "grammatical," "correct," and probably "natural." Style is implicit in "relaxed," "refined," and "unpedantic." Preservation is captured in another principle: that a word or phrase is worse if it "sounds newfangled" or "threatens to displace an established expression (but hasn't yet done so)." The words *effective*, *good* and *bad*, *better* and *worse*, and *undesirable* appear throughout the principles, until the final one: "In the end, the actual usage of educated speakers and writers is the overarching criterion for correctness." Here, standardness, style, restoration, and reform get collapsed into the undifferentiated category of correctness, as established by the actual usage of speakers with an undisclosed level of education in unspecified contexts.

Prescriptivism, as detailed in this chapter, is about more than undifferentiated correctness: it has multiple aims, some of which are clearly more about effective style than standard English, and it does not, in fact, always correspond to any usage by speakers of any education level – be that due to restorative or innovative goals. In criticizing prescriptive approaches to language, linguists will sometimes criticize the first and second strands but use examples from the second and third strands (e.g., split infinitives and the correct meaning of *nauseous* – relatively easy targets), which are not as naturalized as "correct" for most speakers and may in some cases seem quaint to those inside and outside the field of linguistics. In this way, linguists may not be effectively troubling the foundational belief in the correctness of standard English that circulates widely in public discourse and may be adding to the confusion of standards and style, as well as perhaps of spoken and written usage.

By disentangling and clarifying the different strands of prescriptivism and what is at stake with each, linguists can better help educators – as well as prescriptive language mavens generally – sort out the advice they are dispensing. Such an approach could help us to arrive at a more useful "modified prescriptivism," to use John Edwards' (2012) term for an approach to language education that provides shared standards for written (and to some extent spoken) communication without discriminating against speakers. To achieve this end, as I return to in the final chapter, all of the stakeholders – linguists, teachers, students, usage guide writers, and the list goes on – would benefit from differentiating among the kinds of linguistic phenomena that are getting called "correct" in the prescriptive literature.

2   Prescriptivism's lessons: scope and "the history of English"

Lynne Truss's book *Eats, Shoots & Leaves: The Zero Tolerance Approach to Punctuation* was published in November 2003 by the small press Gotham Books, and it became a runaway bestseller, to everyone's surprise. It sold over two million copies in its first two years, and it won the book-of-the-year prize at the British Book Awards. In those first couple of years, the book was a popular gift for English majors and other literary types, as both undergraduate and graduate students in my courses have attested. It also appears that, according to my informal polling, some significant number of the recipients never read the book. This phenomenon raises a tree-falling-in-the-woods kind of question: If a wildly popular prescriptive English usage guide sells millions of copies but significantly fewer people actually read it, is it an important part of the history of the English language in the modern period?

I will argue here that it is an important part of the history of English: its popularity alone speaks to language ideologies and attitudes at play at the beginning of the twenty-first century, which are part of the history of a language; in addition, popular usage guides as well as the attitudes circulating around them have the power, in some instances, to influence English as it is spoken and written. Before developing that argument, though, it is useful to consider two possible counterarguments.

First, some might object that if relatively few people read a popular guide and follow its prescriptions, it may not have much effect on specific points of usage, written or spoken. Truss's advice about "correct" apostrophe use, for example, cannot change apostrophe use if people do not read it and apply it to their own and others' writing. Therefore, the guide should not be seen as an important part of the language's history.

Certainly the direct impact on readers' usage may be limited (less limited perhaps if the readers are teachers). But the discourse itself – the preoccupation with grammar and the linguistic insecurity that allowed Truss's book to sell millions of copies – should be part of the story of Modern English. Joan Beal (2009) calls the rise in prescriptive energy at the beginning of the twenty-first century "New Prescriptivism," a term that may be more applicable in the UK than in the US, given the more continuous history of popular, published prescriptive resources throughout the twentieth century in the US. Whether speakers read Truss's book or not, the sense that speakers and writers need and actively want these books becomes part of a significant number of speakers' understanding of language and how to use it. As a result, one factor in the linguistic choices that speakers and writers make in a given context – from pronunciation to syntax to word choice – can be their awareness of the importance of "correct" ways of speaking, even if they remain uncertain of what choice will be deemed correct. For both speakers who read the book and speakers who hear about the book's message, it reinforces ideologies about the importance of "correct" usage.

Second, skeptics of the importance of popular usage guides in the history of the language may assert that even for the people who read the guide, the prescriptions often focus primarily on written language (*Eats, Shoots & Leaves* targets almost exclusively punctuation issues), so the guide may influence only more formal, edited registers of the written language and have little effect on spoken usage. "Real" change, some argue, happens in the spoken language, often below the level of awareness.

But what is and isn't "real" change when it comes to language? In writing language history, should we accept that changes in the spoken language are more "real" than changes in the written language? And what else goes into language history other than changes in usage? I detail in this chapter why too myopic a focus on change in the spoken language, and change below the level of awareness, is a problematic stance for telling the history of a language. It marginalizes the written language and pays scant attention to the relationship of the written and spoken language. It also privileges changes in language that occur below the radar over changes that are actively debated, contested, prescribed, or proscribed within the meta-discourses circulating around language use in the modern period. These meta-discourses also make up an important part of language history. As Allan Walker Read (2002 [1986], 110) observed nearly thirty years ago, "In addition to the structure and forms of the language itself are the attitudes and beliefs of the speakers, and a full picture of a language must include the linguistic attitudes that the speakers have." This astute observation has not yet fully enough infiltrated the ways in which the history of English is told.

Questions of scope

When I began this project, I was not expecting to end up asking one of the most fundamental scholarly questions one can ask in the field of history of English studies. But examining prescriptivism as a real sociolinguistic factor in the history of English raises the question: What does it mean to tell the "linguistic history" of "the English language"? Or, to put it more prescriptively, what should it mean to tell the history of the English language? Attention to prescriptivism in the telling of language history gives significant weight to writing, ideologies, and consciously implemented language change. In so doing, it highlights some inconsistencies within the field about the focus of study, about what falls within the scope of "linguistic" history.

Re-examining the scope of the linguistic history of English encompasses at least three major issues, all of which will be the focus of this chapter: the relative importance of language attitudes and ideologies in understanding a language's history; the relative importance of the written and spoken versions of the language in constituting "the English language" whose history is being told; and the relative importance of change above and below speakers' conscious awareness (to use standard terminology in the field) in constituting language change.

The field of history of English studies may particularly invite these challenging questions because it lies at a disciplinary intersection, between philology and historical linguistics. These two disciplines rely on different methodologies, privilege different research questions, and rely on different kinds of evidence. I was pointedly reminded of this disciplinary gap at a panel on language, gender, and sexuality hosted at the University of Michigan in 2012. Two colleagues in linguistics presented on how gender and sexuality play out in selected spoken linguistic performances, and I discussed results from Chapter 5 of this book about the effects of nonsexist language reform. In the question and answer period, one of my highly distinguished literature colleagues from the English department remarked that it seemed like all three of us were treating the spoken language as the primary representation of language, as opposed to the written; but, for her, as a scholar of literature, it seemed unquestionable that, as she put it, "the written trumps the spoken." All three of us on the panel tried to contain our surprise at the remark; linguists can, but shouldn't, take for granted what seems like the obviousness of privileging the spoken. Linguistics often presents it as a commonplace that the written language lags behind the spoken in terms of language change, and it is true that the majority of changes in the structure of the language originate in the spoken language. These changes may then slowly work their way into the written, although not all of them will (pronunciation changes, for example, make limited indents on the highly standardized system of English spelling). Yet, as a historian of English, I do not want to dismiss the written as simply derivative. What about changes that begin in the written language, including those that may remain largely restricted to written contexts? It is a mistake to relegate these changes to part of the history of literature or writing as opposed to the history of the language more generally. The written version of the language is an important, not derivative, part of the field of history of English studies.

The field's roots lie in English philology, historically a primarily if not exclusively text-based discipline, often housed in English departments and dedicated to understanding the history and development of the language.[1] Philological research, while spanning different features of language such as word etymology and sound change, has often relied on literary texts for evidence of a language feature's occurrence and has long had close ties with literary studies. Historical lexicographical projects such as the *Oxford English Dictionary*, which documents the historical evidence for specific meanings in its word entries, have relied on written evidence out of necessity for early periods of the language and to some extent out of tradition for contemporaneous periods (in fact, for all periods after the invention of recording devices). With each subsequent edition, the *OED* has expanded the registers of the written language from which it draws, striving to include language outside the literary, from more colloquial language to jargon. But the newest revisions to *OED* for the third edition feature no citations from spoken language, even though those are widely available for current developments in the language.[2] A change in the lexicon has become fodder for historical lexicography once it is solidified in the written language, a clear privileging of the written in the philological tradition.[3]

The philological tradition has undergone sustained challenges from developments in linguistics since the early twentieth century. Starting in the 1980s, the rise of historical sociolinguistics specifically shifted both the focus and methodologies of some of the scholarship in the field of history of English studies, as it encouraged a broader view of what qualifies as "linguistic" developments in the history of a language.[4] Language in use, in social contexts, rises to the same level of importance as language as an abstract system. And speakers trump texts. As Thomason and Kaufman (1988) argued twenty-five years ago, the

---

[1] The title of the first textbook on the history of English captures its philological roots: *Method of the Philological Study of the English Language* (1865), written by Francis A. Marsh, a professor of English Language and Comparative Philology at Lafayette College in Pennsylvania (see Adams 2012b for a fuller discussion).

[2] The journal *American Speech*, for its regular feature "Among the New Words," now includes audio files and transcripts for aural evidence of recent coinages.

[3] Lexicographers are gambling whenever they decide to include or not include a new word or a new meaning of an already existing word. They are aiming to determine whether these lexical innovations will (a) stick in the language, and (b) spread beyond a highly specialized register. Dictionary editors do not want their dictionaries to seem "faddish" and to become quickly outdated. However, there are stark exceptions to both these guiding principles. When working with historical material, the *OED*, for example, includes some words for which there is only one recorded instance, perhaps especially with Shakespeare (e.g., the word *predict* as a noun, which is cited in one of Shakespeare's sonnets but nowhere else). These entries are clearly not lexical innovations that "stuck." The *OED* also privileges the language from some highly specialized registers such as scientific and medical writing for inclusion over other highly specialized registers such as restaurant jargon. In other words, not all words need to spread beyond a highly specialized register to be included – it depends on the cultural value of the specialized register.

[4] See Romaine (1982), Ramoulin-Brunberg (1996), and Nevalainen and Ramoulin-Brunberg (1996, 2003) for useful surveys of the field of historical sociolinguistics.

sociolinguistic history of speakers must be the primary object of study, rather than the structure of language divorced from speakers. Sociolinguistics, as is true of the field of linguistics more broadly, privileges the study of spoken language: spoken language is the essential or fundamental form of the language, the form learned naturally (i.e., intuitively and largely without formal instruction) by children in a speech community. Written language is a cultural product and must be explicitly taught to children for them to acquire it. Spoken language (or signed forms of communication) is universal to human speech communities, whereas many speech communities around the world function without a written form of their primary language(s). The tension around the role of written texts in language history starts to become evident.

Historical sociolinguistics of a language like English draws heavily on written texts, but not as the primary object of inquiry. The field relies on written texts primarily as a vehicle, albeit an imperfect one, for studying the development of the spoken language. For this reason, historical sociolinguistic methods have greatly expanded the range of texts for analysis, with a special interest in forms of writing more colloquial than most literary texts, whenever available. Written texts from the early periods of the English language include mostly more formal registers of language (e.g., religious, legal, and scholarly texts as well as literature), making it difficult to reconstruct the language of the everyday and the messy details of language variation and change. Writing was a highly specialized practice in the medieval period, reserved largely for culturally important texts; these texts were also culturally valuable enough to be preserved. The Old English corpus of written texts is extremely limited (about three million running words), and some of it represents translations from Latin, which potentially affects the syntax and lexicon; poetic texts also contain register-specific grammatical constructions and word choices. Historical sociolinguistics relies on high literature, translations, and other formal texts when it must, but such texts are regarded as a poor mirror of spoken language, the primary object of inquiry. Personal letters and diaries, which start to become available as preserved artifacts for the Early Modern English period, have long been particularly valued for historical language study as their language probably more closely correlates with colloquial spoken language, given the informality of the genre and the range of education of the writers.

Historical sociolinguistics also brings a different set of questions to bear on the historical linguistic data, including how change is implemented within a speech community over time. Histories of a language working in the philological tradition may frame linguistic change in terms of endpoints: in a given period, feature A dropped out of use, replaced by feature B; or form C shifted from meaning P to meaning Q. Such descriptions make linguistic changes sound tidy. Historical sociolinguistics emphasizes that language change is, in fact, variable and messy in its implementation, and that is the stuff of language history. At any given moment during a linguistic change, speakers typically experience the change as variation, with some speakers using one variant and other speakers using other variants or with the same speakers using multiple variants, perhaps in different registers.[5] In this variation, historical sociolinguists can often find evidence of language change spreading from, for example, generation to generation, region to region, or socioeconomic class to class.

As these two brief descriptions capture, the disciplinary differences between philology and historical sociolinguistics can create a picture of competing, perhaps irreconcilable, visions for the field of history of English, from the scope of study to the specific research questions to the methodologies. But, in fact, history of English can comfortably and productively encompass both. I am not the first to argue that the two disciplines share important goals and interests; Donka Minkova (2004), for example, makes a compelling case – "a renewed defense," she calls it – that philology and linguistics cannot be separated; as she points out, philologists tracking spelling changes and rhyme to investigate a sound change are pursuing questions very similar to the historical sociolinguist mining texts for evidence of sound change.

There is another area in which philology and historical sociolinguistics have tended to have more overlap than not: both fields have kept prescriptivism in the margins of language history. The focus on variation and change in historical sociolinguistics has not historically come with sustained scholarly attention to the prescriptive responses to that variation and change as part of understanding the language's development. Early guides to orthography and pronunciation have served as sources of evidence for phonological developments; the early grammars have largely been relegated to "external history," as opposed to being framed as a sociolinguistic factor in speakers' experience with language that could have an impact on usage.

The internal–external binary surfaces in both sociolinguistics and in some history of English textbooks. Internal factors include those considered inherent to the system or structure of the language, such as phonological symmetry, grammaticalization, or ease of articulation. External factors bring in the lived experiences of speakers, who may come into contact with other languages or new phenomena that require changes to the language. The line between internal and external is much blurrier than the binary suggests, as speakers' cognition, beliefs, and lived experience with language are all relevant to language change. Drawing on this binary, C. M. Millward's influential textbook *A Biography of*

---

[5] One of the critical insights of modern variationist sociolinguistics is the concept of orderly heterogeneity (Weinreich et al. 1968, 100) – that variation is often systematically linked to extralinguistic factors such as speakers' age, gender, race or ethnicity, socioeconomic status, and/or region as well as the context and form of their language use. Historical corpora have been invaluable for historical sociolinguists in that they allow scholars to explore correlations between social and textual factors and linguistic features – see Curzan (2009) for a more detailed discussion.

the English Language (3rd edn., revised by Mary Hayes, 2012) structures the story of the language around inner history – "the changes that occur within the language itself, changes that cannot be attributed to external forces" (14) – and outer history – "the events that have happened to speakers of the language leading to changes in the language" (14).[6] The wording itself captures the difficulties inherent in such a distinction. If the outer history is the events, but those events can and do lead to changes in the language, how do those changes fit into the history of the language? And what events are important enough to count as "outer history" as opposed to the day-to-day life experiences that also shape speakers' use of language? In their introduction to *A Companion to the History of the English Language* (2008), Haruko Momma and Michael Matto suggest conceptualizing a "feedback loop" between a language and its environment, which would eliminate the suggestion of a division between the internal and external, a position advocated by Adams (2012b). Prescriptivism as a factor in the history of a language could easily be integrated into such a feedback loop.

This chapter proposes three general principles for telling language history, all of which would help sidestep some unproductive binaries and help integrate prescriptivism into language history, without over-privileging Standard English as the "English" whose history is being told (Milroy 1999). The principles integrate and stretch approaches from the scholarly traditions in philology and historical sociolinguistics. They build on the important work on the history of prescriptivism, historical corpus linguistics, and several other subfields. They call for a more expansive vision of the scope of history of English studies. In forwarding these principles, I am building on work by scholars such as Manfred Görlach (1989, 99), who describes three categories of "purely linguistic" criteria fundamental to describing a language's history: (1) structural; (2) societal (language planning, standardization, etc.); and (3) attitudinal (evaluation by speakers of earlier and current forms of their language). These three categories label sociolinguistic phenomena "purely linguistic," on par with language structure, and recognize the importance of speakers' lived experience with their language as well as structural developments in the language. They blur the traditional line between "inner" history and "outer" history of a language. However, these categories do not address the role of the written language in a language's history or tease out the interplay of language attitudes, processes such as standardization, and structural change. The more expansive view I am proposing accounts for these aspects of speakers' experience with language – the "environment" in

---

[6] Millward and Hayes (2012, 10) also at times privilege the internal as "linguistic history," echoing the roots of the field: "the history of the English language, then, is the record of how its patterns and rules have changed over the centuries." Over the course of the twentieth century and into the twenty-first, scholars have investigated more thoroughly the relationship of language history and the social and political history of its speakers (Cable 2008), yet sometimes the "external" can be too isolated as external to linguistic history.

addition to the language and the relationship of the two – as part of language history.

These principles are not radical. No premises in the principles are entirely new to the field. However, I have never seen these principles brought together and made fully explicit. The principles aim to rectify inconsistencies in terms of articulated scope for the field of history of English studies and the primary object(s) of inquiry. They also show how institutionalized prescriptivism can and should be integrated into language history. The three principles are as follows:

- The history of the English language encompasses metalinguistic discussions about language, which potentially have real effects on language use.
- The history of the English language encompasses the development of both the written and the spoken language, as well as their relationship to each other.
- The history of the English language encompasses linguistic developments occurring both below the level of speakers' conscious awareness – what is sometimes called "naturally" – and above the level of speakers' conscious awareness.

These principles stem directly from my research for this project. In order to examine prescriptivism seriously as a sociolinguistic factor in the history of English and language history more generally, I had to articulate explicitly and, in the end, expand my understanding of what was encompassed under the umbrella of "the history of English." This chapter is devoted to developing the claim of each principle, its links to prescriptivism, and its implications for how scholars study and tell the history of the English language.

Prescriptive discourses and meta-discourses

Humans use language to talk about language. It is one of the remarkable and potentially unique features of human language. The talk about language can be playful, investigative, analytic, poetic, philosophical – or corrective or in other ways censoring. Speakers have likely been talking about language about as long as there has been language, and while strands of language anxiety can be traced far back in the history of English (Machan 2009), the Early Modern English period witnessed a dramatic rise in self-consciousness about language use, which provided fertile ground for the rise of prescriptive language discourses. From prescriptive language discourses are born prescriptive meta-discourses, or conversations about the prescriptive conversations about language (e.g., the lively conversation of Truss's book in the proliferation of book reviews that appeared in 2004). This kind of heightened attention to, including debate about, language conventions encourages the kind of meta-awareness about language that can influence speakers' linguistic performance in specific contexts. And the sustained attention to correctness in institutionalized prescriptivism since the eighteenth century has entrenched a discourse of error into English language education, scholarly and popular usage guides, and less formal conversations about language in the private and public spheres.

Consider the article "This embarrasses you and I" that appeared in the *Wall Street Journal* in June 2012. It starts with a description of office managers correcting employees' grammar "gaffes" such as *There's new people* rather than *There are new people*. The article goes on to assert:

There's no easy fix. Some bosses and co-workers step in to correct mistakes, while others consult business-grammar guides for help. In a survey conducted earlier this year, about 45% of 430 employers said they were increasing employee-training programs to improve employees' grammar and other skills, according to the Society for Human Resource Management and AARP. (Shellenbarger 2012)

This article captures a prescriptive discourse – institutionalized in grammar guides, training programs, and elsewhere – that empowers bosses and co-workers to stop others in the office mid-sentence and correct what they deem to be errors. Whether or not the person corrected actually adopts the "correct" form or not, the act of correction heightens everyone's awareness that there is something grammatically perilous about the construction in question, potentially encouraging speakers to shy away from it or more closely monitor their choice for "correctness" (which can result in a hypercorrect form or some other less predictable result). The appearance of the article itself captures the meta-discourse about prescriptivism circulating in the US. It's striking, if we step back for a bit of critical distance: the phenomenon of grammar correction is, in and of itself, newsworthy, in a publication like the *Wall Street Journal*, which has no shortage of business and other news to cover. And the article certainly does not condemn practicing explicit verbal hygiene in the workplace, perhaps even accompanied by monetary penalties (e.g., the grammatical penalty jar into which speakers must contribute a quarter for each perceived language "error"). Consider the multiple levels of discourse at which speakers can then encounter language prescriptivism, long after their school years: from usage guides to explicit correction based on usage guides to newspaper articles describing the "grammar gaffes" that mar modern workplaces and require intervention.

What if linguists thought about speakers' contact with prescriptive discourses and meta-discourses more the way they think about speakers' contact with other languages/speakers of other languages? I'm not suggesting the two function the same way, but the comparison may be useful. The effects of language contact can range from widespread bilingualism and structural change (including the birth of entirely new languages), to the adoption of a few lexical borrowings, to conscious resistance of contact-induced change (Thomason 2007). Language contact can also lead to different literacy practices (e.g., the introduction of reading and writing, or the introduction of a new genre of writing) or, in the case of English, the adoption of a new alphabet (English was written in runes until the adoption of the Latin alphabet after AD 597). Language contact can change both the spoken and the written form of a language, just as prescriptivism can – a point I will return to with the second principle. The effects of language contact, if bilingualism is framed as part of speakers' cognition and language systems, also usefully blur the idea of a language's "outer history" and "inner history," much the way that effects of prescriptivism can.

Many traditional histories of the English language relegate institutionalized prescriptivism and the discourses it engenders to the "outer history" of English, if it is discussed at all. This is in keeping with the positioning of other historical meta-discourses about language such as the inkhorn controversy about borrowed words in the Renaissance (discussed in more detail in Chapter 4). The "outer history" is intended to describe the historical and social context of a historical period, to situate the discussion of the changes in the language's structure (its inner history). The binary of inner and outer history, while a convenient heuristic, suggests a clear-cut distinction between the two, although discussions of language contact typically blur the boundary. The presence of Old Norse or French or Spanish speakers, just to name a few possible groups, surfaces in both the outer history and inner history of English, although not always with as much attention to grammatical changes, as opposed to lexical changes, as the contact merits (see McWhorter 2008 for a provocative description of how contact with Celtic and Old Norse may have shaped English morphosyntax). Yet prescriptive discourses remain solely in the outer history, for at least two reasons. First, the general dismissal of prescriptivism as an "unsuccessful" enterprise can mean that its impact on usage is not included in the "inner history." Second, the impact of prescriptivism is often assumed to be primarily if not solely on the written language, and the "inner history" of the language assumes a focus on developments in the spoken language – "real" change (a concept already challenged in this chapter). As mentioned earlier, histories of English typically use the evidence from written texts to describe structural changes in "the language," understood as the language as it was spoken, rather than describing observable developments in particular written registers.

In delimiting the field of history of English, scholars have also often been careful to specify a focus on "linguistic developments" – as opposed to social, political, or cultural developments. Scholarly traditions that can be traced back to the Neogrammarians and to structuralism have resulted in one widely accepted interpretation of "linguistic" developments as those in the structure of the language: changes in the sound system, grammar, and lexicon of the language. Sociolinguistic approaches have challenged any such separation of the language system from speakers and the social factors that can influence language change. Görlach's previously mentioned definition of "purely linguistic" criteria, including the social and attitudinal in addition to the structural, embodies this challenge. The past few decades of work in sociolinguistics have provided persuasive evidence for how entangled the internal, social, and cognitive factors are and the critical importance of understanding social motivations for the actuation and spread of language change.[7] Yet some factors, such as contact with prescriptivism, receive less attention than contact with, for example, other languages. Widely circulating language ideologies, such as the ones promoted by prescriptivism, receive little attention at all as part of "linguistic history."

Yet the process of language standardization, an important part of English's history, relies on discourses and meta-discourses about language. As discussed in Chapter 1, prescriptivism helps to maintain a standard language as well as certain class and educational hierarchies, and both the concept and realities of Standard English have been fundamental to the history of Modern English. In this role, prescriptivism has created a range of insecurities in speakers about the correctness of their own language – hence the reliance on published resources for guidance and answers – as well as a range of justifications for disparaging the language of others (and ourselves). As modern sociolinguistics has persuasively argued, speakers' belief systems are part of understanding a language. In this way, circulating attitudes and belief systems represent a key external factor in understanding language variation and change. But that statement, which makes prescriptivism just an external factor, abstracts beliefs away from speakers. These circulating beliefs about language live side by side with all the other knowledge speakers possess about the language(s) they speak, blurring the distinction between internal, external, and cognitive factors in language change.

If speakers' contact with prescriptivism can productively be framed as a factor in language change, in some ways on the model of their contact with speakers of other languages, it is then helpful to think of standardization within the framework of the social factors that provide real-world motivations for speakers to adjust their speech patterns, both consciously and subconsciously. The concept of prestige cannot be extricated from the issue of a standard language. Specific languages, dialects, and linguistic features will carry prestige that may encourage their use in specific contexts. Standard dialects and their specific linguistic features often carry overt prestige, or prestige that is widely recognized across dialect communities and is typically associated with the educational system, professional workplace, and other forms of institutionalized social and political power. Overt prestige, however, represents only one kind of prestige

---

[7] See McMahon (1994) and Janda and Joseph (2003) for detailed summaries of these scholarly traditions.

that influences speakers' choices; it is often challenged by the more localized, sometimes referred to as covert, prestige that can be associated with nonstandard dialects and their linguistic features. Numerous sociolinguistic studies, beginning with Labov's groundbreaking work on Martha's Vineyard, have demonstrated the ways in which nonstandard features can index or signal an affiliation with a local community, a gendered (often masculine) and classed (often working-class) identity, or membership in a social community.

To frame this within Pierre Bourdieu's (1991) theorization of a linguistic marketplace, different kinds of language carry different kinds of cultural or symbolic capital. Very standard language forms can earn a speaker credibility in some contexts and undermine a speaker's credibility as a local community member in others. All speakers move between different styles and perhaps different dialects and languages in order to participate in different communities, many on a daily basis. The range of repertoires that each speaker possesses as a result, both spoken and written, can lead to new patterns of usage as features from one style or dialect are integrated into another context.

The linguistic marketplace establishes the value of different kinds of language through implicit and explicit evaluation. Much of the work in sociolinguistics has focused on speakers' less conscious or unconscious negotiation of linguistic forms as standard or vernacular, masculine or feminine, prestigious or stigmatized, local or supra-local, "in-group" or "out-group." But in the modern period in the history of English, many linguistic marketplaces are also filled with explicit prescriptive discourses that seek to make speakers highly conscious of what usage is valued and not valued. Whenever anyone says, "But that's not a real word," or criticizes another for "bad" speech or writing, they are participating in a meta-discourse about language that makes people self-conscious about their usage. In this way, standardization is not part of an "outer" history divorced from structural changes in the language. The ongoing prescription that is part of standardization is part of many speakers' daily experience with the language, both written and spoken. And while some of that experience is contact with published resources about standard or correct language, part of the experience is also participation in a set of public discourses that are dependent on and perpetuate the belief that there is a right way to speak and write and many wrong ways.

Metalinguistic discussions about "correctness" are relevant to the historical development of *whom*. The gradual replacement of *whom* by *who* began centuries ago, as part of the ongoing loss of case distinctions in the language; there are examples of *who* in object position as early as the fifteenth century. The form *whom* is healthiest after prepositions (e.g., *by whom*), but even in this position *who* appears in spoken discourse. And yet, not only has *whom* not yet died, there is currently some overuse of *whom* in formal contexts (e.g., *the person whom is involved*). Because speakers are aware that they often use *who* where traditional grammars tell them to use *whom*, they can overcorrect in formal contexts. As this example shows, prescriptivism can have unintended, "rogue" consequences. Language history has to take prescriptivism into account to understand the progression of the change as it takes what might otherwise be unexpected turns.

Other meta-discourses about correctness, especially in the twentieth century, have pushed back against established standard forms and advocated the deliberate replacement of established standard forms with new standard forms. An excellent example is the movement to replace generic *he* in formal written prose, as discussed in Chapter 5. This kind of socially and politically responsive prescriptivism, when it becomes institutionalized, has shaped contemporary English usage.

The history of spoken and written language

How important is texting language to the history of Modern English? Does a texting acronym have to become part of the spoken language to become important and included in a historical description? Current linguists' intense interest in the phenomenon of electronically mediated communication (EMC) has meant that texting language often gets included in descriptions of the current developments in the language. This medium, whose speed and informality can resemble the spoken language, but whose form remains written, merits inclusion in the telling of this moment in history. And it should raise – but hasn't yet raised, that I have seen – the more global question of the place of the written language in the history of English.

To tell the history of a language is, or should be, to tell the history of all manifestations of that language: all its spoken dialects and all its written and spoken registers. It has long been recognized that the written language can and does develop separately from the spoken, but this fact should not justify marginalizing the history of the written language in favor of telling the history of the spoken language. A history of "a language" is richer if it tells the history of both the written and the spoken registers of the language and the relationship between the two. There is no need to privilege the spoken language at the expense of the written or vice versa. The historical development of both specific written and spoken registers merits a central place in a language's history as does the shifting distance between them. For any language with a written form, the spoken and written forms change in distinct ways and/or at different speeds; in addition, different registers of the written language and different dialects of the spoken language typically change in distinct ways and/or at different speeds. The development of written registers is an integral part of the history of a language, no matter the relationship of the written to the spoken.

If and when the linguistic understanding of "the language" in a field like history of English comes to encompass the written as an object of study, not just a vehicle for tracking the spoken, then part of the scholarly project becomes understanding the development of specific written registers such as scientific writing and electronically mediated writing, including e-mail and texting. Just these two examples pose interestingly different case studies in terms of, on the one hand, growing distance from colloquial language toward more formal language in scientific writing (Atkinson 1999; Halliday 1993) and, on the other hand, shrinking distance from colloquial spoken language in fast-paced written electronic exchanges. Historical sociolinguistic scholarship that draws from historical corpora has already laid critical groundwork for integrating a more developed focus on written language into the history of the English language. The strategic design of large corpora to be representative of multiple registers in addition to writers' gender, region, etc., as well as the development of multiple specialized corpora of single registers in historical periods, has meant that scholars can track how language changes spread from register to register – including from spoken to written language or vice versa and from informal to formal registers of spoken or written language or vice versa.

The fluctuating distance between written and spoken registers provides one fascinating lens through which to tell the history of English. For the Old English and Middle English periods, scholars assume a much closer correspondence between the written and spoken, with the recognition that the record does not preserve very informal registers of the written. While there were some local written standards, these periods predate widespread language standardization, and spelling and morphosyntactic differences by region suggest that scribes saw the written language as in some way capturing their individual or local pronunciation and grammar. The prevalence of coordinated or paratactic clause structures in these periods is more reflective of the spoken language than the highly subordinated clause structures that come to characterize high written prose in the Renaissance. Consider this heavily subordinated sentence from John Milton's *Areopagitica* (1644):

Another sort there be who when they hear that all things shall be order'd, all things regulated and setl'd, nothing writt'n but what passes through the custom-house of certain Publicans that have the tunaging and poundaging of all free-spok'n truth, will straight give themselvs up into your hands, mak'em and cut'em out what religion ye please.

The Renaissance witnesses a growing chasm between the spoken and written, with the rise of language standardization and the spread of English to more scientific, legal, and other genres that had been formerly written in Latin. To this day, written academic, legal, and medical registers are marked by stark differences from spoken language, from the prevalence of nominalization (e.g., when the verb *enhance* becomes the noun *enhancement*) to the relative paucity of first-person pronouns to highly subordinated sentence structures.

At the turn of the millennium something interestingly cyclical appears to be happening online, in journalistic prose, and in other registers, where the written

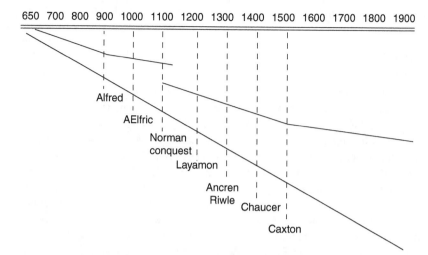

650 700 800 900 1000 1100 1200 1300 1400 1500 1600 1700 1800 1900

Alfred

AElfric

Norman
conquest

Layamon

Ancren
Riwle

Chaucer

Caxton

Figure 2.1 Hockett's (1957) timeline of written and spoken English (the more gently sloping upper line represents the written language, whose rate of change is slowed by standardization in various periods)

language is creeping back toward patterns more characteristic of the spoken language – a process referred to as colloquialization (Leech et al. 2009). In other words, the distance between the structure and style of spoken and written language that has characterized much of the modern period is narrowing, at least in some registers. Current colloquialization of written prose includes the rise of features such as semi-modals (e.g., *have to*), contractions, and the progressive.

More than five decades ago, Hockett (1957) proposed a timeline for the history of English that separated the written from the spoken (see Figure 2.1). In so doing, Hockett aims to capture the discrepancies between the two, often caused by the innovative role of the spoken (that is, language changes often begin in the spoken language) or, from a different angle, the lagging position of the written. As he explains:

With Alfred, the 'writing' line begins to slope downwards more gently, becoming further and further removed from the 'speech' line. This is because Alfred's highly prestigious writings set an orthographic and stylistic habit, which tended to persist in the face of changing habits of speech. The Norman Conquest leads rather quickly to an end of this older orthographic practice; the new 'writing' line which begins approximately at this time represents the rather drastically altered orthographic habits developed under the influence of the French-trained scribes. I have begun this line somewhat closer to the 'speech' line at the time, on the assumption – of which I am not certain – that the rather radical change in writing habits led, at least at first, to a somewhat closer matching of contemporary speech. From this time until Caxton and printing, the 'writing' line follows more or less inadequately the changing pattern of speech, never getting very close to it, yet constantly being modified in the direction of it. But with Caxton, and the introduction of printing, there soon comes about the real deep-freeze on English spelling-habits which has persisted to our own day. (65–66)

Prescriptivism's most obvious effects manifest themselves in the written language. The written language, inherently more planned (although new forms of EMC are challenging that traditional statement), often undergoes editing with a focus on "correctness" – which many writers take to refer to close adherence to prescriptive guides about spelling, punctuation, word choice, grammatical structures, and stylistic alternatives. In this way, one of the effects of prescriptivism is a discrepancy between the written and the spoken caused by speakers editing out spoken features – be those recent changes in the language or long disfavored constructions. Within this framework, the grammar checker in Microsoft Word demands the linguistic historian's attention, as it shapes the prose of many a writer of English. Whether or not these changes infiltrate the spoken language does not make them any less or more important in understanding current developments in the English language, spoken and written.

Sometimes speakers' interaction with the written language does affect the spoken. Perhaps the most obvious examples are spelling pronunciations, which result from a highly literate society and a highly standardized spelling system in which some spellings do not reflect pronunciation. One historical example is the word *adventure*. English speakers borrowed the French word *aventure* in the thirteenth century. The interest in the classical roots of borrowed words in the Renaissance led to the respelling of the word as *adventure*, to reflect the Latin etymon *adventura*, and the respelling led to a pronunciation of the word with /d/. The word *often* provides a current example. Records from the seventeenth century indicate that many speakers no longer pronounced the /t/ in *often*, save perhaps for some speakers in careful speech; a similar loss of medial /t/ occurs in *soften*. Many speakers, perhaps especially in formal contexts, are now putting the /t/ back into *often*, assuming that it should be there and speakers are being lazy in not pronouncing it. The *OED* notes: "The pronunciation with -t- has frequently been considered to be hypercorrection in recent times." In these cases, the spoken language moves closer to the written spelling.

Prescriptivism and/or a sense of correctness can also encourage speakers to distance their writing from their speech, without necessarily affecting their speech. An excellent example is the use of *hopefully* in spoken and written American English in the twentieth through the twenty-first centuries. *Hopefully* started to be used as a sentence adverb meaning 'I hope, it is hoped' in the first decades of the twentieth century. It was not until the 1960s that prescriptive language commentators noticed the change and soundly condemned it as ambiguous and bad usage. The usage note in the *American Heritage Dictionary* recognizes the idiosyncrasy of stigmatizing *hopefully* as a sentence adverb and not *mercifully* or *frankly*; it also notes that the Usage Panel has become more strident in its opposition over the years: "Only 34 percent of the Panel accepted the usage of *hopefully* in our 1999 survey, down from 44 percent in 1969." It appears that this opposition has had little to no effect on spoken usage. A search of the Corpus of Contemporary American English, a collection of over 450 million words of spoken and written English from the 1990s and 2000s, reveals that *hopefully*, while not used as often as *frankly*, appears a healthy 43.1 times per million words in the spoken language.[8] It is easy, therefore, to think of this kind of prescriptivism as an amusing diversion for language pundits, the material of usage notes in dictionaries and style guides with little to no life outside these resources.

However, the prescriptive focus on this construction beginning in the 1960s seems to have had an effect on written usage. To take just one example of formal edited prose, a search of the Time Magazine Corpus reveals a dramatic drop in the use of *hopefully* that seems to coincide with active prescriptivism against it – see Figure 2.2. That the effects may only appear in the written form does not make the change irrelevant to the history of English. A result like this one demonstrates the ways in which prescriptivism can distance formal written from

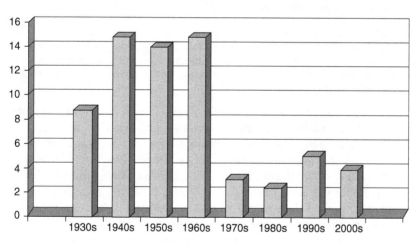

Figure 2.2 Frequency of *hopefully* in Time Magazine Corpus from the 1920s through 2000s

---

[8] Of the first fifty instances of *hopefully* in the spoken register, only one was used to mean 'full of hope'; the other forty-nine instances were sentence adverbs meaning 'I hope', ' we hope', 'it is hoped'.

colloquial spoken usage (as opposed to, for instance, how a spelling pronunciation brings them closer together).

In April 2012 the *Associated Press Stylebook* lifted its prohibition on using *hopefully* to mean 'it is hoped, we hope'. This change made headlines in newspapers such as the *Washington Post* and was featured on National Public Radio. Accepted by some journalists, the decision was fiercely rejected by others, who argued that journalistic prose cannot tolerate the form's ambiguity the way that spoken language can. Historians of the language can watch how long it takes for *hopefully* to rise in formal written usage (editors sometimes demonstrate a lag in picking up the lifting of proscriptions), bringing the spoken and written language closer with regard to this feature.

Change above and below social awareness

The history of the English language encompasses linguistic developments occurring both below the level of consciousness – or what some would call "naturally" – and above the level of consciousness, which is also very "natural" within a speech community. Sarah G. Thomason (2007), in a study of language contact and deliberate change, has also challenged the natural–unnatural distinction in her argument that deliberate choices by speakers can result in nontrivial language change. She concludes:

> speakers are much more able and willing to manipulate their linguistic resources consciously than they have usually been given credit (or blame) for; and I see no way in which one could establish that this type of linguistic behavior, which is actually quite common in individuals and not vanishingly rare in speech communities, is less natural than unconscious linguistic change. (59)

Explicit meta-discourses about a linguistic phenomenon or construction, such as (but certainly not limited to) those involved in prescriptivism, may facilitate speakers making more conscious changes in response. When speakers use a word or grammatical construction and are simultaneously aware of that word or construction as the object of prescription or other ideologically motivated discourses, that fact alone may make the linguistic feature particularly susceptible to change, and the written language is especially subject to conscious monitoring. This self-consciousness may result in speakers avoiding the construction or it may involve a form of self-correction – or it may provoke speakers to comment on the language of others, thereby spreading more widely the linguistic concern. Language ideology and language anxiety play out in day-to-day linguistic decisions by real speakers and writers. In an era of intense prescriptivism, many speakers and writers need to navigate, at least in some contexts, the social perils of breaking – and in some cases of adhering to – prescriptive guidance. Of course, conscious awareness of the social meaning of specific linguistic features can lead to many other results, such as the enregisterment of dialect features as emblematic of a place (Johnstone et al. 2006) or the emphasizing of distinctive dialect features to distinguish one's community and insiders/outsiders.

Certainly many structural changes happen below the level of speakers' consciousness. Current examples include the merger of the vowels /ɑ/ and /ɔ/ in *cot* and *caught*; the shift of the past participle of a verb such as *shave* from an irregular form (*shaven*) to a regular form (*shaved*); and the grammaticalization – that is, the shift of a lexical word such as a verb to a function word such as an auxiliary verb – of *have to* (or *hafta*) such that it can function as an emerging auxiliary verb. But even some of these changes may be affected by speakers' attitudes, by which dialects have prestige in different contexts, by speakers' desires to express membership in particular communities through their language, and other sociolinguistic factors. For example, speakers' participation in the Northern Cities Vowel Shift (a vowel change in cities such as Detroit, Chicago, and Buffalo, as well as surrounding areas, that is resulting in words such as *bag* sounding like "beg" and *block* like "black") is influenced by the communities to which they belong and/or aspire to belong (see, e.g., Gordon 2001).[9]

English speakers' attitudes and linguistic performances in the modern period may also be influenced by processes such as standardization, which have resulted in standard varieties of English carrying institutional prestige. Patterns of which speakers use *-in'* (/n/) for *-ing* (/ŋ/) in what contexts, for example, are often tied to the evaluation of the former as nonstandard; it can function, therefore, as a marker of local vernacular identity, of masculinity in some cases, etc. Politicians who style-shift between more colloquial *runnin' for office* and more formal *running for office* based on audience considerations are typically aware of the formality switch and may or may not be consciously aware of the shift in progressive verb forms specifically.

Other structural changes may be even more overtly legislated or evaluated, sometimes through prescriptive catchphrases such as "gotten is rotten," "*ain't* ain't a word," and "the only thing that can be impacted is a tooth." Such overt prescription does not necessarily mean that any change corresponds to the legislation: for example, American English speakers continue to use the historical form *have gotten*, whereas in the UK speakers tend to use *have got*, but many will avoid it in formal speech and writing due to a sense that there is something wrong with the construction (due to prescriptive efforts over the past two centuries to make American English conform to UK English in this respect). *Ain't* gains some of its expressive power in some contexts due to its condemnation

---

[9] Jeremy Smith (1996) argues that similar factors may have affected the development of the Great Vowel Shift.

as a non-word or at least a very nonstandard one. And the diffusion of *impact* as a verb into written English, given that it is a well-established development in spoken English at this point, is affected (or one might say impacted) by the extent to which this development is on a writer's and/or editor's radar as an inappropriate form for formal written English (as described also with the history of *hopefully* in the twentieth century).

To provide another example, although linguists do not fully understand all the factors involved in the relatively common construction "between you and I" (and its counterparts of PREPOSITION + CONJOINED NOUN PHRASE with at least one personal pronoun – e.g., "for he and I"), the development is likely aided by hypercorrection or overcorrection toward a form that speakers think is right but is actually not prescriptively correct. In some other constructions where the pronoun *me* may feel more natural or intuitive for speakers, such as "My sister's older than me" or "It is me," prescriptive voices dictate that *I* is correct: in the first case, the argument is that *than* functions as a subordinating conjunction not a preposition ("My sister's older than I (am)"); in the second, because linking verbs such as *is* take a predicative noun phrase not an object, the subject case ("I") is required. Both of these corrections are challengeable (for example, French employs the object case in *C'est moi* ('It is me')), but that is irrelevant to the point here. The pervasiveness of the corrections may have caused speakers to think twice as they use these kinds of constructions and other constructions involving object pronouns – and in some cases to change their speech and writing toward a form they perceive as correct (or at least more formal), be that *I* or *myself* (as in *between Yeltsin and myself*). This overcorrection reinforces a construction that makes prescriptivists cringe (as noted earlier, examples of this construction predate institutionalized prescriptivism), but it appears regularly in highly formal spoken discourse.

President Barack Obama's use of phrases such as *a difficult decision for Michelle and I* was examined on the Opinion pages of the *New York Times* by Patricia O'Conner and Stewart Kellerman, authors of the book *Origins of the Specious: Myths and Misconceptions of the English Language* (2009a). The article points out that these constructions have been in the language for centuries and did not become an object of severe critique until the nineteenth century. For all that, however, they conclude, "an educated speaker is expected to keep his pronouns in line," which means no *I*'s as the object of prepositions, even in conjoined constructions (O'Conner and Kellerman 2009b). Nancy Pickelsimer Elkins, from Chapel Hill, North Carolina, responds in a letter to the editor: "I know that President Obama is capable of correcting that in his oratory. Now let's hope that all the rest of our fellow Americans will take note and alter their own usage accordingly." This exchange captures the interaction between meta-discourses about language and the conscious language changes they sometimes strive to promote.

Levels of magnitude of language change

Some may argue that the examples of change mentioned in this chapter, from generic *he* to sentence adverb *hopefully* to the pronunciation of *often*, are just a few words here or there – not fundamental language change. These changes are not the stuff of history. In some cases, it may be more prescriptive talk than anything else. To this argument I have two responses.

First, language change often happens word by word. When histories of English discuss borrowing, for example, even one word borrowed from another language (e.g., *moose*, borrowed from Algonquin into North American English in the seventeenth century) can be seen as noteworthy evidence about language contact. The rise of single semi-modals such as *gonna* and *hafta* have received significant scholarly attention as important grammatical developments in the language. And even more global processes of sound change still may happen word by word through lexical diffusion.

Language change also happens at the level of the individual, although linguists tend to examine it at the level of the community (see Johnstone [1996] for a foundational treatment of the linguistic individual). It is a question of scale and to some extent of agency. Thomason (2007, 45) stresses the importance of the individual in the possibility of linguistic change as well as in innovation, which is brought about by one or more speakers. The change will then spread, or not spread, through a broader community. With regard to conscious agency, Thomason is careful to point out, and I concur, that "the extreme results of speakers' deliberate decisions are – by all the available evidence – very rare" (57) and do not invalidate the comparative method for studying language change and relationships within language families. But, as Thomason makes clear, this caveat is different from asserting that conscious change is always or inherently insignificant in its contribution to language change – or, I would add, to the telling of language history. Single words and individual innovations can make history.

Second, the stuff of language history should include the debates about language being waged publicly in newspapers, online, in reviews of dictionaries and usage guides, and elsewhere. Recall Read's assertion that to understand a language, one must examine speakers' linguistic attitudes. Historians of English have long recognized that the inkhorn debates of the sixteenth century should be included in a textbook (although I will argue in Chapter 4 they should be integrated differently), and current debates about identity terms, the furor over the treatment of *ain't* in *Webster's Third New International Dictionary* (1961), the development of usage notes in dictionaries that have the power to affect editorial style decisions, and the emergence of grammar checkers should be included as well. They have the power to shape usage and to reveal a culture's linguistic preoccupations.

To take just one example, the reviews of Truss's book *Eats, Shoots & Leaves* expose a great deal about current prejudices and beliefs about the English language. The entwining of grammar/usage and morality carries on, and Truss is enmeshed in this discourse. She describes careful punctuation as good manners; punctuation shows courtesy to the reader. So, of course, "bad" punctuation represents bad manners, and reviewers buy right into this analogy. Murray Waldren, in the *Weekend Australian*, stresses "society, as they say, is as lax as its language" (1/24/04). And Michelle Hewitson, in the *New Zealand Herald*, asks: "Because what else is bad grammar and the misuse of apostrophes but bad manners?" (9/4/04). Punctuation is a "casualty in the assault of our uncaring age," another reviewer writes (Janice Kennedy, the *Ottawa Citizen*, 5/2/04). For all these reasons, reviewer after reviewer side with the sticklers, for, as Truss herself states, "they have virtue on their side" (Truss, *Financial Times*, 12/19/03).

Then, in an odd twist, old rivalries between American English and UK English surface in the reviews. One of the most virulent attacks on Truss's book and its style appeared in the *New Yorker* (6/28/04), written by Louis Menand. Menand rants about Truss's mistakes, which was a common strategy for critics – what better way to criticize a prescriptive usage guide on punctuation than to point out its flaws in punctuation? Here is a short sample:

The first punctuation mistake in "Eats, Shoots & Leaves"... appears in the dedication, where a nonrestrictive clause is not preceded by a comma. It is a wild ride downhill from there ... [I]t's hard to fend off the suspicion that the whole thing might be a hoax.

Menand expresses annoyance about the lack of translation into American punctuation conventions and patriotically touts American precision over British laxness:

The supreme peculiarity of this peculiar publishing phenomenon is that the British are less rigid about punctuation and related matters ... than Americans are. An Englishwoman lecturing Americans on semicolons is a little like an American lecturing the French on sauces.

Menand's opening shot elicits rapid return fire from across the ocean, reopening a debate that harks back to Noah Webster and H. L. Mencken about the status of American English compared to its "mother tongue." Andrew Franklin, director of Profile Books, says Menand is jealous and humorless. John Mullan, in the *Guardian*, claims that Menand is xenophobic and threatened that Americans might look to the UK for grammar advice. Michael Skapinker, in the *Financial Times* (7/7/04), provides a more extended response to Menand. He begins:

The New Yorker magazine is famous for its fact checkers, so I would love to see the research that preceded publication of the assertion that 'the British are less rigid about punctuation and related matters ... than Americans are.' How big was the sample? And were the British uniformly sloppy, or did the study reveal national variations?

Bryan Garner, one of the best-known current American prescriptivists, stepped into the fray with a 2005 article in the *Texas Law Review*. "Any experienced editor," he writes, "will probably conclude that, on the whole, British standards of punctuation are somewhat lower than American ones ... Yes, the Brits... have long needed help in punctuation. Not that Americans can't use some as well, but the British need it even more." Clearly this meta-discourse about punctuation was about much more than just the correct placement of commas and apostrophes.

Prescriptivism interacts with the many other factors influencing a language's history, with outcomes that can be difficult to predict. Prescriptive discourses reveal the ideologies speakers come into contact with in their daily linguistic lives. Language does vary and change, and a lot of folks are concerned about that. Linguists do well to take that concern, and its role in the history of the language, seriously. Binaries such as spoken–written, inner–outer, above–below awareness, and natural–unnatural, if they are employed to privilege one part of the pair over the other in terms of what makes language history, hinder fuller explanations of how language changes and fuller accounts of all that constitutes a language's history.

3   Checking grammar and grammar checkers

The sentence which opens this chapter (and which you are reading right now) has made the Microsoft Word Grammar Checker (MSGC) unhappy. It puts a green squiggly line under the string of words *which opens this chapter* and suggests the following rewording: *that opens this chapter*. The Microsoft grammar checker perpetuates the idea that the relative pronouns *which* and *that* are not interchangeable in a restrictive relative clause such as *the sentence ____ opens this chapter*. There are at least three ways to make the green line go away in this sentence: (a) turn off the grammar checker entirely; (b) click "ignore" when the grammar checker suggests changing the sentence; or (c) change the sentence, replacing the word *which* with *that* or revising the syntax so that it doesn't require a relative pronoun (e.g., *this chapter's opening sentence*). A significant number of writers, however, do not know how to turn off the grammar checker, which is on by default, or do not have the confidence to turn off and/or ignore the grammar checker. These writers may feel some compunction to obey the grammar checker, assuming it to be a reliable authority that is alerting the writer to a confirmed error.[1]

The assumed authority of the Microsoft grammar checker, combined with its ubiquity, make it arguably the most powerful prescriptive language force in the world at this point. Any best-selling usage guide pales in comparison, both in terms of the number sold (a few million compared with hundreds of millions) and in terms of the ready availability of the prescriptive guidance. The grammar checker requires no additional purchase; it comes with the Microsoft suite of programs. Writers do not even need to get up from the chair and walk to the bookshelf to consult the grammar checker as it is already available on the

---

[1] The terminology used to describe this program as a "grammar checker" reveals the same confusion between grammar and style discussed in Chapter 1. I will discuss how "grammar" and "style" are addressed in the program in more detail later in the chapter as part of the discussion of specific rules, but the distinction is not entirely transparent, as is true in many published usage guides. Capitalization, for example, is handled as grammar, whereas writing out numerals is considered style. The use of *like* as a subordinating conjunction is grammar, whereas other "informal" choices such as contractions count as style. Sentence fragments in general fall under grammar, but informal fragments such as "A beautiful day!" are treated under style.

computer. The embedding of the grammar checker into the Microsoft Word program, with no author's name attached, can make its rules and advice seem neutral and authoritative; its similarities to published usage guides can become almost hidden.

Histories of English should ensure that the grammar checker does not remain hidden behind the finished written Word products that provide linguists data about Modern English usage. The grammar checker represents an important and powerful continuation of the prescriptive grammatical tradition that took hold in the eighteenth century. As such, it too has the potential to influence actual usage (mostly written) and to perpetuate meta-discourses about language correctness. In sum, given its powerful prescriptive presence in the lives of many English speakers and writers, the Microsoft grammar checker is a sociolinguistic factor that should be taken seriously in the history of Modern English, especially in terms of the development of standard written, edited language. At this point, Microsoft Word is the "most widely used word processing software in the world," with 80–90 percent of the market at the turn of the century (McGee and Ericsson 2002, 454–455). As Baldwin (2002, 6) puts it, "The world runs on Microsoft Word documents"; and those documents all come with the grammar checker not only installed but already on.

The Microsoft grammar checker is now the English teacher that some writers never had or never listened to (just to end a sentence with a preposition, which made the green squiggle appear under the word *to*). It reminds writers of grammar and style rules as they type, aiming to help make their prose conform to accepted standards – or at least to what writers have every reason to assume are accepted standards (and usually are, with a few notable exceptions discussed later in this chapter). This monitoring is not necessarily, in and of itself, a terrible thing. The program can usefully alert writers, both experienced and less experienced, to a potentially infelicitous construction that merits a second look. That said, composition instructors rightly worry that the grammar checker can make students worry about the prettiness of the written product even while they are in the drafting stages and should be focused on process, not product. Instructors should also worry (but this doesn't always seem to be the case) that the grammar checker promotes a discourse of "error" around grammar and style, rather than one of standardness, formality, and context-dependent choices. In other words, it conflates different strands of prescriptivism under the umbrella of "error." The grammar checker also introduces a few "errors" not endorsed by most if any published usage guides. Why, for example, doesn't the grammar checker like the sentence-initial *And* in the second paragraph of this chapter?

Integrating the grammar checker into the history of Modern English requires positioning it in relation to the history of grammatical prescriptivism and in relation to scholarship on the power of prescriptive usage rules – to date those published in usage guides – to influence actual written usage. It is helpful to consider the grammar checker a published prescriptive usage guide that builds on three hundred years of prescriptive grammar advice and that has the power to spread specific prescriptive rules and ideologies around the English-speaking (and writing) world in ways no previous published usage guide ever has. It would be irresponsible to tell the "linguistic history" of English at the beginning of the twenty-first century without considering speakers' and writers' interaction with the Microsoft grammar checker.

In this chapter I describe the rise of grammatical prescriptivism as context for understanding the authority of the grammar checker, which has snuck (or sneaked – the grammar checker allows both the more American, newer past participle form *snuck* and the older form *sneaked*) into English speakers' and writers' lives. The grammar checker continues the three-hundred-year old tradition of hunting for errors in written prose and catching features of spoken language that might appear in written language, from nonstandard constructions to grammatical innovations to colloquialisms. "Young and old alike, cautiously and carelessly," Reva Potter and Dorothy Fuller (2008, 36) stress, "we are all tutored by the word processor's grammar checker." But is it just an annoying thing to be turned off or ignored or does it have the power to change usage? To consider the relationship of grammatical tutoring and actual usage, I examine a selection of the specific rules that the Microsoft grammar checker enforces and the potential implications for written edited English, given scholarship on the historical and current interaction of grammatical prescriptivism and grammatical change. I also stress the importance, in telling the history of English, of the discourse of error perpetuated by the grammar checker.

The rise of grammar checkers in the prescriptive tradition

Computer grammar checkers first became available in the 1980s, and these early versions were stand-alone programs that could be purchased by businesses, academic institutions, and the like (Vernon 2000, 330). At that time, the acquisition and implementation of a grammar checker was a conscious choice – and a reasonably expensive one. The 1980s also witnessed Microsoft shipping out its initial version of Word for MS-DOS 1.00. Current undergraduate students in my courses seem to have trouble imagining that when I entered college in 1987, personal computers were a novelty; I took with me a personal word processor, on which I could see about four lines of type at a time, and I remember going to the computer lab in my junior year to visit the four small Macintosh computers there. I graduated right before grammar checkers became standard in computer word processing programs: it was late 1991 when Microsoft adopted Houghton Mifflin's program CORRECTEXT for integration into Word for Windows 2.0,[2] followed shortly thereafter by WORDPERFECT for Windows 5.2's integration of GRAMMATIK 5 (Vernon 2000, 330–331). In 1995, Word 95, which still employed CORRECTEXT, introduced background spelling, which modern users know as the red squiggly lines beneath words that the program does not recognize and/or believes are misspelled.

Then came 1997, when Microsoft unveiled its own grammar checker, developed by Microsoft's Natural Language Processing group. Word 97 featured "background grammar," which could check grammar with green squiggly lines parallel to the checking of spelling. Doug Lowe effused in *More* WORD *97 for* WINDOWS *for Dummies* (1997): "The first word processor available that comes with a Grammar Checker worth using" (p. 36, quoted in McGee and Ericsson 2002, 459). But the Natural Language Processing (NLP) group, made up primarily of computational linguists, had and continues to have priorities other than creating an editing program. The group's primary goal was focused on automation and usability, on helping users and computers interact through speech recognition. George Heidorn (2000), one of the founding members of the NLP, describes the grammar checker as a beneficial byproduct, "an example of a real-world NLP application that provides intelligent writing assistance" (182). It is a branch of the system: "it has as its heart a full-blown, multipurpose natural language processor, which produces a syntactic parse structure and, when desired, a logical form, for each sentence" (182). As described by Heidorn, the processing in the NLP system occurs in six stages, the first three of which are worth describing in a bit more detail to understand how dictionaries and the grammar checker fit into the system.

The first stage of the natural language processor takes the text and breaks it into individual tokens, typically words and punctuation marks but also some multi-word entries such as phrasal prepositions (e.g., *in spite of*). When it was designed in the early to mid 1990s, this stage generally relied on two dictionaries for word look-up: *The Longman Dictionary of Contemporary English* (1978) and *The American Heritage Dictionary of the English Language* (3rd edn., 1992). The program is transparent about the dictionaries that serve as the source for spelling corrections and part-of-speech information; the same cannot be said for the sources of grammar and style corrections, as I will discuss. The second and third stages result in a syntactic portrait of all the text's sentences. Words are grouped into phrases, which are then understood in relation to each other. The processor, in the third stage, attempts to create "more reasonable attachments" for modifiers, going beyond proximity (Heidorn 2000, 184). For example, this stage sorts through prepositional phrases to determine which should appear at the clause level as opposed to, say, the noun phrase level.

---

[2] CORRECTEXT had a full parsing engine, which analyzed and decomposed sentences, and an error correction facility (Dobrin 1990, 68).

Some of this "reattachment" occurs at the syntactic level (Heidorn provides the example of obvious prepositional phrases of time, which should appear at the clause level – e.g., *we left at noon*) and some at the semantic level, which requires significant additional processing: take Heidorn's example of the sentence *I saw a bird with a telescope* and imagine the semantic work the processor must do to determine that it is more likely that the phrase *with a telescope* is adverbial, describing the act of seeing by the pronoun *I* (I saw with a telescope), than that the phrase is adjectival, describing an accouterment of the bird (a bird with a telescope). The grammar checker, as opposed to the natural language processor, functions without doing the semantic reattachment (Heidorn 2000, 185), which saves it a significant processing burden and time.

The grammar checker, branching off the NLP system, relies on another set of rules that applies to specific syntactic constituents (e.g., a relative clause). Heidorn (2000, 190) explains the process as follows:

Each rule tests for a particular error situation and fires if it occurs. The overall flow of processing is to go through every node in the parse tree, from top to bottom, left to right, and for each node to consider each rule that is relevant for a node of that type. For example, if the node covers a clause, then the clause rules, such as the rule that handles subject–verb number disagreement, would be applied to that node.

In addition, the grammar checker has a special mechanism for handling words that are often confused, such as *its* and *it's*. The syntactic parser is programmed to try both words in the sentence and if the word that is not used parses more logically in the sentence than the word that is used, then the grammar checker will suggest that alternative.

As this description should make clear, the green squiggly line under a word or clause to signal that there is a grammatical issue of some kind with the construction (or an "error" as the program would call it – a problematic label I return to later in the chapter) results from a complex set of processes, most of which involve highly descriptive syntactic parsing, as opposed to prescriptive rule-dispensing. (For the record the grammar checker does not like anything about the length of that sentence: it violates the 60-word length rule, which is certainly not a bad precedent but one that is violated at times in acceptable academic prose and elsewhere.) The grammar checker is, as Heidorn puts it, one application of the underlying language processor. Which grammatical and stylistic rules would go into the grammar checker, and how they would be presented to Word users, seem to have received less expert attention than other parts of the system.

The issue of precisely what kind of expertise underwrites prescriptive rules and the people who publish them harkens back to the earliest days of published grammatical prescriptivism. "The eighteenth-century grammarians were not language experts," Don Chapman (2008, 22) summarizes, "at least not the way we think of them today. Grammars were written not by linguists, but by clergymen, schoolmasters, booksellers and other seemingly self-appointed grammarians." Of course, part of the explanation lies in the fact that linguistics as an expert discipline did not develop until the nineteenth century. At least some of the early grammarians were immersed in the intellectual discussions of language at the time, even if the impetus for some of the grammars was highly commercial as well as educational (see Tieken-Boon van Ostade [2012] for a discussion of the powerful role of booksellers at the end of the eighteenth century). It is unsurprising that eighteenth-century views of language might seem unscientific by today's standards, as do other aspects of eighteenth-century science. Chapman (2008, 35) insightfully points out: "[T]he problem is not that the early grammarians had naïve ideas; the real problem is that those ideas have remained current in our prescriptivist tradition." The Microsoft grammar checker only exacerbates this problem.

Beginning in the eighteenth century, the proliferation of more prescriptive grammar books enshrined some rules about language that were not especially well founded. The scholarly literature is replete with examples, from the rule against stranded prepositions to the condemnation of double negatives as illogical to the prescription of generic *he* (and sometimes implicit proscription of generic *they*). Grammarians and other writers of grammar books (the two are not always synonymous) in the nineteenth and twentieth centuries added more rules than they discarded, including rules about, for example, split infinitives and the use of *that* and *which* in relative clauses. The authority many of these rules have acquired over the decades is only supplemented by their inclusion in the Microsoft grammar checker, where they appear both automatically and without citation, as if this rule is a given for "good grammar." In other words, the grammar checker has become a new nameless, faceless "they" behind the authoritative statements that begin with "They say you can't . . . ," as in "They say you can't end a sentence with a preposition."

The eighteenth century was a watershed moment in the prescriptive grammatical tradition that remains with English speakers and writers to this day. The excellent scholarship written about the rise of prescriptive grammars in this era highlights the rise of two important phenomena for understanding the current historical moment: the growing emphasis on grammatical "error" and the entrenchment of a tradition of grammatical error hunting (see, for example, Michael 1970; Crystal 2006; Tieken Boon van Ostade 2008c). The number of grammars skyrocketed over the course of the late eighteenth century and throughout the nineteenth century, and grammarians during this period changed the tone of the grammatical admonishments: the discourse was no longer just about improving style and rhetoric but also about identifying and eliminating error.

As the Milroys' model of standardization suggests (see Chapter 2), prescriptivism tends to follow on the heels of codification. By the eighteenth century the codification of the language – or the attempt to fix or stabilize it and record it – was steaming ahead, with important lexicographical milestones such as Nathan Bailey's *An Universal Etymological English Dictionary* (1721) – the first effort to create a comprehensive dictionary of the language – and Samuel Johnson's *Dictionary of the English Language* (1755). Johnson's words in the Dictionary's Preface, quoted also in the Introduction to this book, provide a useful reminder of the goals of the era in which Johnson was working:

Those who have been persuaded to think well of my design, require that it should fix our language, and put a stop to those alterations which time and chance have hitherto been suffered to make in it without opposition. With this consequence I will confess that I flattered myself for a while; but now begin to fear that I have indulged expectation which neither reason nor experience can justify.

As discussed in more detail in Chapter 4, the extent to which Johnson envisioned his project as descriptive versus prescriptive has been provocatively debated (e.g., McDermott 2005; Barnbrook 2005), and it appears to have been a bit of both.

The intense interest in scientific classification and taxonomy that characterized a great deal of intellectual inquiry in the Renaissance expanded to include language in the latter half of the seventeenth century into the eighteenth century. The delay in focusing on language as part of this intellectual enterprise may be explained by the comparatively low status of English compared with Latin, Greek, and French through the middle of the sixteenth century. Richard Foster Jones, in his often-cited book *The Triumph of the English Language* (1953), argues for the second half of the sixteenth century as a pivotal time in the shift in attitudes toward English: before this time the language was generally deemed unworthy of use in high literature and academic work as well as of grammatical attention; after this time the language came to be seen as a source of national pride, bolstered by an important literary tradition and worthy of use in domains historically restricted largely to Latin and French. As English started to be written in a much wider range of formal registers (the "elaboration of function" that the Milroys describe as a key part of the standardization process), it adopted a vast number of borrowed terms from Latin, Greek, and other languages in order to be able to fulfill the requirements of these registers (see the discussion of the inkhorn debate in the next chapter). Writers also enjoyed access to a newly published set of rhetorics or manuals on eloquence in English, designed to aid in the flourishing or elaboration of the language.

By the middle of the seventeenth century, the codification of English into grammar books was underway, although these early works appear to be largely attempts to make English conform to Latin grammatical structure rather than attempts to describe the structure of English (Alston 1965; Vorlat 1975). Latin had been the primary focus of grammatical instruction up to that point, so "grammar" to some extent had become synonymous with Latin grammar and the grammatical terminology associated with Latin was applied to English. At this historical moment, the middle class was on the rise, and the eighteenth century witnessed the publication of numerous conduct manuals, written by and for aspiring middle-class writers (Lynch 2009, 45; Fitzmaurice 1998). The advice on writing etiquette in such conduct manuals partly paved the way for more concentrated, sentence-level grammatical and stylistic advice.

Other competitive forces were at work, including the establishment of the Académie française in 1635, whose purpose was to regulate the French language. French had enjoyed significant linguistic prestige for centuries at that point, so it is not surprising that it was deemed worthy of such an academy. By the 1660s there was sustained talk about an English academy, and two of the most famous proposals were made by Daniel Defoe, in his *An Essay on Projects* (1697), and by Jonathan Swift, in his *Proposal for Correcting, Improving and Ascertaining the English Tongue* (1712). Defoe's (1697) discussion of the need for an academy makes clear his interest in correcting the English language (note his use of "polish" and "purge") and then fixing it ("establish"), so that no further changes would mar the language:

The Work of this Society shou'd be to encourage Polite Learning, to polish and refine the *English* Tongue, and advance the so much neglected Faculty of Correct Language, to establish Purity and Propriety of Stile, and to purge it from all the Irregular Additions that Ignorance and Affectation have introduc'd; and all those Innovations in Speech, if I may call them such, which some Dogmatic Writers have the Confidence to foster upon their Native Language, as if their Authority were sufficient to make their own Fancy legitimate. (91)

Swift (1712, 31), in contrast, prioritized the fixing or stabilization of the language over the perfection of it, captured in this famous line from the proposal: "For I am of Opinion, that it is better a Language should not be wholly perfect, than that it should be perpetually changing."

These proposals for an academy came to naught, but the prescriptive energy behind them resulted in the proliferation of projects aimed at codification and improvement of the language beginning in the eighteenth century and leading to what has sometimes been described as the "hyperactive prescriptivism" of the nineteenth century. While there were important grammars that preceded it, Bishop Lowth's *A Short Introduction to English Grammar* (1762) quickly became one of the most popular and influential grammars of the century. Tieken-Boon van Ostade has done invaluable work in debunking modern myths about the unrelenting prescriptivism of the work. That said, Lowth did certainly partake in, and arguably popularize, the error-hunting tradition.

Percy (2008) points out that by the 1750s, book reviewers in book review periodicals like the *Monthly Review* and the *Critical Review* were criticizing contemporaries for specific grammatical errors before similar criticisms appeared in grammars. Lowth then in 1762 writes in the preface to his grammar:

It will evidently appear from these notes, that our best Authors for want of some rudiments of this kind have sometimes fallen into mistakes and been guilty of palpable errors in point of Grammar. (viii–ix)

In the text itself, Lowth uses footnotes to offer often harsh critiques of then-dead authors' grammatical missteps (at least from his perspective). In the preface, Lowth also invites readers to send along their remarks and suggestions for improvement, should they feel that the book is worth a revision. A 1762 letter from Thomas Fitzmaurice to Adam Smith suggests that readers leapt at the invitation (or challenge, as they may have seen it):

Pray have you seen Dr Louths English Grammar which is just come out? It is talk'd of much. Some of the ingenious men with whom this University overflows, are picking faults and finding Errors in it at present. Pray what do you think of it? (quoted in Tieken-Boon van Ostade 2008 b, 197)

Mr. Fitzmaurice goes on to point out what he believes to be a grammatical infelicity in Smith's book. All of this evidence suggests the prevalence of a discourse that encouraged, at least among the learned, the finding and correcting of grammatical error.

In the past decade or so of scholarship on the history of prescriptivism, Lindley Murray has come to replace Bishop Lowth as the arch-grammarian (see, e.g., Chapman 2008; Tieken-Boon van Ostade 2012). Murray's grammar was published at the end of the eighteenth century and had a lasting impact through the nineteenth given its vast popularity. Murray drew heavily on his predecessors but often inserted rigid principles of correctness where there had been more nuanced descriptions of preference. As Lynch (2009, 112) concludes, in his engaging discussion of the rise of the prescriptive tradition, "We would all be happier had Murray and his followers paid even more attention to questions of appropriateness rather than correctness."

In *The Fight for English*, Crystal (2006, 81–82) sums up the resulting belief system, "which would colour our entire way of thinking for the next three hundred years," as follows: Without any guidance, polite (or later "educated") people do not speak or write correctly, so grammars, dictionaries, and usage manuals must provide that guidance on correctness; the fact that even the most famous authors fall into "error" in their literary works only reinforces the idea that those of us who are not famous literary authors cannot be trusted to know good usage. Within this framework, the act of identifying "grammatical errors" for others is a kindness, a way to rescue them from the foibles of common usage that might not be approved by manuals and other institutionalized authorities. The Microsoft grammar checker becomes a benign force, transmitting institutionalized, seemingly neutral knowledge of error to users through its red and green squiggly lines. The "errors" range from spelling and punctuation to word choice and syntax.

Language is most standardized at the level of spelling, which provides readers and writers with a clear sense that there is a right way to spell a word (and in a few cases, perhaps two – e.g., *advisor* and *adviser*) – and many wrong ways to spell it. Gone are the days when medieval scribes could spell the same word in different ways, even on the same manuscript page, and still be writing down "the same word." (The analogy I use to explain this medieval perspective on spelling variation, which can seem very foreign to modern writers, is my own handwriting, which utilizes both print and script versions of letters like "f" and yet readers understand that I mean "f" whichever form I use.) The educational system focuses on correct spelling early in a child's school career, and spelling tests, spelling bees, modern dictionaries, and the Microsoft spell checker all reinforce a belief that spelling does not and should not tolerate variation. Variation is "misspelling," or error. This is standardizing prescriptivism at its most concentrated and effective.

Interestingly, punctuation probably follows right after spelling as the most popular object of prescriptive error hunters. Yet, as Crystal (2006, 131) points out, punctuation was one of the last issues that prescriptive grammarians of the eighteenth and early nineteenth century paid attention to as they codified the standard variety of English. With her call "Sticklers Unite!" in *Eats, Shoots & Leaves* (2003), Lynne Truss encourages error hunting on grocers' signs, where plural apostrophes such as *apple's* might appear. And reviewers of Truss's book found hunting for punctuation errors in her work to be an appropriate response to reviewing the quality of the book's argument(s). Chastisement over punctuation pops up at the beginning of the twenty-first century in some unexpected places, as the exchange between neighbors through the names of their wireless networks in Figure 3.1 captures.[3]

Prescriptivism about punctuation encompasses different strands of prescriptivism, including issues of standardization, such as apostrophe use in *your* versus *you're*, and issues of stylistic differentiation, such as what punctuation is deemed elegant or less so (e.g., the comma after an introductory phrase such as *In addition*). The entrenched language of correctness subsumes them both.

Word choice and morphosyntax are not exempt from the ideology of correctness and error, despite the complexity inherent in different conventions

---

[3] Some readers will undoubtedly notice the use of the plural verb *are* with the technically singular indefinite pronoun *none* ("None of your preferred networks are available"), which is criticized as a lack of agreement in many usage guides. The Microsoft grammar checker flags it as an error of subject–verb agreement. For many speakers and writers, the plural meaning of a phrase like "none of your preferred networks" governs the verb.

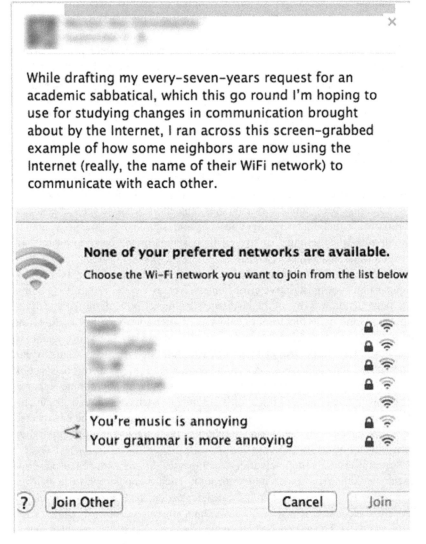

While drafting my every-seven-years request for an academic sabbatical, which this go round I'm hoping to use for studying changes in communication brought about by the Internet, I ran across this screen-grabbed example of how some neighbors are now using the Internet (really, the name of their WiFi network) to communicate with each other.

None of your preferred networks are available.

Choose the Wi-Fi network you want to join from the list below

You're music is annoying

Your grammar is more annoying

Join Other   Cancel   Join

Figure 3.1 A neighborly exchange about correct punctuation (circulated on the Internet in Fall 2012)

and expectations across genres and in distinctive authorial styles. Double negation, the conjunctive use of *like*, and singular generic *they* can all get lumped together as error, making no distinctions between (or among – depending on how one feels about the prescriptive rule about *between* and *among*) standardizing prescriptivism, stylistic prescriptivism, and politically responsive prescriptivism.

The modern field of composition studies has been plagued by conflicting understandings of "grammar teaching" and by the tradition of error hunting. The two are, unfortunately, often seen as almost synonymous in education: to teach grammar is to help students identify and eliminate "errors" in their sentences, rather than to think about how language is structured and what grammatical choices are appropriate in which contexts (see Hartwell [1985] for a good discussion of the different meanings of "grammar" in composition). Even scholars such as Mina Shaughnessy, who famously and valuably challenged prevailing attitudes toward basic writers in her foundational book *Errors and Expectations* (1979), calling on writing teachers and scholars to look beyond surface issues to read for arguments, did so within the discourse of error. Linguists have emphasized the social construction of "error," trying to demonstrate how stylistic choices and nonstandard dialect features are inaccurately subsumed under "error," but they are all too rarely in direct conversation with scholars and teachers in composition classrooms. And the Microsoft grammar checker only perpetuates the already widespread focus on "error" rather than on variation among dialects and registers; it participates in a discourse of right and wrong rather than of context-dependent stylistic and rhetorical choices.

Many of the rules that have been embedded into the grammar checker can be traced back to published grammar and usage books, with varyingly persuasive rationales for the prescriptions. With the grammar checker, unlike most usage guides, users must pursue the cause of the green squiggle at least two additional steps to see if any rationale is provided. And in some cases, the digging can produce little to no explanation beyond a straightforward replacement of a construction deemed "an error." It can also unearth advice about formal versus informal discourse, but the informal variant has still been flagged as "an error." In other words, any nuance buried in the grammar checker that might differentiate among strands of prescriptivism is largely erased by the more prominent use of the language of error, which continues a long-standing tradition in the dispensing of prescriptive rules in school contexts and far beyond.

Microsoft Word Grammar Checker rules

The grammar checker promotes the practice of error hunting that dates back to the eighteenth century, helping English speakers and writers to remain immersed in the language of correctness and error. The published grammars and usage guides that contain most of the rules in the Microsoft grammar checker were written for educational and reference purposes; the grammar checker more often than not streamlines the rules to fit into the program, a process that can strip rules of much if any flexibility or nuance they may once have had. Like the eighteenth-century grammars that laid down some of the rules in the program, the grammar checker does not cite its sources and in some cases seems to promote idiosyncratic rules of its own (not unlike published usage guides over the past three hundred years).

In critically examining this powerful new prescriptive force, it is important to ask who is writing the rules in the MSGC (computational linguists versus educational linguists versus English teachers); it is equally if not more important to examine how the rules are presented. As scholars in education have noted, the grammar checker feeds students' desire for a right answer. I would add that it isn't just students who desire or believe in "right answers" when it comes to usage. In fact, many English speakers and writers, including a significant number of English teachers at all levels, believe in right answers around grammar and style, in the same way that there are right answers about spelling. And, really, what is the difference between a red squiggly line and a green squiggly line?

The answer is that there is a big difference in terms of the transparency of the authority on which that squiggly line rests. In addition, as discussed above, spelling is much more standardized than grammar and style. But this answer requires a critical perspective that many users do not bring to the program.

Many users of Microsoft Word assume that just as the red squiggly lines correspond to a standard dictionary's judgment that a spelling is incorrect, the green lines must similarly correspond to a reputable usage guide. The reality appears to be more complicated. Microsoft is completely transparent about the two dictionaries from which it draws for the parsing and the spell-checking function. It is much more difficult to get a definitive answer about the source of the grammar and style rules. Yet the rules are more strict than some of the most prescriptive of published usage guides, without any of the subjective and sometimes moral commentary of traditional usage guides. As a result, the advice in the grammar checker can seem even more like it comes from nowhere, with authority derived from the brand name behind it.

A Microsoft employee who worked in the NLP group, when my research assistant interviewed her in 2010, indicated that the group used a combination of popular style guides that were available to them as well as what was already in available grammar checkers. There was an attempt to arrive at "consensus" about good style and good grammar.[4] Heidorn (2000, 192) describes sometimes allowing usability testing to change the rules. For example, the program offers revision of passive sentences into the active voice. In earlier versions it offered revision for sentences with a *by*-clause (e.g., *The paper was written by Susan* > *Susan wrote the paper*) as well as without a *by*-clause (e.g., *The street was*

---

[4] In 2012, Microsoft turned down my requests for further interviews.

plowed this morning > *Someone plowed the street this morning*). Users did not like the latter *someone*-oriented revisions of passive sentences without a *by*-clause (who can blame them?), and now the program only offers revisions for passive sentences with a *by*-clause.

The program draws on the *American Heritage Dictionary of the English Language,* but not on its detailed usage notes about contested usage and the history of prescription on grammatical and stylistic issues. The usage notes would not have been input into the processor because they are not coded under a word entry and would not have aided in lexical identification and disambiguation. In these usage notes, the editors of the American Heritage dictionaries seek to provide some context and perspective on what might be commonly thought of as an "error." Microsoft Word, however, uses the term *error* with no context and no explicit troubling of the issue.

The grammar checker has about two hundred descriptor rules, to use Heidorn's terminology. About half of these handle issues at the clause or phrase level (e.g., agreement in number) and half address lexical features (e.g., contractions) (Heidorn 2000, 192). There is also the file containing over one hundred pairs of easily confusable words (e.g., *its* and *it's*). A savvy user can select among five different writing styles for the grammar checker: casual, standard, formal, technical, and custom. Within each style option, the user can further customize which of twenty-one features they (just to use singular *they,* which the grammar checker does not like) want activated, such as capitalization, passive sentences, first-person, etc. In the Help menu for Word 2010, users who know to look there can find a list of "grammar errors" and "style errors" that the grammar checker includes. Some issues under grammar could be argued to be stylistic: for example, the use of *like* as a conjunction and run-on sentences. And many of them should not be categorized as "errors" at all.

The published scholarship on the Microsoft grammar checker is limited, and what is available focuses primarily on the reliability of the checking function, as opposed to its power to reinforce already strongly held beliefs about grammatical correctness and error (see, for example, Haist 2000). The issue of reliability has received the most attention from scholars concerned about the impact of any inconsistency on students who are learning to write formal prose. Vernon (2000) argues that "the unreliability of grammar checkers, given their ubiquity, becomes a reason to address them in the classroom" (331). Any and every resource that helps teachers encourage critical engagement with prescriptive usage rules represents a valuable pedagogical turn, and Vernon explores some of the potential of the Microsoft grammar checker for facilitating discussion of the politics of grammar rules: "For a number of us grammar checkers might be more pedagogically intriguing less for teaching final draft editing skills than for deconstructing the authority of grammatical rules, thus challenging students with a conversation about the determinants of written language conventions"

(331). He proposes strategies including: having students compare the grammar checker's rules with published handbooks (although he does not raise the question of where the grammar checker rules originate); examining with students how the grammar checker has parsed the sentences it flags; and asking students to write "bad" sentences that will trigger the grammar checker flag. With all of these suggestions, Vernon advocates a valuably critical pedagogy, although he continues to use the term "error," as the grammar checker does. The pedagogical approach he advocates also requires that teachers themselves are thinking critically about the grammar checker, which many of them are not.[5]

The design of the grammar checker has the power to propagate more prescriptive beliefs about language than it dispels. Many of my colleagues in the English department, who have advanced degrees in English, say that they turn the grammar checker off, but English professors tend to have more confidence in their ability to write good prose than the average user of the Microsoft grammar checker. My colleagues also often explain turning off the grammar checker as indicative of the fact that they know the rules of written English well enough to bend them, if not break them, in ways that make the grammar checker unhappy. When I raise the question of where the rules come from to begin with, colleague after colleague look at me with that look that says, "I had not considered that before." And informal polls of undergraduate students suggest that their secondary school teachers are not offering them a critical perspective on the grammar checker. From what I can determine, McGee and Ericsson (2002, 463) are exactly right in their assertion:

Given that their school-based language instruction is largely prescriptive and that few, if any, precollege students have been let in on the secret that the prescriptions of Standard English are neither natural, nor logical, nor productive of language that is 'better' (in any meaningful sense of the word) than nonstandard Englishes, most simply accept the authority of this smart machine to police their grammar, just as they have heretofore accepted the authority of their smart teachers.

In other words, the grammar checker reinforces prescriptive pedagogy rather than challenging its authority. McGee and Ericsson add: "Although many might smart from this power relationship, for most, it has operated invisibly, as just one of the many givens of the school environment. For them, the situation simply could not be otherwise. It is just what is. 'Good grammar' is a fact of school life, and the MSGC is licensed to check their grammar by the same

[5] Vernon (2000, 333) notes: "Today's more flexible grammar checkers are less monolithic than those of the past; a teacher who does not consider the split infinitive taboo simply does not have the program check for split infinitives." But this assumes savviness on the part of teachers; many users of the program do not realize they can be selective about what constructions will get a green squiggly line.

invisible authority that licenses the rest of the adult world they are being socialized into" (2002, 463).

McGee and Ericsson offer some of the most critical analysis of the Microsoft grammar checker rules to date. For example, with the grammar checker's attempt to distribute the use of *that* and *which*, they ask whether this results from the program's preference for binaries or from its adherence to Strunk and White's *Elements of Style*, but they do not pursue the question further. They also make the following important observation: "not acting on the line's recommendation or not bothering to inquire into its meaning is not the same as being uninfluenced by it" (462). In other words, every student and professor who ignores the green squiggly line has still seen the green squiggly line, which suggests that by some authoritative standard, the construction in question is problematic.

The Microsoft grammar checker divides the "errors" into "Grammar Errors" and "Style Errors." What the program identifies as "grammar" reinforces the conflation discussed in Chapter 1 about what counts as grammar. For example, included on the list of eleven "Grammar Errors" in the Help menu from Microsoft Word 2010 are capitalization and punctuation (including use of commas and colons, multiple spaces between words, and punctuation in quotations). What the program calls "nonstandard questions" seems to be more about punctuation: "He asked if there was any coffee left?" and "She asked did you go after all?" Fragments and run-on sentences fall into the category grammar, although informal fragments such as "Why?" are identified as a style error.

The use of the label "error" categorically relegates nonstandard forms to the realm of error. The grammar checker targets nonstandard grammatical features under several categories. It identifies multiple negation as error, and while multiple negation is nonstandard, it is fully systematic in the dialects in which it is used. Also categorized under error are "number agreement problems in noun phrases (e.g., 'five machine' instead of 'five machines')." This kind of agreement pattern occurs in African American English among other nonstandard dialects: when a plural noun is preceded by a number, it does not require the plural -*s*. I do not want to suggest that it is not helpful for writers to be alerted to the fact that this construction is nonstandard and that it may be judged by readers in any formal document; the grammar checker, however, uses the term "error" with no further explanation. As another example, the nonstandard construction such as "he talk" is described as "disagreement between the subject and its verb," as opposed to a systematic but nonstandard grammatical feature. In other words, the most powerful prescriptive force in the world serves to reify attitudes about nonstandard grammar being "error."

Like as a conjunction (as in the prescriptively condemned cigarette ad "Winston tastes good like a cigarette should," first introduced in the 1950s) pops up as a grammatical "error." In this case, the grammar checker appears to adopt a prescriptive stance similar to that in Strunk and White's *Elements of Style*, as opposed to the more forgiving discussion in Joseph Williams' *Style: Ten Lessons in Clarity and Grace* (2005). With *like* the grammar checker targets an incoming grammatical change. With *who* and *whom* the grammar checker participates in the effort to prop up *whom* as an object form. The fact that the grammar checker catches the use of *who* in object position (most of the time – it can be thrown by complicated syntax) and suggests replacing it with *whom* may help keep *whom* alive in written English a while longer and reinforce distance between spoken and written usage with this pronoun.

The grammar checker perpetuates the idea that there is something wrong with sentence-final prepositions. If a user asks the grammar checker to explain the "error," the pop-up box makes an attempt at nuance, distinguishing between formal versus less formal prose: "Although a preposition at the end of a sentence may be used informally, consider deleting or repositioning the preposition for a more formal or traditional tone." But, in fact, most reputable style guides provide even more nuanced advice, which allows more wiggle room in formal prose for the sentence-final preposition. For example, consider this from Fowler's *A Dictionary of Modern English Usage* (1965, 473–475):

It was once a cherished superstition that prepositions must be kept true to their name and placed before the word they govern in spite of the incurable English instinct for putting them late ... 'A sentence ending in a preposition is an inelegant sentence' represents what used to be a very general belief, and it is not yet dead ... The fact is that the remarkable freedom enjoyed by English in putting its prepositions late and omitting its relatives is an important element in the flexibility of the language ... The legitimacy of the prepositional ending in literary English must be uncompromisingly maintained; in respect of elegance or inelegance, every example must be judged not by an arbitrary rule, but on its own merits, according to the impression it makes on the feeling of educated English readers ... If it were not presumptuous, after that, to offer advice, the advice would be this: Follow no arbitrary rule, but remember that there are often two or more possible arrangements between which a choice should be consciously made. If the final preposition that has naturally presented itself sounds comfortable, keep it; if it does not sound comfortable, still keep it if it has compensating vigour, or when among awkward possibilities it is the least awkward.

Of course the grammar checker cannot judge the respective elegance or inelegance of every sentence with a final preposition in context. So, instead, it applies the rule to all sentence-final prepositions.

Under "style errors," the grammar checker flags many features that readers might agree are colloquial, such as *get* passives (e.g., *the book got reviewed immediately*) and *kind of* for *somewhat*. There might be less consensus about the recommended replacement of *scared of* with *afraid of*. Gender-specific language such as *councilman* and *councilwoman* can be flagged as problematic if users selects this feature in the menu (it is not necessarily on by default); even with this feature selected, the word *freshman* is not flagged, as is true of many published usage guides as well (see Chapter 5 for more discussion of nonsexist language reform).

Other style "errors" are more mystifying. For example, under misused words, the grammar checker flags "angry at" instead of "angry with." The phrase *angry at* has been employed in the written language since Shakespeare's time (Gilman 1994, 97). While historically there have been some attempts to distinguish between *angry with* and *angry at* in terms of the animacy of the object of one's anger (persons vs. inanimates), the wholesale disparagement of *angry at* seems to be idiosyncratic to the grammar checker. As Gilman summarizes: "It does not seem reasonable, on the basis of the evidence here and in the OED, to make rigid distinctions about which prepositions are proper in which uses" (97). The construction is not included in Strunk and White, nor is there a usage note in the American Heritage dictionaries. Yet the grammar checker tells writers to change this – an unreasonable demand, as Gilman sees it.

Because the grammar checker cannot distinguish an effective passive from a less effective one, it targets all of them. Contrast this highly prescriptive approach with Strunk and White's (1979, 18) discussion: "The active voice is usually more direct and vigorous than the passive ... This rule does not, of course, mean that the writer should entirely discard the passive voice, which is frequently convenient and sometimes necessary ... The habitual use of the active voice, however, makes for forcible writing."[6] The passive is common not only in scientific prose, where it helps maintain a tone of scientific objectivity, but it also occurs regularly in other disciplines in staples such as the phrases *it could be argued* or *must be considered.*

Then there is the construction that first tipped me off to the potential source problems with the grammar checker: its dislike of sentences beginning with *and* and *but*. Simply put, there is no reputable style guide that espouses this rule. As Gilman (1994, 93) summarizes: "Everybody agrees that it's all right to begin a sentence with *and*, and nearly everybody admits to having been taught at some past time that the practice was wrong. Most of us think the prohibition goes back to our early school days ... [T]he prohibition is probably meant to correct the tendency of children to string together independent clauses or simple declarative sentences with *ands*." Fowler (1965, 29) writes: "That it is a solecism to begin a sentence with *and* is a faintly lingering superstition. The OED gives examples ranging from the 10th to the 19th c.; the Bible is full of them" (29). The grammar checker, if asked for explanation, suggests that

---

[6] Strunk and White's treatment of the passive was one of several targets in Geoffrey Pullum's (2009) vigorous critique of the book in the *Chronicle of Higher Education,* on the occasion of the book's fiftieth anniversary. Pullum points out that several of the sentences that Strunk and White identify as passive are not, in fact, passive, which he frames as evidence of the authors' incompetence with grammar. Pullum concludes about the book's legacy: "Its enormous influence has not improved American students' grasp of English grammar; it has significantly degraded it."

Figure 3.2 The Microsoft Word Grammar Checker's explanation of sentence initial *and*, *but*, *or*, or *plus*

sentence-initial *and* and *but* constitute an issue of formality, not of superstition (see Figure 3.2). And again, users must request an explanation to move beyond the green "error" line to a pop-up box that makes a formality distinction with these constructions.[7]

The grammar checker rejects the "or not" in "whether or not" as wordy. Its model for doing so is, once again, unclear. Fowler's *Dictionary of Modern English Usage* notes no problem with the construction; Williams does not mention the issue in *Style* nor do Strunk and White. Recent American Heritage dictionaries contain no usage note. Gilman (1994) mentions it in terms of a general sense among language commentators that fewer words make better prose, but his conclusion would not support putting this rule into the grammar checker: "It should be noted, however, that this use of *or not* is more than 300 years old, and is common among educated speakers and writers. It is, in short, perfectly good, idiomatic English" (956). In addition, when the clause is adverbial, the *or not* cannot be avoided: for example, *Whether or not you agree, the proposal will go forward*, and not **Whether you agree, the proposal will go forward*.

The split infinitive provides one final example where the grammar checker stands on fairly unprecedented prescriptive ground. The prohibition against split infinitives was publicly "lifted" – and made newspaper headlines for doing so – in 1998 when the new edition of the *Oxford American Desk Dictionary* stated that not splitting infinitives could lead to "awkward, stilted sentences." The prohibition dates back to the nineteenth century, and while many modern

---

[7] The grammar checker also flags sentence-initial *hopefully* as a problem, in all likelihood based on the premise that sentence-initial instances of *hopefully* are likely to be functioning as sentence adverbs meaning 'it is hoped'. At the time of this book's publication, it remains to be seen if the grammar checker will follow the *Associated Press Stylebook* in no longer flagging this use of *hopefully* as an error.

commentators blame the prescriptive rule on false analogies to Latin and the elevating of Latin as the model for good English (in Latin, the infinitive is one word and so cannot be split), the earliest criticism of the split infinitive found to date is in a letter to the editor of the *New England Magazine*, which describes it as "uneducated" (Bailey 2006). Perales-Escudero (2011) cites the British editor John Taylor then arguing that not splitting infinitives would make English more like its Germanic roots (not like Latin). In any case, the prohibition is now technically lifted, although anecdotal evidence suggests that not all English teachers have received the news. The grammar checker allows split infinitives with one word between *to* and an infinitive verb, but not with two or more words (so *to boldly go*, but not *to very boldly go*). Fowler (1965), in contrast, allows flexibility for the stylistic possibilities of split infinitives and does not mention any strict parameters for how they are split. He concludes the entry by quoting a review that cites a "deafeningly split" infinitive, but the example goes far beyond a two-word split: "A book... of which the purpose is thus – with a deafeningly split infinitive – stated by its author: 'Its main idea is to historically, even while events are maturing, and divinely – from the Divine point of view – impeach the European system of Church and States'" (582). It is hard to disagree with Fowler that this particular split infinitive is over the top.

It is too early to evaluate the full ramifications of the Microsoft grammar checker on written English in the twenty-first century. But the grammar checker may well matter for the development of written usage as well as for the perpetuation of a discourse of error. In recent years scholars have begun to investigate whether the institution of a discourse of error around grammar and style as well as the specific prescriptions in the eighteenth, nineteenth, and twentieth centuries have had an impact on actual usage. From the research to date, the answer is a mixed bag – which provides a helpful context for considering the potential effects of the grammar checker on written English in the twenty-first century. If the case studies described below of the effects on usage of earlier prescriptive attempts at controlling English prose are any indication, the effects of the Microsoft Word Grammar Checker will be variable and to some extent unpredictable, but they will be a factor in the development of contemporary English.

Prescriptive usage rules and patterns of actual usage

Does grammatical prescriptivism matter for actual usage? With recently created historical corpora, history of English scholars have unprecedented opportunities for evaluating the effects on written prose of prescriptive attempts to stigmatize one variant (or more) of a construction and elevate another variant (almost always singular, given the desire to minimize variation). To begin, these resources allow scholars to evaluate the pervasiveness of a feature that started to be pre- or proscribed at an earlier historical moment. They can then examine whether, once prescriptivism on a grammatical or stylistic feature began in earnest, written usage changed in any discernible way. Of course, if it did, any conclusions about cause and effect must be drawn carefully, but patterns may be suggestive of prescriptive influence. In addition, as detailed in Chapter 1, prescriptive efforts have multiple aims, including delineating standard from nonstandard usage, elevating some stylistic choices over others, and restoring older forms. Given the different stakes involved in adherence, different kinds of prescriptive regulation have differential power to affect usage.

This section, while far from comprehensive of research carried out on the effects of prescriptivism, highlights some fascinating recent studies addressing the interaction of concerted prescriptivism on specific points of usage and writers' concurrent and subsequent use of that linguistic feature in the history of Modern English. There are no easy answers about cause and effect, but the studies, taken together, make it clear that prescriptivism should not be dismissed as a factor in the development of formal written English.

In the case of double or multiple negation, concerted prescription seems to have occurred after this feature had largely fallen out of educated writers' use (certainly written use, and perhaps also to some extent in spoken use). While the stricture against double negation is generally associated with Bishop Lowth and *A Short Introduction to English Grammar* (1762), Tieken-Boon van Ostade (1982, 2008b) has shown convincingly that Lowth was not the first grammarian to address the issue and that Lowth was significantly more descriptive than subsequent grammarians such as Lindley Murray, who modified his treatment. Tieken-Boon van Ostade dates the first published discussion of double negation to James Greenwood's *Essay towards a Practical English Grammar* (1711), in which he writes: "*N.B.* Two *Negatives*, or two *Adverbs* of *Denying* do in *English* affirm" (160, quoted in Tieken-Boon van Ostade 2008b, 199). Lowth does not address double negation in the first edition of the grammar (1762), and Tieken-Boon van Ostade hypothesizes that the addition in the second edition (1763) must have been prompted by reader response (i.e., correction). Lowth's words on the subject are strikingly descriptive, even if their descriptive validity can be legitimately questioned: "Two Negatives in English destroy one another, or are equivalent to an Affirmative."[8] However, Lowth then makes the move of singling out dead authors for critique, in this case Shakespeare and Chaucer. The examples from Lowth (from Shakespeare) involve double negation with

---

[8] In some instances, typically within a phrase, one negative can mitigate the effect of another, as in *not unhappy* or *it hasn't never happened*. But more often, two or more negative adverbials and/or pronouns in a clause reinforce each other: *I don't know nobody in this school* has a meaning equivalent to the standard construction *I don't know anybody in this school*.

the conjunction *nor* (e.g., *She cannot love, nor take no shape nor project of affection*). Lowth writes of Shakespeare's frequent use of double negation: "It is a relique of the antient [*sic*] style abounding with the Negatives, which is now grown wholly obsolete."

Joseph Priestley adds a note about double negation in the second edition of his grammar (1768), writing that double negatives "often occasion embarrassment to a writer" (quoted in Tieken-Boon van Ostade 2008b, 202), which suggests the social class judgment that may have come to accompany this construction by the eighteenth century (much as it does today). It is then Murray who adds the prescriptive advice: "But it is better to express an affirmation by a regular affirmative than by two negatives" (Murray 1795, 121).

It does not appear to be the case that prescriptivism against double negation drove the construction into becoming regarded as a lower-class, stigmatized feature; indeed, it appears to be the reverse. Working with data from letters from the Early Modern English period, Nevalainen and Raumolin-Brunberg (2003, 71–72) conclude that double negation was falling well out of use in the standard variety by the end of the sixteenth century. Tieken-Boon van Ostade (2008b, 209) explains "the obsession" with multiple negation in the eighteenth century as part of the strong desire for upward mobility: "Thus, anyone who wished to rise in society had to be made aware of the social stigma attached to its usage [multiple negation], but at the same time those who employed servants had to be on their guard against possible contamination from their language in this respect." Prescriptivism institutionalized the nonstandardness of double negation; it also provided intellectual rationales for calling the construction a grammatical "error," contravening the logic of language. Of course, there is nothing illogical about double or multiple negation as a way to express negation within the clause and many languages, including many varieties of Modern English, express negation this way. But the label of error, and the stigma that comes with it, have stuck with remarkable success.

Unlike prescription about double negation, which confirmed the nonstandard status of a construction that had already largely fallen out of standard usage, prescription on the subjunctive has sought to preserve a construction falling out of standard usage – and it has witnessed some success. Auer and González-Díaz (2005, 323) suggest that prescriptivism on the subjunctive caused "a blip in its development": a slight rise in usage in the second half of the eighteenth century in written prose and a more notable increase at the beginning of the nineteenth century. The eighteenth-century grammars that Auer and González-Díaz survey for the study often explicitly recognize the decline of the subjunctive and the use of the indicative in constructions that would traditionally take the subjunctive. In these guides, the subjunctive comes to be associated with polite speech and writing, an incentive for "careful writers" to use it. Auer and González-Díaz conclude: "Apart from suggesting that the prescriptivists' concerns regarding

the inflectional subjunctive and the invitation to use it more frequently might have paid off, this result also shows that there is a time lag before we can see any results" (323).[9]

The relationship of double comparatives and superlatives (e.g., *more happier*, *most best*) to prescriptivism more closely resembles double negation. As Auer and González-Díaz (2005, 325–326) point out, scattered comments in histories of English suggest that prescriptivism abolished the construction from written English. Their study indicates that the stigmatization of the double forms as uneducated or more vulgar usage was fairly well complete by the end of the seventeenth century – before severe prescriptivism against the construction kicked in. Prescriptivism was then a "reinforcing factor" (336). In comparison, González-Díaz (2008) argues that eighteenth-century prescriptivism may have been a factor in the drop in usage of the doubly inflected comparative *lesser* (originally used synonymously with *less*). The word *lesser* is now lexicalized with a specialized meaning in contrast with *greater* and not stigmatized; but as a double comparative, it was described as a "mistake," "ungrammatical," "barbarous," and "a most disgusting fault" in eighteenth-century grammars. (The influence of prescriptive condemnation of *worser* by the middle of the eighteenth century remains more tentative, according to González-Díaz. Interestingly, the word *worser* was described neutrally as a variant of *worse* in early eighteenth-century grammars.)

Another highly stigmatized form in grammar books has been irregular past tense forms (e.g., *the phone rung a few minutes ago, I drunk a whole glass of water*). So has that had any effect on actual usage? Anderwald (2012) suggests that with verbs like *sing, swim*, and *shrink*, American grammar books in the nineteenth century actually lagged behind usage, generally being more permissive than trends in usage. For example, many of the grammars remained tolerant of forms such as past tense *swum, sung*, and *shrunk* through the late nineteenth century, even when usage was trending strongly toward the *a*-form (*swam, sang, shrank*). British grammars were prescribing the invariant *a*-form earlier. The grammar books Anderwald surveys also promoted the fallacious argument that the *u*-forms (e.g., *the phone rung*) are an overextension of the past participle form, which facilitates the stigmatization of them as error. In fact, the *u*-forms reflect the legacy of the Old English plural past, as opposed to the singular past with *a*. Anderwald notes that with another set of verbs like *swing, slink, sling*, and *spin*, there was almost no variation in usage: the *u*-form was used in the

---

[9] The status of the subjunctive remains complicated to this day. Leech et al. (2009) find that in the second half of the twentieth century in American and British English the mandative subjunctive (e.g., *I insist she go*) is spreading (again) while the subjunctive in conditional or counterfactual clauses (e.g., *If she were an alien*) is receding. In terms of the relatively more common use of the *were*-subjunctive in American English, they raise the question of whether the strong prescriptive tradition in the US might be a factor.

past tense. And American grammars tolerated very little variation from this. British grammar books often described or allowed the use of both *a*-forms and *u*-forms, which Anderwald reads as a kind of prescriptivism: an attempt to reinstate a distinction between the past tense and past participle with verbs that had obliterated the distinction by using the *u*-form for both. It was unsuccessful restorative prescriptivism. Anderwald concludes:

Even if grammar writers did not cause the nonstandardization of past-tense *u*-forms, then, by condemning past-tense *u*-forms in moral terms, they must have contributed to this process by actively promoting past-tense *a*-forms as a shibboleth of educated speech, which was seen as the linguistic equivalent of morally irreprehensible behavior, and by generally acting as linguistic (and social) gatekeepers . . . At the same time, the continual repetition of this dictum ("do not use the past participle for the past tense") over the course of the nineteenth century practically unchanged in form is probably a good indicator that this syntax rule did not have much effect (apart from contributing to speakers' linguistic insecurity, of course) and may indirectly indicate the survival of variation in this area of morphosyntax at least in spoken language, with the past-tense *u*-forms relegated by this time to the realm of nonstandard grammar. (284)

The interaction of prescriptivism and usage defies straightforward cause–effect relationships.

Turning from standardizing to stylistic prescriptivism, let's return to one of the best-known prescriptive rules in circulation to this day, one included in the Microsoft grammar checker: do not end a sentence with a preposition. Has three hundred years of prescription on this construction caused any change in how prepositions are used (especially in writing)? Bishop Lowth was far from the first to comment on stranded prepositions, but his words have become famous, as he is typically given credit for canonizing the preference for not stranding the preposition. John Dryden (who also proposed a language academy in the 1660s) is usually cited as the first to notice and disparage the stranded preposition, in 1672 picking out for critique the prose of Ben Jonson and subsequently not only avoiding stranded prepositions in his own prose but going back and revising earlier work that contained stranded prepositions (Lynch 2009, 31). Yáñez-Bouza (2006) notes multiple rationales for the dislike of the construction that grew over the course of the eighteenth century: Latin does not allow preposition stranding; the etymology of the word *preposition* suggests that the preposition must come before (*pre-*) the word it governs; and the drive toward standardization aimed to eliminate variation, such as the ability to strand or not strand a preposition, hence selecting one form as "better" in a construction that showed variation. Lowth then helped make this preference into grammatical law. In a passage from the first edition that remained unchanged in subsequent editions, Lowth writes:

The Preposition is often separated from the Relative which it governs, and joined to the Verb at the end of the Sentence, or of some member of it: as, "Horace is an author, *whom*

I am much delighted *with*." "The [2] world is too well bred to shock authors with a truth, *which* generally their booksellers are the first that inform them *of*." [Pope, Preface to his Poems] This is an Idiom, which our language is strongly inclined to; it prevails in common conversation, and suits very well with the familiar style in writing; but the placing of a Preposition before the Relative is more graceful, as well as more perspicuous, and agrees much better with the solemn and elevated Style. (1762, 127–128)

A subsequent critique of the construction by John Fell, in *An Essay towards an English Grammar* (1784), contains the suggestion that the prescription had already influenced the decisions of "respected authors":

This mode of ending a sentence, or clause, with a preposition, is an idiom that our language is strongly inclined to; yet it seems to be studiously avoided of late by many respectable authors; and, indeed, it is censured by one of our best grammarians.

It is said to be a violent transposition, but, perhaps untruly; for if we examine this idiom we shall find it to be perfectly consistent with the greatest simplicity of arrangement. The preposition, when thus placed, is always used to express the relation which the word governed bears to the word governing; and it appears that, to make the preposition follow the word governing, is more suitable to the genius of our language, than to place it next to the word governed. (129, quoted in Yáñez -Bouza 2008a, 261)[10]

To the detriment of all subsequent writers who might wish to use this idiom that the language is inclined to, Murray copied Lowth's words in his influential grammar (except that he unstranded Lowth's preposition in "which our language is strongly inclined to" and started the clause with "to which"). Over time, the prescription became less about the benefits of fronting the preposition to create a construction like *to which* (also known as pied-piping) and more about the inelegance of the stranded preposition (Yañez-Bouza 2008a, 258); in other words, it became more of a proscription of "bad usage" than a commentary on especially elegant usage.

Some eighteenth-century authors even reversed the description of preposition stranding as common and describe pied-piping as "the regular and natural construction" (Brittain 1788, 73, quoted in Yáñez-Bouza 2008a, 265). And by the end of the century there was a proliferation of strict proscriptions such as: "Never close a sentence, or member of a sentence, with a preposition, when it may be conveniently avoided" (Benjamin Dearborn, *The Columbian Grammar* (1795, 74), quoted in Yáñez-Bouza 2008a, 273); and "At all events, never close a sentence with a 'preposition', for it destroys the strength and harmony of the period" (Philip Withers, *Aristarchus, or The Principles of Composition*, 2nd edn. (1789, 391), quoted in Yáñez-Bouza 2008a, 273).

---

[10] The strikingly similar wording across some of these grammars, which today might well be called plagiarism, was sometimes recognized by the authors through an expression of indebtedness to previous works, and sometimes not.

In this case, prescription seems to have affected usage. Yáñez-Bouza (2006) demonstrates that the construction dropped in written use dramatically between the period from 1680–1740 and the period from 1740–1780 (as prescriptivism set in). The drop may result in part from the shift in preferences from the plain style of the seventeenth century to the "elegant" and elaborated style endorsed by much eighteenth-century prescriptivism, and in part from the concerted attempt by writers to avoid being stigmatized for error-ful prose. Yáñez-Bouza concludes, based on the study of six genres: "In my view, this shift was not so much an expression of a genuine grammatical change internal to the language, but rather the result of the chief prescriptive ideals of correctness and politeness. On the basis of the findings obtained in this study, there seems to be a certain parallelism in the development of these ideals and the process of stigmatisation of end-placed prepositions" (n.p.).

As one final case study, the recent rise of the relative pronoun *that* in restrictive relative clauses in written, edited American English may well also show the effects of concerted prescriptivism. A restrictive relative clause provides essential information about the preceding noun or antecedent, thereby restricting or defining the precise referent: for example, in the noun phrase *the book that I read last week*, the *that*-clause distinguishes the book being referred to from other possible books. In speech, English speakers use both *which* and *that* in restrictive relative clauses (e.g., *the book that/which is on the table*); *that* may be perceived as more colloquial and *which* more formal. Leech et al. (2009, 230) hypothesize that the increased use of *that* in restrictive relative clauses in written American English results from the strong American prescriptive tradition with respect to relative clauses over the course of the twentieth century. A study by Bendikt Szmrecsanyi and Lars Hinrichs supports this theory (Szmrecsanyi 2012). Comparing written data from the Brown Corpus (1960s) and the Frown Corpus (1990s), Szmrecsanyi and Hinrichs determine that non-prescriptivism-related predictors are least explanatory for the patterns in the written American English of the 1990s. In other words, it is difficult to explain the distribution of *that* and *which* based on language-internal factors (e.g., complexity of antecedent, animacy of antecedent, embedding of relative clause within another) and stylistic factors; prescriptivism seems a more likely explanatory factor. In contrast, internal and stylistic predictors are more explanatory in the written data from the 1960s, the relatively early days of prescriptivism on the construction.

Prescription on *that* and *which* in relative clauses represents an attempt to create order through a clear and complementary distribution of the two relative pronouns. Given that only *which* can be used in non-restrictive relative clauses (e.g., *She kept her eye on the car, which was in the driveway*, but not **She kept her eye on the car, that was in the driveway*), it creates a neat binary distribution if only *that* can be used in restrictive relative clauses – despite the fact that

English speakers do not seem to require such a distribution and regularly use both *which* and *that* in this construction. The prescription goes back to H. W. Fowler's *The King's English* (2nd edn., 1908):

This confusion is to be regretted; for although no distinction can be authoritatively drawn between the two relatives, an obvious one presents itself. The few limitations on 'that' and 'who' about which every one is agreed all point to 'that' as the defining relative, 'who' or 'which' as the non-defining ... 'Who' or 'which' should not be used in defining clauses except when custom, euphony, or convenience is decidedly against the use of 'that'.[11]

In his influential *A Dictionary of Modern English Usage* (2nd edn., 1965), Fowler clarifies his preference for complementary distribution and yet shows his awareness that actual usage and his preferred order do not necessarily align:

What grammarians say should be has perhaps less influence on what shall be than even the more modest of them realize; usage evolves itself little disturbed by their likes and dislikes. And yet the temptation to show how better use might have been made of the material to hand is sometimes irresistible. The English relatives, particularly as used by English rather than American writers, offer such a temptation. The relations between *that, who,* and *which* have come to us from our forefathers as an odd jumble, and plainly show that the language has not been neatly constructed by a master builder who could create each part to do the exact work required of it, neither overlapped nor overlapping... It does not follow that the use we are now making of it is the best it is capable of; and perhaps the line of improvement lies in clearer differentiation between *that* and *which*... The two kinds of relative clause, to one of which *that* and to the other of which *which* is appropriate, are the defining and the non-defining; and if writers would agree to regard *that* as the defining relative pronoun, and *which* as the non-defining, there would be much gain both in lucidity and in ease. Some there are who follow this principle now; but it would be idle to pretend that it is the practice either of most or of the best writers. (625–626)

Fowler's recognition of "ideal usage" versus real usage, and the idealistic motives behind the rule for complementary distribution, are lost in Strunk and White's (1979) version of the rule. It has become a rule in *Elements of Style*:

That is the defining, or restrictive pronoun, *which* the nondefining, or nonrestrictive ... the use of *which* for *that* is common in written and spoken language ("Let us now go even unto Bethlehem, and see this thing which is come to pass."). Occasionally *which* seems preferable to *that*, as in the sentence from the Bible. But it would be a convenience to all if these two pronouns were used with precision. The careful writer, watchful for small conveniences, goes *which*-hunting, removes the defining *whiches*, and by so doing improves his work. (59)

---

[11] It has long been recognized that *which* must replace *that* when a preposition is pied-piped: *the book to which I referred*, not **the book to that I referred.*

That kind of definitive advice is repeated in university press style sheets and guides such as the *Associated Press Stylebook*: "Use *that* for essential clauses, important to the meaning of a sentence, and without commas: *I remember the day that we met.* Use *which* for nonessential clauses, where the pronoun is less necessary, and use commas: *The team, which finished last a year ago, is in first place*" (259). While rigid, the rule comes free of judgment. In contrast, in the well-respected *A Dictionary of Modern American Usage* (1998), Bryan Garner writes these strong words about the grammatical distinction and those who choose to care about it (note the moral language in this characterization):

You'll encounter two schools of thought on this point. First are those who don't care about any distinction between these words, who think that *which* is more formal than *that*, and who point to many historical examples of copious *whiches*. They say that modern usage is a muddle. Second are those who insist that both words have useful functions that ought to be separated, and who observe the distinction rigorously in their own writing. They view departures from this distinction as "mistakes." Before reading any further, you ought to know something more about these two groups: those in the first probably don't write very well; those in the second just might. (647)

The Microsoft Word Grammar Checker enforces this distinction between *which* and *that*, with no overt judgment but also with little explanation and no flexibility (see Figure 3.3).

The list of style errors in the Microsoft Word Help menu summarizes the relative pronoun issues as "questionable use of 'that' or 'which'," but the correction that pops up within the text itself does not suggest that *which* in a restrictive clause is "questionable," but that it is wrong. Every writer who subsequently changes the restrictive *which* to *that* will be contributing to the rise of restrictive *that* in written English, a phenomenon historians of English are already tracking and trying to explain.

Figure 3.3 The Microsoft Word Grammar Checker's explanation of *that* and *which*

The most ubiquitous prescriptive grammatical force in the world at the beginning of the twenty-first century is not teaching grammar but rather flagging "errors" and offering "correct" alternatives with little and sometimes no explanation. To be fair, the grammar checker was never designed to be a grammar teacher, but it has become one because its rules are the ones many writers of English encounter more regularly than any others. The message of the grammar checker echoes the grammatical tradition from which it is born: left to their own devices, even the most educated writers are prone to falling into error; this predilection reinforces the need for the grammar checker to monitor written prose and allow writers to change their sentences in adherence to a fixed set of rules at the click of a button. Histories of English, constructing the "linguistic history" of the period we are all currently living through and seeking to explain developments in the spoken and written language, need to heed this clicking of buttons in telling not only the history of prescriptivism but also the history of usage itself.

4 Dictionaries and the idea of "real words"

The second edition of the *New Oxford American Dictionary*, published in 2005, featured a made-up word that began with the letter *e-*. Henry Alford, a contributing writer for the *New Yorker*, took the leak of this information as a challenge to sort through the 3,128 *e-* entries in the dictionary, consult with six lexicographers, and determine the culprit. The playful made-up word, confirmed by editor-in-chief of the second edition Erin McKean, was *esquivalence*, defined as 'the willful avoidance of one's official responsibilities'. The word was included in the dictionary in order to catch any rogue editors at competing dictionaries who might be plagiarizing from the *New Oxford American Dictionary*.

This sleuthy (to make up a word of my own) enterprise was deemed worthy of two and a half columns of text in the "Talk of the Town" section of the *New Yorker* (Alford 2005). I note that fact not as a critique: it was a wonderfully entertaining piece, and, as a linguist, I am always happy to see lexicography (the work of "harmless drudges," to quote Samuel Johnson's definition of the word *lexicographer*) get a bit of the limelight. My interest in Alford's piece, in the context of this book, is the discourse that makes this bit of news possible as news. For *esquivalence* to be noteworthy, the dictionary's readers must have accepted the idea that there are "real" words and "not real" words and that dictionaries are the arbiters that decide on which side of "real" a word falls. The notion of "real words" can be so commonsense to Modern English speakers and writers that it may seem odd to question the validity of this concept. But for the real-word discourse to be meaningful, there have to be accepted arbiters on the status of words. Dictionaries have come to be such arbiters, although they certainly did not always function this way.

In introducing a new slang word to me, students sometimes say, "Well, it's not a real word, but. . . " With that preamble, they then tell me about a word that is fully meaningful for them as speakers, even if it does not appear in a standard dictionary (yet, or perhaps ever, depending on the shelf life of the slang term). As a linguist, I can say that at some level this attitude toward the slang word does not make sense: the slang word is in every way a real word because it is a freestanding lexical unit that carries conventional meaning within a speech community. But, as a linguist who has spent a lot of time studying the history of dictionaries and who takes speakers' ideologies seriously, I know that this attitude toward the slang word makes complete sense to Modern English speakers, who take for granted the institutionalized authority of dictionaries. Dictionaries' purpose is – at least as far as most speakers are concerned – to record "the language"; and if dictionaries include more peripheral words (e.g., slang), they should mark them as such. If speakers work from this understanding, it is perfectly logical for them to discuss whether or not a word is "a real word." Real words are in dictionaries, without usage labels. Words not in dictionaries have a questionable status as words at best, and usage labels such as "nonstandard" can shake speakers' sense of a word's full legitimacy.

In contrast, consider the seventeenth century and some of the first dictionaries of English ever published, which seem to have regularly included what Arthur Kennedy (1927) calls "hothouse words." Hothouse words, unlike ephemeral words from slang or other colloquial language, appear to have been created by lexicographers themselves, perhaps as part of an attempt to elaborate the lexicon of the language. Kennedy came up with this term through a close examination of Thomas Blount's *Glossographia* (1656), a dictionary of "hard" English words. He was struck by just how many of the terms no longer had any currency at the beginning of the twentieth century (about 25 percent); at first, he thought they were ephemeral words like any others, but he came to discover "they more nearly resemble those exotic or newly hybridized plants of the hothouse which most of us at one time or another have admired, have unwisely attempted to transplant into our outdoor gardens, and have hopefully but unsuccessfully cherished to an untimely but inevitable end" (418). These are the kinds of words that Johnson gave the label *Dicts.* for *Dictionaries* and wrote of them in the Preface:

of these I am not always certain that they are read in any book but the works of lexicographers. Of such I have omitted many, because I have never read them; and many I have inserted, because they may perhaps exist, though they have escaped my notice; they are, however, to be yet considered as resting only upon the credit of former dictionaries. (quoted in Kennedy 1927, 422)[1]

The lexicographic game with *esquivalence* highlights the modern assumption that dictionary editors no longer take the liberty of adding hifalutin words that they think "should be" words in English, as opposed to hifalutin words that are actually used in some written register of English. The game "Fictionary" or "The Dictionary Game" works only because dictionaries are filled with obscure words that the typical speaker and writer does not know; the goal of the game

---

[1] Read (2003) dates hothouse words back at least as far as John Bullokar's *English Expositor* (1610), including *hamkin* ('a pudding made vpon the bones of a shoulder of mutton, all the flesh being first taken off'). The only other citation for the word in the *OED* is the entry from Blount's *Glossographia*, with exactly the same definition.

is to make up the most believable fake definition of the word (determined by a vote of the game's participants). Players assume that someone other than the dictionary editors has actually used this word in a meaningful context, even if they are not sure who that someone might be; in other words, the word is obscure but not "phony."

This chapter highlights the prescriptive meta-discourse about "real" words that now seems thoroughly ordinary. It is so ordinary, in fact, that speakers often do not realize that the lexicographers behind modern dictionaries are, for the most part, no longer participating. As this chapter demonstrates, prescriptive impulses show up early in English dictionaries, but, at this point, the prescriptivism that aims to limit flexibility in terms of accepting new words into the language is perpetuated by users and reviewers of dictionaries more than dictionaries themselves. This second case study focuses on the history of prescriptive meta-discourses about the legitimacy of words, starting in Early Modern English; the next two chapters highlight actual changes in words Modern American English speakers and writers use.

In histories of English, Shakespeare's legendary creativity with the language is often studied and celebrated. Not often enough is his creativity contrasted with the lexical creativity of, for example, modern politicians, who are often as not questioned if not criticized for their innovative creations (consider George W. Bush's *misunderestimate*). Yet the continuities and shifts in the meta-discourse about new words – in dictionaries, the press, and other public commentary – merit attention in the way we tell language history.

Shakespeare's creativity took place in a time period of intense debate about borrowed words, not as much about novel creations using native word-forms – although those would come under scrutiny by the eighteenth century. The sixteenth and seventeenth centuries are often framed as a time of increasing self-consciousness about language, and one focal point was the effects of the massive influx of borrowed words into the language, especially from Latin and Greek. This controversy over borrowings, now known as the "inkhorn controversy," provides useful historical context for the development of dictionaries and the conversations modern speakers have about "real" words today. Those early conversations get attention in textbooks, but today's concerns about the legitimacy of words that swirl around dictionaries, politicians, and public neologisms remain marginalized as part of speakers' experience with the spoken and written language.

The inkhorn controversy

The inkhorn controversy constituted, at least at face value, a debate about linguistic innovation: whether to use "proper and commonlie used wordes" or the new "strange and *inkhorne* tearmes" (this contrast is Roger Ascham's, *The*

Scholemaster [1570, 127]). The language purists of the day battled what they saw as an overly exuberant rash of overly opaque borrowed words – these long words that took too much ink from the inkpot to write (hence the name inkhorn terms). The purists advocated instead native English formations such as *gainstrive* for 'oppose', *awkness* for 'perversity', *outborn* for 'foreign', and *onwriting* for 'inscription' (not that the native forms were not always shorter, just more Germanic). The last of these, *onwriting*, was an Old English word revived in 1557 by Sir John Cheke, an adamant language purist, in his translation of the Gospel of St. Matthew. In this work, Cheke also employed *hundreder* where the King James version in 1611 would use *centurion*, *foresayer* for *prophet*, and *gainrising* for *resurrection*. Today, a good number of the inkhorn terms are so familiar that it is hard to imagine they were contested. But contested they were (see Baugh and Cable [2002, 200–233] for an excellent discussion).

Thomas Wilson, in *Arte of Rhetorique* (1560), provides a famous critique of the new, obscure words – or "darke" as he calls them – coming into English in the period. He begins with this assertion:

Among all other lessons this should first be learned, that wee neuer affect any straunge ynkehorne termes, but to speake as is commonly receiued: neither seeking to be ouer fine, nor yet liuing ouer-carelesse, using our speeche as most men doe. . . Some seeke so far for outlandish English, that they forget altogether their mothers language. And I dare sweare this, if some of their mothers were alive, thei were not able to tell what they say: and yet these fine English clerkes will say, they speake in their mother tongue, if a man should charge them for counterfeiting the Kings English. (quoted in Mair 1909, 162)

Wilson then goes on to quote a letter that he claims was written by a Lincolnshire man asking for an unoccupied benefice. I quote here the first few lines:

Pondering, expending, and reuoluting with my selfe, your ingent affabilitie, and ingenious capacity for mundaine affaires: I cannot but celebrate, & extol your magnifical dexteritie aboue all other. For how could you haue adepted such illustrate prerogatiue, and dominicall superioritie, if the fecunditie of your ingenie had not been so fertile and wonderfull pregnant. Now therefore being accersited to such splendente renoume and dignitie splendidious: I doubt not but you will adiuuate such poore adnichilate orphanes, as whilome ware condisciples with you, and of antique familiaritie in Lincolneshire. (Mair 1909, 163)

Some of the new terms that Wilson identifies as inkhorn terms have fallen out of use – if they ever were in much use – such as *accersited* and *adnichilate*. Many others, however, have become commonplace, such as *dexterity*, *extol*, and *superiority*. And some of the words that endured harsh critique in these kinds of forums appear to have been hothouse words promoted by dictionaries but perhaps few others.

Defenders of borrowing pointed out how embedded some of the loanwords already were in the language, as well as the ways in which English needed more words to be able to express complex material in the new scientific, academic, and literary registers in which it was being deployed. Baugh and Cable (2002, 221) quote George Pettie as providing a nice summary of the position in the preface to his translation of Guazzo's *Civil Conversation* (1581):

And though for my part I use those words [inkhorn terms] as litle as any, yet I know no reason why I should not use them, and I finde it a fault in my selfe that I do not use them: for it is in deed the ready way to inrich our tongue, and make it copious, and it is the way which all tongues have taken to inrich them selves ... it is not unknowen to all men how many woordes we have fetcht from thence [Latin] within these fewe yeeres, which if they should be all counted inkepot termes, I know not how we should speake any thing without blacking our mouthes with inke: for what woord can be more plaine then this word *plaine*, and yet what can come more neere to the Latine? What more manifest then *manifest*? and yet in a maner Latine: What more commune then *rare*, or lesse rare then *commune*, and yet both of them comming of the Latine?

Pettie's rhetorically savvy hedge about how rarely he himself uses inkhorn terms captures the power of these terms to do rhetorical damage to a writer who used them inelegantly, even for their defenders and even when used in moderation.

Baugh and Cable (2002) devote extended attention to the inkhorn controversy in their history of the English textbook, as part of a discussion of new conditions or factors that affected the development of English in the Modern period, beginning in the Renaissance.[2] They list the factors as follows: "the printing press, the rapid spread of popular education, the increased communication and means of communication, the growth of specialized knowledge, and the emergence of various forms of self-consciousness about language" (200). As Baugh and Cable note, this self-consciousness, both at the individual and more broadly public level, remains with English speakers to this day, creating a sense of need to conform to accepted language standards in some situations (or at least an awareness that there are standards) and an impetus for language policy and planning. This link to the present day is important, but self-consciousness about language and then full-fledged prescriptivism receive much more attention in their pre-twentieth-century manifestations. In a later chapter on American English, the authors include a section on purist attitudes and Americanisms, mentioning the controversy over *Webster's Third New International Dictionary* and its sparing use of usage labels. The link of the highly self-conscious discussion of Americanisms and their merits, both in the UK and the US, with the self-consciousness about language that arose in the Renaissance, in this case specifically about new words, is left largely implicit.

---

[2] The controversy receives even more extended attention in books focused specifically on the Early Modern English period, such as Jones (1953) and Barber (1997).

C. M. Millward's *A Biography of the English Language* similarly emphasizes the heightened awareness of language that characterized the Renaissance. In the first and second editions (1989 and 1996), a multi-page section about the inkhorn controversy, spelling reform, the movement for an English academy, and the emergence of dictionaries and grammars is called "The Self-Conscious Language"; in the third edition (2012), this heading is revised to "English Comes of Age." The perceived importance of this "outer history," as Millward calls it, is captured by the number of pages it receives: at twenty-five pages in the third edition, the section is over three times longer than the outer history for Old English and four times longer than the outer history for Middle English (despite the presence of the Norman Conquest and its aftermath). The outer history of Present Day English is more extensive than Old or Middle English (at fourteen pages) and covers the growing acceptance of borrowing, spelling reform, text messaging, calls for an academy, and dictionary making. The section on dictionaries, however, is an entirely descriptive historical account of important lexicographical projects, beginning with the *OED*; there is no discussion of the ideologies and meta-discourses that the meteoric growth of dictionaries in the modern period has promoted. Millward's division of language history into the "outer" and "inner" does not allow the text easily to make the important point that Baugh and Cable include about how speakers' awareness of standards has become part of their social consciousness, which can affect language usage.

If anything, this awareness, including a preoccupation with the authority of dictionaries and style guides, has become more pronounced and more widespread since the Renaissance, with the introduction of universal education and rapidly rising literacy rates, as well as cheaper, more accessible printed texts. And yet because this self-consciousness about usage and about language authority is no longer new, it tends to fall out of the limelight in telling the history of Modern or Present Day English.

It can be tempting to think that prescriptive impulses came later in the history of English lexicography, but they seem to have been present from the very beginning. In fact, contemporary dictionaries have become less prescriptive since the undertaking of the *OED* at the end of the nineteenth century and in keeping with prevailing trends in linguistics; but dictionaries continue to be coopted into the prescriptive project, now by users and by reviewers. Today, users of dictionaries often talk about "real" words; earlier the language was often about "legitimacy," employed by the dictionary makers themselves. The discourse of legitimacy, authenticity, and purity in relation to words has been circulating since the very first dictionaries were created, as this chapter will discuss. Early on, the legitimacy of borrowed terms was a primary focus; today other kinds of neologism receive critique, not from dictionaries but from published pundits, often worried that dictionaries are not fulfilling their responsibilities in drawing the lines around the English lexicon.

Prescriptivism and the earliest dictionaries

The first English dictionaries were designed to record and help literate folks, perhaps especially the aspiringly literate or "educationally insecure" (McArthur 1986, 86) such as women and young people, with "hard words." The first English–English dictionary – in contrast to the earlier bilingual dictionaries (e.g., English–Latin) – is usually said to be Robert Cawdrey's *A Table Alphabeticall, conteyning and teaching the true writing, and vnderstanding of hard vsual English words, borrowed from the Hebrew, Greeke, Latine, or French. &c. With the interpretation thereof by plain English words gathered for the benefit & helpe of Ladies, Gentlewomen, or any other vnskilfull persons* (1604). Cawdrey's dictionary has only 3,000 entries, a paltry number compared with the 150,000 or so entries in today's college dictionaries. This slim volume doesn't even look like a dictionary to modern eyes. The entries are typically very short: for example, *agilitie* is defined as "nimblenes or quicknes," and *fantacie* as "imagination." Of the hard words included in this work, some are surprising given how mundane they now are (e.g., *fact, idiot, ocean*). Cawdrey includes no usage labels or notes in the entries;[3] while the Preface contains a warning against "strange ynckhorne Termes," Cawdrey does not judge specific hard words in the dictionary as good or bad, legitimate or illegitimate, which can make it seem like these early English dictionaries were purely descriptive in purpose.

However, Allen Walker Read's survey of the beginnings of English lexicography highlights evidence of prescriptive aims in dictionaries significantly before the rise of concerted prescriptive language efforts in the eighteenth century. For example, William Bullokar's plan for a dictionary in his *Bref Grammar of English* in 1586 contains the following line: "A dictionary and grammar may stay our speech in a perfect use for euer" (quoted in Read 2003, 190). Read comments: "I regard this as a landmark statement, as it so boldly proclaims (in 1586, mind you) the dictionary as law-giver" (190–191). He adds that the statement shows that "English speakers were ready to put implicit faith in dictionaries even before there were any English dictionaries" (224). By the time John Webster's play *The Duchess of Malfi* was performed in England around 1614, it appears that references to "a dictionary" had become standard fodder in conversation: in response to a physician's statement about a "very pestilent" disease, "They call lycanthropia," the Marquis of Pescara replies, "What's that? I need a dictionary to't" (quoted in Read 2003, 196).

Read dates the first English dictionary back to the list of hard words at the back of Edmund Coote's *The Englishe Scholemaister* (1596); he sees

---

[3] The only two labels given to words in the dictionary indicate word origins: *[fr]* for French, and (*g.*) or *[gr.]* for Greek.

Cawdrey's work as derivative. Perhaps most obviously, these early dictionaries aimed to standardize and legitimize particular spellings. Coote states that the word list allows users to know the "true writing" of words (Cawdrey stressed "true Orthography"), even when no definition is provided; this idea of "true writing" echoes Richard Mulcaster's emphasis on "the right writing of our English tung" in *Elementarie* (1582), described by Baugh and Cable (2002, 212) as "the most extensive and the most important treatise on English spelling in the sixteenth century." In *The Englishe Scholemaister*, Coote includes a dialogue in which two students reinforce the value of the word list for knowing correct spelling:

IOHN. How spell you Iesus?
ROBERT. I, e, s, u, s.
IOHN. How know you that it is not written g, e?
ROBERT. Because it is not in the table at the end of my booke: for all that be written with ge, be there, and our maister taught us that all other of that sound must bee written with Ie.
IOHN. How write you Circle?
ROBERT. S, i, r, c, l, e.
IOHN. Nay, now you misse: for if you looke in the table, you shall find it Circle . . .

(Coote 1596, 32–33)

This passage captures the growing intolerance for variability in English spelling with the idea that there is one right way to spell a word.

Even before dictionaries aimed to be more fully comprehensive of the lexicon in the eighteenth century, some dictionary makers were concerned with establishing the boundaries of "legitimate" usage. Edward Phillips, in *The New World of Words* (first published in 1658, with four subsequent editions in the next forty years), was the first to use a mark or stigma (an "obelisk") to mark words he disapproved of "on any appreciable scale" (Osselton 1958, 3).[4] In the Preface, Phillips writes:

besides, that even of these sorts of words there were many wanting before, which were requisite to be inserted, many not so properly rendred as was convenient, divers cram'd in by the head and shoulders without any distinction, but as if they had been as good as the best; whereas in works of this nature men ought to fly all Pedantismes, and not rashly to use all words alike, that are met with in every English Writer, whether Authentick, or not, this is a bad example to the unadmonish't Reader, and might incourage him to suck in barbarisme as soon as Elegance, but by long experience out of a continued course of reading the best Authors, and conversation with the better sort of company to examine throughly what words are natural, and legitimate,[5] and what spurious, and forc't; nor is it

---

[4] Osselton notes that Henry Cockeram in the *English Dictionarie* (2nd edn., 1626) marked twenty-four words as obsolete with an asterisk. Read (2003) critiques Cockeram for significantly increasing the number of hothouse words in his dictionary.

[5] This word "legitimate" comes up again in Webster's plan for his dictionary in the early nineteenth century.

proper to quote an Authour for a word that long custome hath sufficiently authoriz'd, but either such as are grown out of use, or such as are used onely upon special occasions, or as terms of Art; and not upon the credit of every one neither, nor to quote any modern, or trivial Authour for words used by those more ancient, or of greater credit: I do not deny indeed, but that there are many words in this book (though fewer then in other books of this kinde) which I would not recommend to any for the purity, or reputation of them, but this I had not done, but to please all humours, knowing that such kinde of words are written, & that the undistinguishing sort of Readers would take it very ill if they were not explained, but withal I have set my mark upon them, that he that studies a natural and unaffected stile, may take notice of them to beware of them, either in discourse, or writing; and if any of them may have chanc't to have escap't the Obelisck (as such a thing may happen in spight of deligence) there can arise no other inconvenience from it, but an occasion to exercise the choice and judgement of the Reader, especially being forewarned. (c2)

Phillips employs the language of legitimacy, authenticity, and purity – terms that permeate prescriptive discourse to this day.

Stigmata continued to be used in four other major lexicographic works, leading up to Samuel Johnson's Dictionary: John Kersey's revision of *The New World of English Words* (edns. 1706, 1720); Kersey's *Dictionarium Anglo-Britannicum* (edns. 1708, 1715, 1721); Nathan Bailey's *Universal Etymological English Dictionary* "Vol. II" (1727); and Benjamin Martin's *Lingua Britannica Reformata* (edns. 1749, 1754) (Osselton 1958). Osselton argues that the practice of using stigmata to relegate words to the realm of the inelegant, pompous, or otherwise unworthy had received little attention before his book because the practice was discontinued after Johnson's dictionary. It was a lexicographic practice that lasted about one hundred years, later replaced with usage labels. For the purposes of this chapter, it is important to realize that the tradition of differentiating legitimate from illegitimate words goes back to the seventeenth century, and its echoes surround English speakers in the UK, the US, and else-where today, even though contemporary dictionaries themselves rarely if ever talk about legitimacy.

In 1664 a committee of the Royal Society planned to compile "a Lexicon . . . of all the pure English words" (quoted in Read 2003, 208), and John Evelyn reiterated this idea of purity in 1665, calling for "a Lexicon or collection of all the pure English words" (quoted in Lynch 2009, 73). A review of William Lloyd's *An Alphabetical Dictionary* (1668) critiqued the inclusion of words "very questionable as to their . . . propriety" and was concerned about the leaving out of the original asterisk (Read 2003). In his 1697 *An Essay on Projects*, Daniel Defoe wrote of his hope that with an Academy: "'twou'd be as Criminal then to *Coin Words, as Money*" (Lynch 2009, 60). This metaphor clearly signals Defoe's belief that there are legitimate words and illegitimate, or illegal, words. Jonathan Swift, in his *A Proposal for Correcting, Improving and Ascertaining the English Tongue*, also expressed concern about the ability of unworthy words to make their way into the language. Jack Lynch (2009, 73) concludes: "But even after the first English lexicons had been written, the public wasn't satisfied – there may have been English dictionaries, but there was still no authoritative English dictionary. These new books did nothing to settle disputes, and to many the language still seemed frustratingly chaotic."

In sum, it is not that prescriptivism was absent from dictionaries in the seventeenth and the first half of the eighteenth century. But, clearly, their approach did not yet fulfill readers' desire for prescriptive guidance on the legitimacy of words. Lord Chesterfield, who supported Samuel Johnson's plan for the dictionary, wrote in the magazine *The World* about the need for Johnson's dictionary (to which Johnson responded angrily because Chesterfield had not provided financial support to match his rhetorical support):

It must be owned, that our language is, at present, in a state of anarchy, and hitherto, perhaps, it may not have been the worse for it . . . The time for discrimination seems to be now come. Toleration, adoption, and naturalization have run their lengths. Good order and authority are now necessary. But where shall we find them, and at the same time the obedience due to them? We must have recourse to the old Roman expedient in times of confusion, and chuse a dictator. Upon this principle, I give my vote for Mr. Johnson, to fill that great and arduous post, and I hereby declare, that I make a total surrender of all my rights and privileges in the English language, as a free-born British subject, to the said Mr. Johnson, during the term of his dictatorship.

Johnson himself approached the project with the goal of drawing lines between legitimate and illegitimate words. He wrote in the plan for the dictionary:

By tracing in this manner every word to its original, and not admitting, but with great caution, any of which no original can be found, we shall secure our language from being over-run with cant, from being crouded with low terms, the spawn of folly and affectation, which arise from no just principles of speech, and of which therefore no legitimate derivation can be shewn. (quoted in McDermott 2005, 114)

The dictionary that Johnson and his editorial aids produced was both prescriptive and descriptive, as usefully detailed in contrasting takes on the question "Johnson the prescriptivist?" in McDermott (2005) and Barnbrook (2005). McDermott points out that Johnson's rhetoric about the need for lexicographic prescriptivism may have been stronger than his actions. For example, he states in the *Plan*: "Barbarous or impure words and expressions, may be branded with some note of infamy, as they are carefully to be eradicated where they are found" (quoted in McDermott 2005, 121). Johnson excluded obscenities and marked unassimilated borrowings with italics. He did not use the dagger though. How "sparing" (to use McDermott's term) Johnson's use of usage labels was is open to debate. According to Barnbrook's calculations, over 10 percent of the headwords in the first and second editions contain usage notes of some kind, but only a percentage of the usage notes (perhaps about

25 percent) put forward prescriptive judgments such as "a barbarous corruption" or "in low and ludicrous language." These statistics justify for Barnbrook the assertion of a "significant prescriptive element" in the text. Wild (2009) challenges these statistics, calculating that less than 2 percent of headwords receive prescriptive labels in the first edition – and even this number, she argues, may be high given that the usage label often applies only to one sense of a word, not the entire headword. Johnson's use of literary quotations within entries could be read as an acknowledgement of the importance of usage or as a prescriptive selection of what constitutes "English undefiled."

The debate about the extent of Johnson's prescriptivism can seem arcane, but Barnbrook argues that Johnson's practices shaped subsequent lexicographical projects:

dictionaries after Johnson, with one or two notable exceptions, seem to take prescription as a natural and thoroughly positive aspect of lexicography, growing effortlessly into their new powers as linguistic guardians. Johnson did not create the environment that transferred power in this way, but he colluded with it and, in so doing, helped to change the attitudes of lexicographers and dictionary users, as well as the nature of lexicography, in ways which can only be seen as negative. (110)

The late nineteenth and twentieth centuries witnessed key changes in lexicographical practices[6] – but not necessarily in the attitudes of dictionary users.

Contemporary debates about dictionaries

History tells us that dictionary users have come to care deeply about dictionaries' responsibility to differentiate good usage and good words from bad – and dictionary users care perhaps especially deeply about usage labels, as demonstrated by the controversy over Webster's *Third New International Dictionary, Unabridged*, published in 1961 (for excellent descriptions of the uproar, see Sledd and Ebbitt 1962; Morton 1994; Skinner 2012). The dictionary itself strove to be a model of descriptive lexicography and to capture the informality of much twentieth-century usage, in contrast to the second edition, which was commonly seen as an arbiter on usage. The third edition eliminated most usage labels (e.g., *colloquial*, *proper/improper*, *erroneous*) and relied only on *nonstandard*, *substandard*, *slang*, *obsolete*, and *archaic*. Most famously, it included no usage label for *ain't*, although it did note "disapproved by many and more common in less educated speech, used orally in most parts of the US. by many cultivated speakers esp. in the phrase *ain't I*." The new edition of the dictionary was slammed in the press as overly permissive and accelerating the deterioration of the English language; the treatment of *ain't* in particular was thought to

---

[6] For excellent scholarship on the history of modern dictionaries, see Landau (1991), Green (1996), Lynch (2009), and Bejoint (2010).

show approval "for the mediocre" and to "comfort the ignorant." The *New York Times* publicly rejected the third edition and pledged continued allegiance to the second edition, published in 1934.

While no dictionary or new edition of a dictionary since has spurred this level of public protest, the decisions of dictionary makers still regularly make the news and spark public assertions of disagreement if not downright disgust about the "legitimizing" of "illegitimate" words (or, for example, pronunciations of words). No matter how hard contemporary lexicographers may protest that their work is descriptive, no matter what the prefaces of contemporary dictionaries say about their role in tracking language change and actual usage, users and reviewers still tend to see dictionaries as largely prescriptive. I have an entire file in my office of newspaper articles about dictionaries, which includes reviews of new editions and commentary about new words "admitted into" the electronic *OED* and other dictionaries.[7] Because admittance into a dictionary suggests to the reviewers that the word is being legitimized, the value of the word and the legitimacy of the dictionary's authority are both up for debate.

I have selected just two examples to provide a flavor of the commentary. The first, by *Washington Post* columnist Gene Weingarten, appeared in 2001 in the feature "Below the Beltway." While Weingarten's tone is humorous, the sense of grievance and injury are designed to resound with readers who share his concern about the decline of linguistic standards (and once again, the question of the pronunciation of one word is deemed worthy of an entire newspaper column):

I recently wrote a list of my personal grievances against the human race, including "idiots who say Feb-you-erry." An alert copy editor at the Washington Post deleted this line, pointing out that according to the dictionary, Feb-you-erry was now an accepted pronunciation.

Sure enough, he was right. Sometime in the last few years, the Merriam-Webster Dictionary decided that this particular befouling of the English language was okay.

This was not my first such disappointment. I discovered not long ago that after years of misuse by the ignorant, dictionaries had caved in and were now defining "infer" to be a synonym of "imply," a word that is essentially its *opposite*. But this Febyouerry thing was too much.

So I called Frederick Mish, the editor of the Merriam-Webster Dictionary. Mish is a giant of American lexicography, and I did not wish to offend him, so I phrased my question delicately: "What the hell are you doing to the English language, sir, and why should you not be thrashed to within an inch of your life?"

---

[7] For example, in May 2011, the Collins English Dictionaries, which serve as the basis for the Collins Official Scrabble Words List, added 3,000 new playable words, including *thang*, *grrl*, and *fiqh*. This change made headlines.

"We are doing nothing to the language," Mish said. "We don't make it happen. We are recording what *you* are doing to the language."

The anecdote captures dictionary users' prescriptive expectations and lexicographers' descriptive practices colliding, published as part of an ongoing public conversation in the twenty-first century about the perceived misuse of the English language and the presumed responsibility of dictionaries to do something about it.

A few months earlier, Edward Rothstein (2000) attacked the newly published fourth edition of the *American Heritage Dictionary* with more seriousness, and a fundamental misunderstanding of the goals of the *OED* and of American Heritage:

In England in 1857, an ambitious proposal was made to create an encyclopedic concordance of English words. Such a dictionary, it was argued, would be a "historical monument"; it would represent "the history of a nation" recounted from a distinctive "point of view." The result, completed 70 years later, was the first edition of the Oxford English Dictionary. In that work's 441,825 words and 1,827,306 quotations, the grandeur of the English language was displayed in all its expanse, every transformation chronicled by citations from English poetry and prose.

Times have changed. In the fourth edition of the American Heritage Dictionary, the monument is dismantled, multiple points of view are proffered and the authority of the past is rejected along with the privileged position of written poetry and prose . . . Though many authorities are consulted for this dictionary, the ultimate authority is the ordinary person's ordinary speech . . . "Incentivize," a variety of boorish bureaucratic misspeak, has an entry simply because the word has come into use (meaning 'to motivate').

If any lexicographic project could be described as fundamentally descriptive in its principles, it is the *OED*. It is true that the *American Heritage Dictionary* was originally conceived as a response to the kerfuffle over *Webster's Third*, and it incorporated a Usage Panel and usage notes as a way to insert more prescriptive guidance into the dictionary. However, as Adams (2012a) concludes, that more prescriptive impulse gave way by the third edition to a more descriptive approach to usage notes and other elements in the dictionary. The privileging of poetry and high prose over other forms of language – a practice Rothstein glorifies – was productively challenged by most standard dictionaries long before the fourth edition of the *American Heritage Dictionary*. And the *OED* does not include the past as the authority on meaning but rather as key material in the tracing of semantic change. Rothstein's concern about the authority of the "ordinary person" and his desire for dictionaries to exercise more authority in delineating "good" or "legitimate" words echo the calls for Johnson's dictionary some 250 years earlier.

Once dictionaries established their presence in the lives of English speakers and writers, and English speakers and writers came to trust their authority, it became possible for speakers to have discussions about whether a word, simply because it "has come into use" (to quote Rothstein), is "really a word" – that is, whether it is a legitimate word. And while speakers may still say a word that their dictionary does not endorse, as writers they may hesitate to write it down in any more formal contexts (especially if Microsoft Word does not recognize it – such as *writerly* in the next sentence). In describing this writerly decision, I do not have in mind informal slang, which writers might avoid in formal contexts for multiple reasons. There is another set of more formal lexical creations, such as *misunderestimate* and *normalcy*, whose legitimacy has come under very public scrutiny.

It is helpful to return to a contrast with Shakespeare. Shakespeare had a penchant for creating new words: he liked to verb things (e.g., *to tongue*), to *un-* things (e.g., *uncurse*), and *be-* things (e.g., *bemonster*). For this lexical creativity with native English words and affixes (as well as the incorporation of some never-before-cited borrowings), Shakespeare is celebrated rather than mocked. He is the most cited author in the *OED*, and he typically receives significant attention in histories of English for his prolific contributions to the English lexicon – even in Crystal's *Stories of English* (2004), which devotes an entire chapter to debunking myths about how many thousands of words Shakespeare created in order to show that Shakespeare is too prominent in histories of English. Crystal takes the number of coinages down to about 1,700, and Metcalf (2002, 59–62) notes that some of these are getting predated in the revised version of the *OED*. Of note, Shakespeare started writing his plays before Cawdrey's English dictionary even became available, and the contemporaneous debates about inkhorn terms focused on hifalutin borrowed words. His creativity escaped criticism at the time and in modern times. But the prescriptive discourse around dictionaries now changes the playing field for high-profile neologizers, and that story, along with Shakespeare's, is worth telling as part of the history of English to highlight current meta-discourses about "not real" words and the ways that dictionaries get invoked in the critiques.

The modern politics of "not real" words

The word *misunderestimate*, which George W. Bush famously used in November 2000 after the presidential election ("They misunderestimated me"), made headlines as "a Bushism" – a word already in the *OED* in reference to an idiom or peculiarity of speech associated with George H. W. Bush or George W. Bush. The word, along with others seen to be of its ilk, was used as fodder for critiquing Bush's intelligence and competence – on both sides of the Atlantic. Take, for example, this line from the *Leicester Mercury* ("Read Dubya's Unwise Words," December 16, 2000): "For a hair-raising peek into the cob-webby mind of the most powerful man on earth take a look at The Complete Bushisms [the online magazine *Slate*'s running list of Bushisms]. It's full of garbled utterings from the man who told America that his detractors had 'misunderestimated me.'"[8]

In a significant number of the mocking discussions of this blend of *misunderstand* and *underestimate*, commentators harkened back to earlier presidential neologisms, perhaps the most famous of which is *normalcy*. Some twenty-first century commentators mistakenly credit Woodrow Wilson with *normalcy*, but, in fact, it was President Harding, before he became president. And the controversy over *normalcy* showcases some of what is at stake in the twentieth and twenty-first centuries for presidents who neologize (whether intentionally or not). Neologisms can prove slogan-worthy as well as demeaning to their author, as the word's legitimacy stands in for the speaker's legitimacy; and in both cases the neologisms can be distracting to the press and the public, stealing part of the spotlight from the issues to which they refer.

On May 14, 1920, Warren G. Harding supposedly misread the word *normality* in a draft of a campaign speech, saying *normalcy* instead.[9] So what he said is as follows:

America's present need is not heroics, but healing; not nostrums, but normalcy; not revolution, but restoration; not agitation, but adjustment; not surgery, but serenity; not the dramatic, but the dispassionate; not experiment, but equipoise; not submergence in internationality, but sustainment in triumphant nationality.

The word *normalcy* quickly attracted attention, and Harding harnessed that publicity and incorporated the word into a campaign slogan: "Return to Normalcy." This kept the word *normalcy* in the limelight, and over the next year, the *New York Times* addressed the legitimacy of the word *normalcy* multiple times, including in letters to the editor from concerned readers (on both sides of the issue). In other words, not only the word but also the conversation about the word were considered newsworthy. It demonstrates an ongoing and widespread interest in the legitimacy of select, often new words, now spread far beyond an inner circle of dictionary makers and language mavens. In this case, the *New York Times* and other newspapers fed the public's appetite for talking about new words.

On July 21, 1920, the *New York Times* ran a story about asking then Senator Harding about the meaning of *normalcy*, after he used the line "normal times and a return to normalcy" in a homecoming speech. The piece quotes Harding as follows:

"I have noticed that word cause considerable newspaper editors to change it to 'normality,'" he said. "I have looked for 'normality' in my dictionary, and I do not find it there. 'Normalcy,' however, I did find, and it is a good word.

---

[8] Michael Adams (2008, 207) defends the blend as a "wonderful" one, "one that simultaneously captures a range of meanings – misestimated, misunderstood, and underestimated."

[9] See also Metcalf (2004, 134–137) for a treatment of Harding's use of obsolete words, including *bloviate* and *normalcy*, and the public reception of those words.

"By 'normalcy' I do not mean the old order, but a regular, steady order of things. I mean normal procedure, the natural way, without excess. I don't believe the old order can or should come back, but we must have normal order, or, as I have said, 'normalcy.'"

The very next day, the *New York Times* ran a mixed defense of the word. On the one hand, it was not his coinage, which gave it legitimacy; on the other hand, it might not be a good rhetorical choice for a politician:

If Senator Harding likes the word "normalcy" he has the perfect right to use it. Mathematicians used it before him long ago, and nobody can question successfully either the propriety or the comprehensibility of the term. The word, however, is unfamiliar to most people, and therefore its employment in a political campaign is of dubious wisdom, as it will distract attention from what the Senator says to the way he says it . . .
    Why either a mathematician or a candidate for the Presidency should consider "normalcy" better than the familiar "normality" is a puzzle beyond the solution of an inquirer who is neither, but such a preference does not need explaining. There are even people who like "abolishment" better than "abolition."

But that was far from the end of the story. On September 27, 1920, this headline appeared in the *New York Times*: "Gompers Assails Harding Position: Declares 'Normalcy' Means 'Going Backward,' While Cox Is for 'Going Forward.'" Gompers was the President of the American Federation of Labor, and the *Times* quoted from his piece called "'Normalcy' versus Progress" in *The American Federationist*. In that, Gompers wrote: "He [Harding] speaks of 'normalcy.' The word is obsolete, and so is the condition to which he would return."

Harding won the election, but that also was not the end of the story of *normalcy*. The mere fact of the word stuck as one way to use language to critique Harding. On March 14, 1921, the legacy of Harding's resuscitation of *normalcy* was mentioned as part of a critique of his splitting infinitives:

Just as President Harding gave wide currency to the word "normalcy," which till he went to its assistance was slowly dying at the hands of a few mathematicians, so now, by dividing an infinitive in one of his official letters, he will revive the perishing controversy as to the rights and wrongs of that locution.

While the newspaper itself does not condemn the split infinitive, the fact that it mentions the stylistic feature at all calls into question its legitimacy.
    Just over a month later, on April 29, 1921, the *New York Times* brought in the British to join in the critique of Harding's language ("Says Harding's Style Jolts King's English: London Newspaper Thinks World Might Have Done Very Well Without Some of His Phrases"). While the piece starts with other linguistic outrages (according to the Brits), it returns to the word *normalcy*:

London, April 28. – The Daily Chronicle, in criticism of the English used by President Harding in his first message to Congress as disclosed on the full text which has reached here in American newspapers says:

"The message contains several passages that could cause a shudder in academic circles. He describes America as 'illy prepared for war's aftermath.' He says she is 'ready to co-operate with other nations to approximate dis-armament.' He refers to the overlapping of functions 'which fritters energies' and talks of 'protesting outlay' when what he means is protesting against outlay.

"Mr. Harding is accustomed to take desperate ventures in the coinage of new words. In his election addresses he invented the hideous 'normalcy.' This message gives us 'hospitalization' which the English speaking world might surely have done very well without."

As often happens, some of the linguistic "atrocities" blamed on Harding have much longer histories: *illy* is cited in the *OED* back as far as 1546 (although the Microsoft spellchecker underlines the word in red); and *hospitalization* was already in *Webster's New International Dictionary of the English Language* by 1909. But, in the end, the language is an excuse for a critique of the President, as some readers pointed out.

A bit more than a week later, on May 8, 1921, the *New York Times* published a letter to the Editor ("In the Dictionary") that came to Harding's defense, with at least a hint of patriotism:

Please permit me to enter a protest against the unreasonable criticism of President Harding's use of the English language. For instance, a London paper writes that "Mr. Harding invented the hideous normalcy" and sneeringly refers to "hospitalization," while a writer from New Jersey speaks of "barbaric normalcy and hospitalization."

As both words may be found in Webster's New International Dictionary, 1920 edition, it can hardly be truthfully said that President Harding invented them ... I think the criticism of the above words, and of some of President Harding's phrases, is unjust and entirely unwarranted.[10] (F. T. B., Hunger, N.Y., May 5, 1921)

Another *New York Times* reader, Gilbert M. Tucker of Albany, New York, chimed in with proof that Harding did not invent the word *normalcy*: "The word was at least eight years old when Mr. Harding was born. It occurs on page 386 of the Davies & Peck Mathematical Dictionary, published in 1857: 'If we denote the co-ordinates of the point of contact, and normalcy, by' certain symbols" (April 29, 1921).

A subsequent letter to the editor captures the ongoing attention and energy at least some readers were giving to this question of the origins of *normalcy*. On May 13, 1921, the *New York Times* published this response from the New Jersey writer, claiming to have been misquoted on May 3:

Mr. Harding did not invent a word. What he did invent was a new meaning for an old word which is to be found in the dictionary, indeed, but concerning which two facts should be noted. First, the sub-definition, "as the point of normalcy," indicates a specialized use.

---

[10] This point is repeated in a letter printed a full year later (July 23, 1922); the conversation about *normalcy* had not yet completely died out.

This was made plain in a letter from Mr. Tucker in THE TIMES of May 9, which proves that the word had, in it's [*sic*] day, a mathematical signification. Moreover, the Standard says, "used specifically in mathematics." Second, since 1913, the date of the latest general compilation of the New International, "normalcy" has been included among obsolescent words, &c., at the bottom of the page. Nor is it in the addenda of new words in the 1920 edition of the 1913 compilation.

Thus it appears that the habitat of the word is in the field of mathematics. It broke out last June, however, and has been roaming the jungle of politics these eleven months, setting a bad example for other respectable, superannuated words.

Probably the word will remain in usage after its very spectacular resurrection. Indeed, its euphony recommends it. University "Dry-as-dusts" of 2021 will amuse their classes in philology with its history, and will point to the heroic part played by a loyal partisan press in saving a situation and reanimating a dying word. JAMES A. BIGGS, Mahwah, New Jersey, May 10, 1921

It's not yet 2021, and I hope not to be a Dryasdust – a wonderful but now obsolete word coined by Sir Walter Scott that came to refer in the nineteenth century to one who studies antiquities and is interested in the uninteresting. As Biggs predicted, I am pointing to the importance of the press in the story of this word, but I am less interested in the history of the word *normalcy* per se than in the very public conversation about the word's legitimacy. Throughout this back-and-forth in published letters, writers are turning to dictionaries as a way to legitimize words. At no point do the critics of the word make the argument that they do not understand the word *normalcy* (or *illy* or *hospitalization* for that matter); in that way, the word is clearly understood to be a meaningful unit of language. At issue is whether it is a real, legitimate word, and Harding's skill, with language at least, and perhaps also his abilities more generally, are being judged through the lively discussion of the word. This prescriptive meta-discourse is part of the sociolinguistic context in which speakers and writers, both famous and not famous, are making choices about what words to use.

George W. Bush's word creations, as mentioned above, were similarly scrutinized publicly by the press, taken as in some way indicative of his intelligence and qualifications for leadership. On his heels came Sarah Palin, the Vice Presidential candidate in 2008, whose language – especially her choice of idioms and some of her grammatical constructions – was regularly ridiculed by the press during the presidential campaign. Then she created a word. Or at least many thought she did. On January 27, 2010, Sarah Palin responded to President Barack Obama's State of the Union address on Fox News and said the following:

Ever since about August. . . Americans have paid more attention to what is in this health care bill, and more and more Americans are becoming more concerned about what we see in there, so it hasn't been a matter of he not being able to explain his policy, with government takeover and mandation of health care.

The Twittersphere and blogosphere went atwitter about this "new word": *mandation*. And it wasn't celebratory buzz. Much of it was along the lines of "Is mandation even a word?" And to answer that, tweeters and bloggers turned to dictionaries. Take this example from the Mudflats:

> After Sarah Palin's excruciating exchange with fellow Fox News talking head Sean Hannity, America was introduced to a brand new word – "mandation." Seconds later it entered the Twittersphere, and Facebook, and blogs across the cyber universe. Liberals adored it, and Mandation Nation was born. When writing my post, I looked it up in the dictionary and announced on the blog that acording [*sic*] to Dictionary.com, "mandation" meant "no dictionary results."

Note the reference to "the dictionary," which suggests that all dictionaries are equally authoritative, and then the equating of "the dictionary" with Dictionary.com, which draws from various published dictionaries and other sources (not always clearly citing its sources). The blog post continues:

> In the wee hours of the morning, I got this little gem in the moderation queue. . . :
> Submitted on 2010/01/28 at 1:02am
> Sorry AKM, Palin just punked you. mandation is a word, moron.
> mandation: "another form of involuntary servitude"
> 1: a condition in which one lacks liberty especially to determine one's course of action or way of life
> 2: a right by which something (as a piece of land) owned by one person is subject to a specified use or enjoyment by another
> http://wiki.answers.com/Q/What_is_mandation

The respondent once again turns to a dictionary-like source for authority on the issue. (This source now reads: "The problem is that it is unclear if 'mandation' is even a word. It cannot be found in any dictionaries. Some websites claim 'mandation' is another form of involuntary servitude.")

Now, of course, almost all viewers of Palin's interview understood exactly what Palin meant by "mandation of health care": *mandation* is a straightforward derivation of the verb *mandate*, using the nominal suffix *-ion* (e.g., *legislate* > *legislation*). The sport was to see if it was a "real word" – not a meaningful word derived from rule-governed processes in the language but rather a word recognized by dictionary editors in standard dictionaries. It was not (it is in the *OED* but as obsolete with the meaning 'the act of committing a speech to memory'), which gave commentators fodder for critique. Never mind that Palin was far from the first person to use the word, and others had even used it in print (e.g., some commentators quickly located a 1989 article in the *Compensation and Benefits Review* titled "Healthcare for the Uninsured: Is Mandation the Answer?").

A few months later, Palin made headlines again, this time for her innovative blend *refudiate*. As with *mandation*, this word formation was not entirely innovative – the blend of *refute* and *repudiate* had popped up before, but

Palin made it famous. She used it first on July 14, 2010, in an interview on Fox News, again with Sean Hannity, and commentators in the blogosphere poked fun at the word. Then on July 18, she tweeted: "Ground Zero Mosque supporters: doesn't it stab you in the heart, as it does ours throughout the heartland? Peaceful Muslims, pls refudiate." The tweet was quickly removed, after almost instant ridicule, and later in the day, Palin posted a tweet that cited *refudiate*, *misunderestimate*, and *wee wee'd up* (an expression President Obama used in 2009) as evidence of English as a living language. She then added: "Shakespeare liked to coin new words too. Got to celebrate it!" The comparison to Shakespeare once again lit up the Twittersphere. The word *refudiate* got so much buzz over the next few months that the *New Oxford American Dictionary* named it their word of the year for 2010, although the announcement on the Oxford University Press blog added the caveat that the Press and its lexicographers had "no definite plans to include 'refudiate' in the NOAD, the OED, or any of our other dictionaries." Several critics of this decision argued that *refudiate* was a speech error, not a coinage (and not new to Palin).

Zimmer (2013) raises the question of why presidents no longer lead in creating or popularizing new words. Thomas Jefferson is credited in the *OED* for *neologize* (1813), as well as *belittle* (1785) and *Anglophobia* (1793). Of course, Jefferson was carrying out his neologizing before Webster's dictionary had been published in the US. Zimmer concludes:

Presidential language, while still closely watched, no longer exerts the impact it once did. In part, that is because modern presidents are exceedingly careful about what they say, which puts a damper on linguistic innovation. But we are also swamped with so many forms of creative public discourse, online and in the mass media, that "words from the White House" don't stand out as much.

It is certainly true that we are swamped with creative public discourse, and it's important that part of that discourse focuses on presidential neologizing, usually as illegitimate. Consider the ridicule that George W. Bush endured for his use of the word *embetterment*, formed through regular morphological processes from the verb *embetter*, which the *OED* lists as obsolete, but would still be transparent for English speakers through analogy with a verb such as *embitter*. *Embetterment* as a neologism is arguably no more radical than Jefferson's creation of *belittle*. Yet while *belittle* appears in the *OED* with Jefferson as the first citation, *embetterment* appears in *Urban Dictionary* with this definition: "A non-existent word that George W. Bush frequently uses in speeches and at press conferences."

Jefferson wrote: "Necessity obliges us to neologize." What counts as "necessity" is open to debate. And Jefferson was not living in the age of blogs and tweets and 24/7 news cycles, which raise the political stakes of neologizing. It is no wonder that modern presidents are exceedingly careful about what they say – not only in terms of the content but also in terms of the perceived legitimacy of the words. As Ben Jonson wrote centuries ago in *Discoveries Made upon Men and Matter* (1640): "A man coins not a new word without some peril and less fruit; for if it happen to be received, the praise is but moderate; if refused, the scorn is assured."

At the beginning of the twenty-first century, the new words created by famous people are regularly debated publicly online and in the press. For politicians, the question of a word's legitimacy can be a way to debate the person's legitimacy. For others, the discussion of the new word can be more of a fun diversion or a useful form of publicity. For example, in February 2013 Fred Wilpon, the principal owner of the New York baseball team the Mets, described real estate as having "gone zimmo"; this phrase and the question of the word's etymology (no one had any answers) earned him a headline in the *New York Times*.[11] Companies like Subway can play with the idea of neology and "real words": in 2012, Subway released a series of ads about "turkeytopia," and in one, professional boxer Mike Lee asks, "Turkeytopia: is that even a word?" And decisions about words' inclusion in well-known dictionaries, from the *OED* to the Scrabble dictionary, appear in the news with startling regularity. This conversation about words is part of many speakers' and writers' everyday experience with language and, therefore, an important a part of the history of English, which should tell both the intertwined stories of words and of the meta-discourses around words.

---

[11] The coverage of words in newspapers can provide invaluable evidence for lexicographers and other word sleuths. For example, the *Los Angeles Times* headline "Ben's Jazz Curve," and the quote in the article from Portland Beavers pitcher Ben Henderson about his "jazz ball," is the earliest recorded instance of the word *jazz*. It helps solve the puzzle of that word's etymology and links its origins to baseball (see Zimmer 2012).

Nonsexist language reform, or the set of efforts to make the English language more equitable to and inclusive of men and women, falls under the more general heading of "politically correct" language reform. The scare quotes around "politically correct" in that sentence are highly intentional, designed to emphasize the charged and problematic nature of this term at the beginning of the twenty-first century. The phrase "politically correct" has undergone semantic pejoration (that is, its meaning has become more negative) such that it no longer refers neutrally to efforts to reform language in order to make it more respectful and inclusive of all persons, but instead suggests overly sensitive if not silly and unnecessary efforts to change language "at the whim" of underrepresented groups and their advocates.

Politically correct language and the efforts to promote it are regularly ridiculed in the public arena. Fabricated language reforms such as *personhole cover* for *manhole cover* and *vertically challenged* for *short* are held up as symptomatic of the movement's excesses. I call these fabricated because I have never actually heard any advocate of nonsexist language reform seriously propose *personhole cover* or anyone proposing any kind of language reform make a serious case for *vertically challenged*. Yet they can show up side by side with more common, even at this point mainstream reforms such as *Native American* for *Indian*, *African American* for *Black*. If *Urban Dictionary* provides a snapshot of attitudes about the term *political correctness*, the term's negative connotations have gone beyond silly and unnecessary and now include manipulative, harmful, and silencing. The first definition in *Urban Dictionary* in Fall 2012 (which means it had the best ratio of thumbs up to thumbs down) read: "Organized Orwellian intolerance and stupidity, disguised as compassionate liberalism." It goes on to note: "Political correctness is most well known as an institutional excuse for the harassment and exclusion of people with differing political views." Subsequent definitions link politically correct language to censorship and "the death of comedy."

The explicit complaints about politically correct language often focus on specific words, but the underlying resistance taps into a deeper issue. At least in part it is speakers' resistance to having their language and their day-to-day linguistic choices politicized (Cameron 1995, 119). Politically correct language efforts highlight some words as problematic if not offensive to a specific social group. As a result, a speaker's choice to use or not to use those words can become a political act in relation to that group and perhaps in relation to the movement for social equality more generally. Individual word choices thus can carry a lot of weight: it's not just a question of a word's denotation (its most direct meaning) but also its social connotations or associated meanings. Perhaps especially disconcerting for some speakers is that the repercussions of the choice weigh heavily on the connotations an audience may bring to a word. That is, it is not a question only of speaker intention but also of audience reception. This fact defies a common belief that words are the medium of the message, not the message itself (Cameron 1995). Politically correct language efforts force speakers to confront the fact that words are not neutral conveyors of intended meaning; words in and of themselves carry information about speaker attitudes and much more. Politically correct language asks speakers to use care in avoiding bias in their language choices and to respect the preferences of underrepresented groups in terms of the language used to refer to them.

Given that the politically correct language movement has gained momentum rapidly over the past few decades and its language recommendations have shifted over time, speakers can feel uninformed, frustrated, or even angry at not being sure what is currently "correct." Those emotions can lead speakers to cry censorship, to capture the sense that their freedom of speech has been curtailed. Such a claim confuses censorship and censoring, two concepts that Keith Allan and Kate Burridge usefully disentangle in *Forbidden Words* (2006). Censorship typically involves suppression of language by groups in power claiming to act for the public good; censoring can be institutionalized and by the powerful or it can be local and by the less empowered. One key point is that all of us self-censor in our everyday speech (consider politeness conventions) as well as censor others. As Allan and Burridge (2006, 110) put it: "Certain restrictions must be observed for everyone to have the freedom to speak. We are rarely at liberty to say exactly what is in our minds in the plainest and most explicit terms." Nonsexist language reform provides a fascinating example how this kind of censoring, promoted by the less empowered, has become institutionalized and enforced by the powerful. Censorship, Allan and Burridge point out, is usually futile, but it can be effective "when it coincides with what individuals would choose to censor for themselves (hence the comparative success of non-discriminatory language guidelines)" (238). In other words, in this case prescriptive language reforms responded to social and political conditions and aligned with broader social and political agendas.

In this chapter and the next, I will use the term *politically responsive prescriptivism*, rather than *politically correct prescriptivism*, in order to avoid the now negative connotations of the latter. The description "politically responsive" captures the ways in which these rules for usage occur in reaction to and/or as a reflection of political and social developments in the culture.[1] And the discussion in these two chapters will focus not on the merits of any specific proposed change to the language but instead on the real stakes involved in these efforts to consciously change usage. The serious efforts to reform language to be more inclusive and less derogatory toward marginalized social groups are fundamentally about respect: an explicit request for respectful language and, if taken up, a respectful acknowledgement of the request.

The not-seriously proposed compound *personhole cover* is funny because it sounds outlandish – we notice it in a way that we probably would not notice the now standard alternative *streethole cover*. And there are many more gender-neutral language alternatives that are now standard enough to be fully unremarkable. Consider the lyrics of the 2010 song "Flyover States" by the country singer Jason Aldean:

> A couple of guys in first class on a flight
> From New York to Los Angeles,
> Kinda making small talk killing time,
> Flirting with the flight attendants, . . .

Even in this sexualized context of men engaged in flirtation, the objects of the flirting are not identified by gender – they appear in the song as "flight attendants," the generic, nonsexist term. This song's use of *flight attendant*, even when gender may be very relevant, is standard, unremarkable. (Aldean did not need *attendants* for the rhyme scheme; if anything, if Aldean had female flight attendants in mind, *stewardesses* would have provided more rhyme in the stanza. Perhaps Aldean wanted the gender of the flight attendants to be ambiguous.)

The speed with which some politically responsive language efforts have changed Modern English usage is remarkable and the focus of this chapter. While linguists have often defended such efforts to make language more inclusive and less biased (I will talk about the Linguistic Society of America's policy on nonsexist language use later in the chapter), they have not yet examined these efforts seriously enough as an important factor in understanding language change in the modern period. This chapter takes up one specific case study

---

[1] As part of this study and publishing this book, I could try to reappropriate the term *politically correct* – to take this term that has become a negative description of conscious efforts to reform language to be more respectful and inclusive and deliberately use it with positive meanings. I have, however, chosen to use the umbrella term *politically responsive* both because it may help readers shed some of the connotational baggage that comes with *politically correct* and because I am examining politically correct efforts as an example of politically responsive prescriptivism, which could encompass other kinds of language change efforts. (Given that I have resisted the term *correct* throughout this book in relation to prescriptivism, it also would feel odd to employ it here.)

of conscious efforts to change the language in response to political and social movements: nonsexist language reform. The next chapter turns to the reappropriation of negative terms for underrepresented or marginalized social groups.

Nonsexist language reform

In the second decade of the twenty-first century, it can be easy to lose perspective on the surprisingly rapid success of nonsexist language reform. Nonsexist language reform gained momentum in the 1970s with second-wave feminism, but even in the 1970s, it was hard to see how effectively efforts to change sexist words would infiltrate many corners of the language, including the personal pronoun system.

An excerpt from Robin Lakoff's foundational work *Language and Woman's Place* (2004 [1975]) nicely captures the perspective of some of even the most progressive feminist thinkers about what was possible. Lakoff's book is often cited as the spark for modern language and gender research and Lakoff herself has been a pioneer in the field. In this 1975 publication, when addressing the issue of generic *he*, she wrote:

I have read and heard dissenting views from too many anguished women to suppose that this use of *he* [as a generic] is really a triviality ... Perhaps linguistic training has dulled my perception, and this really is a troublesome question. If so, I don't know what to advise, since I feel in any case that an attempt to change pronominal usage will be futile. My recommendation then would be based purely on pragmatic considerations: attempt to change only what can be changed, since this is hard enough. (71)

Lakoff is certainly right that changing the pronominal system is hard at best. Personal pronouns are key building blocks in the language's grammar, or the "linguistic glue," as some linguists call these kinds of function words. They are very common and typically play a supporting role in the grammar; as a result, it is difficult to highlight them for speakers in such a way that they can actually change their usage consistently.

Yet, in this case, nonsexist language reform did change usage, specifically in the written language – and this specification is important. There are probably a couple of reasons that generic *he* was successfully driven out of standard usage. First, this linguistic effort was backed by a highly successful social movement in second-wave feminism. Feminists pointed out that generic *he* is sexist in its implications that the generic person is male by default; feminist linguists began to run studies and write articles arguing that the pronoun *he*, like the pronoun *she*, is not gender neutral. These linguists had more chance of being heard and influential – that is, that their proscription of generic *he* might get picked up and institutionalized in usage guides – given the inroads that feminism was making in social and political arenas more generally. Second, the effort to change generic *he* was focused primarily on the written language, which is more easily regulated than the spoken language. In the spoken language, speakers have a long history of not consistently using generic *he*: they have for centuries used singular *they* in addition to or often rather than generic *he* or generic *he or she* (Curzan 2003; Balhorn 2009).[2] There is a website dedicated to Jane Austen's use of singular *they*; Shakespeare employed it at times, and he was breaking no new ground given that there are examples at least two centuries earlier. At this point, singular generic *they* is the majority form for modern speakers of American English (Newman 1997), despite prescription to the contrary. So the written use of generic *he* in the 1970s was already often a conscious decision for writers (even if highly naturalized) in order to adhere to codified rules of formal, "correct" usage.

Explicit prescription of generic *he* rather than singular generic *they* or any other option dates back to the eighteenth century and Ann Fisher's *A New Grammar* (1745), the first grammar known to be written by a woman. According to Ingrid Tieken Boon van Ostade (2000), the citation of John Kirby's *A New English Grammar* (1746) as the source of the rule in Bodine (1975) does not account for Kirby's plagiarism of Fisher's earlier grammar. The rule was then more widely disseminated by Lindley Murray's extremely popular *English Grammar*, first published in 1795 (see also Curzan 2003). The prescription became firmly entrenched over the next 150 years as "correct grammar." A glance at usage guides from the 1970s quickly demonstrates why Lakoff might have been pessimistic about making any inroads with this specific grammatical rule. For example, in the 5th edition of the *Modern English Handbook* (1972), by Robert M. Gorrell and Charlton G. Laird, the use of *he or she* is described as "not usual," with the comment that "*He*, alone, is usually preferred" (619).

In the third edition of William Strunk and E. B. White's extremely influential *Elements of Style* (1979), the authors discourage any use of *they* as a singular, calling it "a fault," and then write:

> The use of *he* as pronoun [*sic*] for nouns embracing both genders is a simple, practical convention rooted in the beginnings of the English language. *He* has lost all suggestion of maleness in these circumstances. The word was unquestionably biased to begin with (the dominant male), but after hundreds of years it has become seemingly indispensible. It has no pejorative connotation; it is never incorrect. (60)[3]

---

[2] Proposals for a new, "artificial" singular generic pronoun (e.g., *thon*, *hisser*, *e*) have been put forward for a couple of hundred years; see the chapter "The Word That Failed" in Baron (1986) for an excellent discussion. These pronouns have, generally, failed to take hold; speakers have instead opted to take a pronoun already in the language (*they*) and adapt it for a new use. At the current moment, there is some energy to use the created pronoun *ze* for transgender individuals. Given the more specific environments for this pronoun, as compared with a singular generic pronoun, the odds are better for some success.

[3] See Curzan (2003), specifically ch. 3, for a detailed discussion of the extent to which generic *he* is "rooted in the beginnings of the English language." It is difficult to talk about generic pronouns in

The absolute tone of the final prescription, with the negatives "no" and "never," is strikingly assured, especially given that this edition was published in the late 1970s, when feminist efforts to reform just this kind of construction in the language had gained momentum. In fact, Strunk and White go on to dismiss contemporaneous efforts to replace so-called generic *he*:

No one need fear to use *he* if common sense supports it. The furor recently raised about *he* would be more impressive if there were a handy substitute for the word. Unfortunately, there isn't – or, at least, no one has come up with one yet. If *you* think *she* is a handy substitute for *he*, try it and see what happens. Alternatively, put all controversial nouns in the plural and avoid the choice of sex altogether, and you may find your prose sounding general and diffuse as a result. (61)

The commonsense rhetoric of the pronouncements in this passage is typical of the discourse of standard language ideology, the widely circulating belief system that promotes the standard language as better than other varieties and the only correct option. In the Strunk and White passage, one option, in this case generic *he*, is made to sound "natural" and uncontroversial while other options are in various ways clearly inferior. The treatment of generic *she* dismisses its political power to disrupt the supposed naturalness if generic *he*. The phrasing "try it and see what happens" assumes readers will see the obvious misstep and its negative if not ridiculous consequences. The rejection of plural nouns as creating more "diffuse" writing does not hold up under scrutiny. And the two most common alternatives, *he or she* and singular *they*, are not addressed at all – they evidently do not qualify as "handy substitutes." The tone and content of Strunk and White's prescription emphasize the challenge nonsexist language reform faced in its early stages.

And yet today, it is a rare style guide that embraces generic *he*. A notable exception is the *Associated Press Stylebook*, as I will discuss later in the chapter. Many style guides now advise instead a range of options: the conjoined pronominal phrase *he or she*; alternation between *he* and *she* by sentence, paragraph, or example; revision of the sentence to make it plural (in which case the writer can use *they*); or omission of the pronoun entirely. And this new prescription has been so successful that published academic prose in the US, UK, and elsewhere seldom uses generic *he*; as notably, older quotes with generic *he* often receive a [*sic*] after the pronoun to indicate that the usage is no longer acceptable. Journalistic prose does not appear to be far behind, if behind at all.

Old English because the language still maintained a grammatical gender system such that all nouns, including those for people, carried a grammatical gender. By Middle English, there is a noticeable tendency to talk about a generic teacher or citizen, for example, with *he*, but it is hard to determine the extent to which the pronoun was intended to be generic or the teacher or citizen was assumed to be male.

To show the rapidity of the changes in prescription on nonsexist language, I will review the relevant revisions to the style manuals of two major academic associations: the American Psychological Association (APA) and the Modern Language Association (MLA). I then compare the shifting guidelines in these manuals to evidence from the Corpus of Contemporary American English (COCA) and the Corpus of Historical American English (COHA) about changes in usage in spoken and written English over the past two hundred years. The manuals pay much attention to the singular generic pronoun issue, which will be the first example of changes in prescription and usage. They give increasing attention over the years surveyed to potentially sexist nouns, which will constitute the second example of how socially responsive prescriptivism takes hold, in guides to usage as well as in usage itself.

With politically responsive prescriptivism like nonsexist usage guidelines, the directionality of change between guides and usage is difficult if not impossible to determine definitively. In all likelihood, the process is bidirectional, with changes in one encouraging changes in the other and vice versa. In other words, the feminist push for nonsexist terms – be those pronouns or nouns – eventually infiltrated the editorial boards that create these kinds of manuals and influenced the prescriptions. Changes in prescriptions resulted in more nonsexist language in publications. More nonsexist language in publications changed what people read and saw as acceptable for formal usage, which has the power to influence standards of acceptability for spoken usage as well. At the same time, the feminist push for nonsexist terms may have had an impact on spoken usage directly, and, as spoken usage changed, the guides were revised to reflect the shifting sense of what constituted appropriate nonsexist usage in everyday language. The success of these conscious language reforms is remarkable, and the alignment of the efforts with powerful social and political forces helps to explain how the changes gained momentum in both written prescription and actual usage, both written and in some cases spoken.

Generic pronouns: changing prescriptions

In forty years, prescriptive advice on singular generic pronouns in formal written prose has taken a fairly radical turn, although it has yet to embrace fully (if at all) the spoken usage of singular *they*. The standard generic pronoun guidelines have moved from the acknowledgment of a potential issue to quite strong prescriptions about equitable language, which leave no room for the unquestioned use of generic *he*.

The *Publication Manual of the American Psychological Association*, the reference manual for publications in many social sciences and beyond, provides a valuable map of the changes. It has gone through six editions since its original publication in 1952. The first edition, which was revised in 1967, does not address potential gender bias in the text at all.

The second edition, published in 1974, adds a short paragraph about possible gender bias at the end of a section called "Consideration of the Reader." It alerts writers to the "current move to avoid generic use of male nouns and pronouns when content refers to both sexes"; it does not explicitly prescribe a nonsexist practice but instead notes that writers "may wish to use alternatives to words such as *chairman* and to avoid overuse of the pronoun *he* when *she* or *they* is equally appropriate" (28).[4] This wording reflects a growing awareness of the movement afoot to avoid potentially sexist language, but it sidesteps any strong prescription along these lines. The advice to "avoid overuse of the pronoun *he*" suggests that some use of *he* as a generic may be acceptable.

The third edition (1983) seems to mark the turning point for this publication, with the addition of a new section entitled "Guidelines for Nonsexist Language in APA Journals," which first appeared as a Change Sheet for the second edition, after the APA Publications and Communications Board approved the policy in 1977. But even before this new section, the paragraph under "Consideration of the Reader" has been significantly strengthened in tone and policy. It reads:

APA as a publisher accepts journal authors' word choices unless those choices are inaccurate, unclear, or ungrammatical. Because APA as an organization is committed both to science and to the fair treatment of individuals and groups, however, authors of journal articles are required to avoid writing in a manner that reinforces questionable attitudes and assumptions about people. (43)

Here, unbiased or equitable language becomes a requirement, not a suggestion; it reflects a policy adopted by the APA Board in 1982.[5]

The guidelines for nonsexist language tackle the issues as ones of accuracy, clarity, and absence of evaluation and bias. While long-established cultural biases are described as "insidious," the advice itself is hedged with modals such as *can* and *may*, as in the following:

[T]he use of *man* as a generic noun can be ambiguous and may convey an implicit message that women are of secondary importance. You can choose nouns, pronouns, and adjectives to eliminate, or at least to minimize, the possibility of ambiguity in sex identity or sex role. (44)

---

[4] Compare this position with the entry for *chairman* in Frederick T. Wood's *Current English Usage: A Concise Dictionary* (1962): "Used for both sexes. *Chairwoman* is not recognised as correct English" (44).

[5] Two of my colleagues in the School of Education at the University of Michigan who were publishing in the 1980s have distinct memories from this period of filling out forms to accompany articles submitted for journal publication that confirmed the author(s) had edited the work to remove bias. Such forms may strike some as quite heavy-handed politically responsive prescriptivism.

The opening hedges leave open the possibility that *man* might be generic in some circumstances, alongside advice about how to eliminate the ambiguity and the potential negative message for women. The subsequent table presents "Examples of common usage" in the left-hand column and "Alternatives" in the right-hand column. For example, "man's search" could be replaced with "the search," and "mankind" could be replaced with "people, humanity, human beings, humankind, human species."

These prescriptive guidelines for nonsexist usage are distinguished as somehow more artificial than other grammatical or stylistic prescriptions in the manual with the following note: "The task of changing language may seem awkward at first" (44). It is rare that other new guidelines for usage, such as the proscription of *hopefully* meaning 'it is hoped' that was added to many usage guides in the 1960s, receive such a caveat, even though using *it is hoped* for *hopefully* may strike many writers as awkward. It may be that nonsexist guidelines so clearly consciously respond to a social and political movement, even though they are also justified on rhetorical grounds such as the reduction of ambiguity. In that way, they may strike editors and readers as a more artificial imposition on written usage than equally artificial impositions that carry no political baggage – that seem like purely grammatical or stylistic issues.

The fourth edition of the APA manual, published in 1994, combines gender and ethnic bias under one section about reducing bias in language, and the language introducing the guidelines becomes more prescriptive. The stated requirement for authors is strengthened to: "avoid perpetuating demeaning attitudes and biased assumptions about people in their writing" (as opposed to "questionable attitudes and assumptions" in the previous edition). The paragraph goes on to offer an unhedged prescription: "Constructions that might imply bias against persons on the basis of gender, sexual orientation, racial or ethnic group, disability, or age should be avoided" (46).

The language is toughened elsewhere as well. In stressing accuracy, the manual states: "For example, using *man* to refer to all human beings is simply not as accurate as the phrase *men and women*" (47). Not only are there no hedges in the statement, the intensifier *simply* emphasizes the common sense of the preference for the phrase *men and women*. The use of *he* as a generic becomes "careless" and *man* as a generic becomes (potentially) incorrect:

[S]exist bias can occur when pronouns are used carelessly: when the masculine pronoun *he* is used to refer to both sexes, or when the masculine or feminine pronoun is used exclusively to define roles by sex (e.g., "the nurse . . . *she*"). The use of *man* as a generic noun or as an ending for an occupational title (e.g., *policeman*) can be ambiguous and may imply incorrectly that all persons in the group are male. (50)

The manual presents various options for replacing generic *he*, including rephrasing a sentence so the pronoun is unnecessary (e.g., making the antecedent and pronoun plural). It notes that *he or she* can become "tiresome," and alternating between *he* and *she* may be "distracting" and "is not ideal"; the subsequent note adds that alternating pronouns "implies that *he* or *she* can in fact be generic, which is not the case" (51). This statement stands in striking contrast with Strunk and White's earlier pronouncement that *he* is fully generic while *she* is clearly not.

Prescription is everywhere in the fourth edition of the manual. The table that summarizes the guidelines for unbiased language with examples now labels the right-hand column as "Problematic" and the left-hand column as "Preferred." The manual compares these rules for unbiased language with more familiar kinds of prescriptive rules when it aligns different kinds of editing practices: "Just as you have learned to check what you write for spelling, grammar, and wordiness, practice reading over your work for bias" (46). Given the overt prescriptivism of this powerful style manual, it should not be surprising to see a shift in the published written usage it governs.

Interestingly, the *MLA Handbook for Writers of Research Papers* has not taken as strong a prescriptive stand on these issues historically, although it has consistently addressed them. The first edition, published in 1973, takes a descriptive stance about the "careful writer," who "gives consideration to the implications of language." It then generalizes to the practices of "many writers," with the implication that the careful writer will consider the practices of the many writers:

> For example, many writers now avoid the use of the generic pronoun 'he' in referring to a person whose sex is not specified so as to avoid the possible implication that only a male person is intended. For advice on current practices, consult an instructor or one of the more recent guides listed below. (6)

These "many writers" remain in the second edition, published in 1984, but the handbook adds a stronger statement about avoiding bias: "Your language, in other words, should not suggest bias or prejudice toward any group" (30).

In the third edition of the MLA handbook (1988), the many writers become conscientious, a rhetorical move in a more prescriptive direction:

> Your language, in other words, should not suggest bias or prejudice toward any group. Discussions and statements concerning nondiscriminatory language have focused particular attention on avoiding language that could be labeled sexist. For example, conscientious writers no longer use *he* to refer to someone of unspecified sex – a doctor or an executive, say – lest readers infer that the statement can apply only to a man. To avoid this use of *he*, they recast sentences into the plural, specify the sex of an individual under discussion, and occasionally, if all else fails, use *he or she* or *her or him*. (34)

The conscientious writers have returned to being "many writers" in the fourth edition (1995) and subsequently. In each edition, there has been a list of other guides to consult, with the advice that writers would do well to consult them, and the list has been growing over time. Many of these guides take a stronger stand, more similar to the APA than the MLA.

The Executive Committee of the Linguistic Society of America (LSA) first approved nonsexist guidelines in 1995 (published in the *LSA Bulletin* in 1996). The Committee on the Status of Women in Linguistics (COSWL) was instrumental in advocating guidelines and subsequent revisions. The introduction to the current guidelines reminds writers of the power of readers/listeners to determine what is sexist: "[S]exism is often not a matter of intention but of effect." Of course, the guidelines themselves are also identifying specific constructions as inherently problematic, no matter the audience or context. The first guideline addresses generic *he* and *man*:

> Whenever possible, use plurals (*people, they*) and other appropriate alternatives, rather than only masculine pronouns and "pseudo-generics" such as *man*, unless referring specifically to males.

The term *pseudo-generic* leaves little room for ambiguity about the (non-)generic status of *man*.[6]

These guidelines are now cross-referenced in the Unified Style Sheet for LSA's flagship journal *Language*. But were one to look for the guidelines on the LSA website, as LSA's position statement on the issue, they are not especially easy to find. On the LSA website, the link to the nonsexist guidelines is found under "Selected Projects" of the Committee on the Status of Women in Linguistics, even though the Committee's work was to recommend changes to the LSA Executive Committee, which had ultimate authority to approve, and the guidelines are LSA's, not COSWL's. One possible interpretation is that the guidelines have been marginalized within the organization as a "women's issue." A more positive interpretation is that the guidelines have become mainstream enough that they can now be a cross-reference rather than a centerpiece for the organization and its journal.

I may be biased by my own experience as a journal editor, which I found myself reflecting on as I did the research on the history of nonsexist guidelines. I co-edited the *Journal of English Linguistics* for nine years (2002–2011), the last six with my colleague Robin Queen. We both pursue scholarship in the area of language and gender studies and are proponents of nonsexist usage. We did not, however, explicitly state guidelines for nonsexist usage on the journal's webpage. For the first few years the journal followed the *Chicago Manual of Style* and then switched to the *Language* Unified Style Sheet – for citations and, by implication, for guidelines about unbiased usage. I think that at this point

---

[6] In addition to sexist words, the guidelines address how bias can arise in the selection of examples in linguistics scholarship. For example, all the examples can focus on male subjects. Or the examples can perpetuate sexist stereotypes (e.g., an example sentence like "His wife nags him about taking out the garbage").

nonsexist language usage in published scholarship is naturalized enough for both of us that we never noticed the omission of the guidelines on our site; and in all nine years, I remember having to change only a handful for pseudo-generics in articles I was copy-editing for publication (and I did feel fully authorized to change them to nonsexist forms).

In light of these dramatic changes in academic style guidelines, the *Associated Press Stylebook*'s stance on generic pronouns seems oddly conservative (Christian et al. 2012).[7] Newspaper prose is typically slightly less formal, slightly more colloquial than academic prose; yet in this case, the guidelines adhere to the older prescription. The *2012 AP Stylebook* continues to support generic *he* if the sentence cannot be rewritten to avoid a singular pronoun (which is framed as the preferred option). The entry on "his, her" states: "Do not presume maleness in constructing a sentence, but use the pronoun *his* when an indefinite antecedent may be male or female: *A reporter tries to protect his sources*." (Not *his or her* sources, but note the use of the word *reporter* rather than *newsman*.)

The entry for "every one, everyone" in the 2012 version provides an example sentence with a generic *he*: *Everyone wants his life to be happy*. The entry stresses that *everyone* requires singular agreement in the noun and pronoun. The implication here is that *they* would not be singular in such a context. But counterexamples can be found in the *Stylebook* itself. In the Ask the Editor section of the online guide, a writer from Piscataway, New Jersey, asks in April 2007 whether the sentence "Everyone should have access to the prescription medicines they need" is incorrect. The answer accepts *they* in this context: "Until someone comes up with a better term, 'they' is acceptable in these cases (and better than he/she)." In this case, the guide appears to contradict itself in the advice. And a user from Atlanta notices this contradiction and writes the following to Ask the Editor in May 2012:

> I found conflicting responses to the question of if "everyone" uses a plural or singular pronoun. "Everyone will receive training that meets their needs" versus "Everyone will receive training that meets his or her needs." Which is correct?

The answer disowns the earlier response, but also contradicts the entry on "his, her" in endorsing *his or her* rather than *his*:

> Yes, I see the 2007 response, though it wasn't from me. The Stylebook entry on "every one, everyone" remains our guidance: everyone takes singular verbs and pronouns. Your second example is correct.

This response maintains the idea that the indefinite pronoun *everyone* is singular and the personal pronoun *they* is not; it also promotes *he or she* as a nonsexist

---

[7] The *Associated Press Stylebook* has made other notably conservative decisions about usage, including the decision to ban the use of *homophobia* in 2012, claiming the word was "imprecise."

singular alternative. In this way, it keeps the written language at a distance from common spoken practice but does support nonsexist usage. But another quoted example in the *Stylebook* shows the prevalence of generic *they* in reference to *everyone* even in formal written discourse: in the discussion of libel and the right of fair comment, the guide quotes a New York court in the case *Hoeppner* v. *Dunkirk Printing Co.* (1930): "Everyone has a right to comment on matters of public interest and concern, provided they do so fairly and with an honest purpose."

The indefinite pronoun *everyone* may not be a completely fair example to pinpoint because the pronoun is semantically plural – that is, its meaning encompasses a group of people, so it may be less surprising to see it in conjunction with the pronoun *they*. The indefinite pronoun *someone* is more clearly singular both grammatically and semantically. The pronoun *someone* is not addressed specifically as an entry in the *Stylebook*, so one must infer that the advice for indefinite antecedents holds. But, in fact, the *Stylebook* itself does not follow its own advice on this. The section "Business Guidelines" contains the following sentence in the first paragraph:

No story we write is too small or routine to meet this standard: Each has meaning for *someone*, because *they* own a stock, are buying some consumer product, have a job or some other connection to the news we are providing. (italics added)

Singular *they* can seem naturalized enough that even the most astute copyeditors may miss it.

Given how widespread nonsexist usage guidelines are at this point, entrenched in some of the most powerful style books and usage guides, what has happened to written usage? Almost forty years after Robin Lakoff's comment about the potential futility of changing a form such as generic *he*, it turns out that the effort was not futile at all.

Generic pronouns: changing usage

Tracking generic pronoun use in written language is no easy task. Pronouns are common enough forms in the language that it would take many months at the least to go through all the instances of, say, *he, him,* and *his* in the Corpus of Contemporary American English to determine which ones were used generically (647,132 instances in newspapers alone). That said, there are ways to exploit the databases available to get at the question of the extent to which prescriptivism on generic pronoun usage has affected actual written usage.

To begin, the alternative construction *he or she* and its related forms *his or her*, now often promoted by well-respected style guides, have grown dramatically in usage since the 1970s. In other words, prescription seems to have had an effect on usage. Figures 5.1 and 5.2 summarize the frequency of usage in the

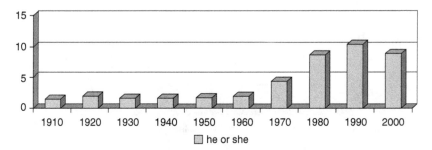

Figure 5.1 The frequency of "he or she" in COHA by decade (frequency calculated per million words)

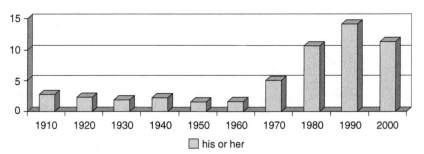

Figure 5.2 The frequency of "his or her" in COHA by decade (frequency calculated per million words)

Corpus of Historical American English over the course of the twentieth century; the charts both show a sizeable increase from the 1970s to the 1980s, with subsequent growth in the 1990s and them some decrease in the first decade of the twenty-first century.

This shift in usage appears to be largely a written development. Usage guides are not wrong in noting that *he or she* can seem cumbersome, and while speakers sometimes use it, perhaps especially in more formal registers, they more often turn to singular *they* (Newman 1997). A search of the Corpus of Contemporary American English shows the preference for *he or she* in more formal written registers, with relatively low use in fiction and spoken discourse (Figure 5.3).

The low use in fiction may be explained by less need to refer to people generically. In other words, fictional works are largely populated by people of identified genders and often require less discussion of abstract worlds with people of unknown or unidentified gender. The lower use in newspapers may be a result at least in part of the *AP Stylebook*'s recommendation against the

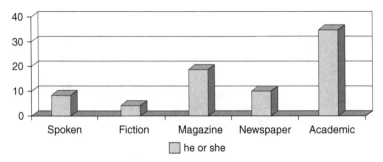

Figure 5.3 The frequency of "he or she" in COCA by register (frequency calculated per million words)

he or she construction. But even writers for the Associated Press don't consistently abstain from using *he or she*, as demonstrated in the following sentence from Dave Carpenter's 2011 article "Penn State Image Damaged; What Can University Do?," published in *Business News*:

If they get *a trustworthy, top-quality president* who cares about the students and the faculty, *he or she* can go a long way toward healing the hurt that's surrounding the program. (italics added) (11/20/11)

Another Associated Press report, this one by Paul Haven in *International News* and entitled "Still No Layoffs in Cuba 5 Months after Announced," shows the infiltration of the more spoken singular *they* into newspaper prose, here with *someone* as the antecedent:

More than five months after the government announced that a tenth of Cuba's work force would be laid off by March 31, it is difficult to find an unemployed person, or even somebody who knows *someone* who has lost *their* job. (italics added) (2/20/11)

The significant resistance to singular generic *they* in formal written prose itself provides an interesting case of the effects of prescription on usage. Despite the regular use of singular *they* in speech, the pronoun is regularly edited out of formal prose, by writers themselves or by copy-editors. As discussed in Chapter 2, this editing creates the kind of distance between spoken and written usage that should be of interest to historians of the language. The prescriptive condemnation of singular *they* has been so successful that a good number of English speakers and writers believe that not only is singular *they* not appropriate in formal written prose but it is also ungrammatical and bad usage in general.

In my own work, I have been struck by the sometimes vehement response to my argument that the pronoun *they* functions as a singular in the language and is, therefore, not ungrammatical by linguists' definition of ungrammatical. The columns and interviews I have done on this question have generated more – and more heated – response than almost anything else I have ever discussed; I have been targeted on a conservative political blog for my opinion on singular generic *they*. While non-linguists may be open to my perspective on many grammatical questions, they seem less open on this one, arguing that I am wrong in my analysis ("*they* simply cannot be singular") and promoting bad usage. The argument that another pronoun in English, *you*, functions as both a singular and plural is not enough to justify the use of *they* as a singular and a plural pronoun.[8] And even I succumb to the prescriptive forces in my own formal writing, either footnoting my first use of singular *they* in order to explain my choice and show that I know the prescription or by opting for the more accepted *he or she*.

The larger point in terms of this book's argument is that widespread prescription on singular generic pronouns has had a significant impact on usage, from the dominance of generic *he* in formal written prose after the eighteenth century to the subsequent rise of *he and she* after the 1970s to footnotes like mine that justify a deviation from accepted prescription to make the written language behave more like the spoken in this regard. In order to understand the patterns of usage, both spoken and written and then the differences between them, historians of the language must take into account the long-standing and often lively conversation about this construction in style guides and now in chat rooms, response forums, grammar resource websites, and the like on the Internet.

Gender-specific terms: changing prescriptions and usage

The "generic pronoun problem" can steal the spotlight in style guides and in linguistic scholarship, but other gendered constructions such as *-man* and *-ess* words as well as compounds such as *female professor* have also been the target of nonsexist language reform. Once again, politically responsive prescriptivism has changed usage, and this time it has significantly affected spoken usage as well as written usage. Two questions are intertwined in these nonsexist language reforms. First, can gendered words (typically masculine, such as *chairman*) function generically? And, second, does gender specification facilitate

---

[8] The argument that singular *they* can sometimes be ambiguous has merit; it certainly can be, as is true of many constructions that pass muster in spoken English but become overly ambiguous when written down, without the context of a speech event. In those instances, the pronoun should be revised to avoid unhelpful ambiguity. The fact is that spoken language is often ambiguous; speakers tolerate and even exploit ambiguity in language. And many uses of singular *they* are not ambiguous at all (e.g., *A teacher should learn their students' names*). The pronoun *you* can also be ambiguous, and some dialects of spoken English have developed alternate second-person plural pronouns such as *y'all*, *yinz*, and *you guys*. None of these plural forms is yet acceptable in formal written prose. The use of *you* to address readers in published prose, therefore, is often ambiguous in terms of whether it is addressing the reader individually or readers as a group.

gender-specific and potentially sexist readings of otherwise generic nouns (e.g., *professor*)?

Nonsexist language reform has historically taken one of three different approaches to changing usage (Pauwels 1998). First, reforms may promote generic alternatives to words with gendered endings such as *-man* and *-ess*. Those generic alternatives may employ a word-final *-person* or replace the gendered word with a nongendered one such as *firefighter* for *fireman*; as I will discuss shortly, the latter option seems to have been strikingly more successful than the first. Second, the reforms can promote symmetrical gender specification, so that just as *actor* is paired with *actress*, *chairman* is paired with *chairwoman*, *stewardess* with *steward*. One potential problem with these reforms is that one term, usually the masculine one, may continue to serve as the generic when the gender is unknown or unspecified, unless speakers or writers carefully specify both the masculine and feminine in such instances (e.g., *when an actor or actress joins the union*). In these gendered pairs, one term also is typically marked, in this case carrying an additional suffix (e.g., *-ess*) or a feminine compounded form (e.g., *-woman*). What does it mean, feminist scholars have asked, to call a woman an authoress? Does it lower her status to specify her femaleness, make her less respected than the generic and/or assumed-to-be-male author? It marks femaleness, bringing it to attention rather than assuming that it could be inherent in the profession of author. And to talk about a female author and not a male author allows the word *author* to be assumed to be male unless otherwise specified. The third tack for nonsexist reform has been the least often deployed: linguistic disruption. The common example of substituting *herstory* for *history* shows how this linguistic maneuver can highlight perceived problems with a male-centered version of history and a male-centered language. It reinterprets etymology (*history* is borrowed into English from the French *histoire*, unrelated to the pronoun *his*) in order to make a broader social and political point. This third category has tended not to have a significant impact on everyday usage. To this point, the most successful solution to sexist gendered terms is a proliferation of generics.

By the 1980s, both the APA and MLA guides address gender bias beyond the generic pronoun and generic *man*, and they both generally recommend generics. The table introduced in the third edition of the APA manual includes, among other issues: (a) the use of gender-marked compounds such as *woman doctor* and *male nurse* (recommending that sex designation should occur only if necessary); and (b) nouns ending in *-man* such as *chairman* (recommending the use of *chairperson* or *chair*). Reforms of the gender-marked compounds aim to combat assumptions about the gender of otherwise generic terms such as *doctor* and *nurse*, allowing them to retain or perhaps regain generic status – and in this way often better reflect the reality of who occupies these professional roles. The targeting of *-man* words tackles a more explicitly sexist construction. The table in the APA manual offers alternatives for *chairman, foreman, policeman,* and *mailman.* The word *freshmen* receives a separate entry and in the column "Alternatives" appears the following: "No alternative if academic standing is meant." Oddly, an additional comment is added: "*First-year student* is often an acceptable alternative to *freshman,* but in these examples, *freshmen* is used for accuracy." It is not clear why *first-year student* cannot be accurate in the plural. I continue to be struck to this day by how resilient *freshman* has been in the face of nonsexist language reform. I receive many memos every term about "freshman seminars" and the like; recently I saw a poster for a psychology study that was recruiting "female freshmen." The word *freshman,* unlike any other -*man* word I can think of, remains widely used in academia, which has been on the forefront of many other language reform efforts, including non-sexist language reform and specifically revision of (other) -*man* words.

The third edition of the MLA handbook contains this description of careful practice: "Careful writers also avoid designating sex with suffixes like -*man* and -*ess* and substitute nonsexist terms (*police officer, flight attendant, poet, author*)" (34). In the LSA guidelines, the third guideline reads: "Whenever possible, use terms that avoid sexual stereotyping. Such terms as *server, professor,* and *nurse* can be effectively used as gender neutral; marked terms like *waitress, lady professor,* and *male nurse* cannot."

Once again, the *Associated Press Stylebook* takes a different and more conservative stance. The guide prefers gender specification when the gender of a person is known and asserts that -*man* words can and should function generically if the gender is not known. The entry on -*person* captures the general rule:

Do not use coined words such as *chairperson* or *spokesperson* in regular text. Instead, use *chairman* or *spokesman* if referring to a man or the office in general. Use *chair-woman* or *spokeswoman* if referring to a woman. Or, if applicable, use a neutral word such as *leader* or *representative.* Use *chairperson* or similar coinage only in direct quotations or when it is the formal description for an office.

It is not entirely clear when a neutral word would be applicable. The entry for *chairman* specifies that *chair* and *chairperson,* both neutral words, are not acceptable in AP style. However, *representative* rather than *spokesman* is acceptable.

The fact that some major style guides still present words like *chairman* and *spokesman* as generic serves as an important reminder of just how ensconced -*man* words have been as generics in the written, if not also in the spoken, language. Some -*man* words are common enough that Robin Lakoff's pessimism in the 1970s about pronoun change could easily have extended to these words as well. Changing written usage, in the face of pervasive resistance to the "feminist furor," would have seemed a challenge indeed. And even if it was possible to change written usage, what were the odds of changing how people

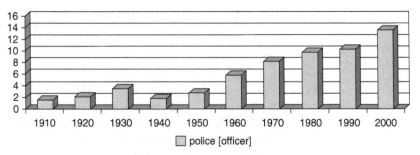

Figure 5.4 The frequency of "police officer" in COHA by decade (frequency calculated per million words)

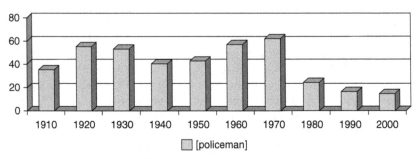

Figure 5.5 The frequency of "policeman" in COHA by decade (frequency calculated per million words)

spoke about, for example, the police and the people in charge of passenger safety on airplanes? A few decades after the initial concerted efforts to change the use of these gendered terms, the results show surprising success, not only in written usage but also in spoken. A few selected examples speak volumes about the rapidity of change, as well as the range of generic solutions.

Words used to refer to the police show the replacement of the *-man* form, *policeman*, with the generic alternative *police officer*. Figure 5.4 captures the rise of *police officer* in written English, based on COHA data, starting in the mid-twentieth century and gaining momentum in the 1970s.[9] Forms of *policeman* drop precipitously in written use after the 1970s (Figure 5.5). The generic option *police officer* was selected over a parallel feminine term, *policewoman*; *policewoman* enjoyed a bit of experimentation in the 1970s but never became preferred usage (Figure 5.6).

[9] The use of the brackets around a search term in COHA and COCA indicates that all forms of the word were searched. For example, the search string "[officer]" retrieves instances of both "officer" and "officers."

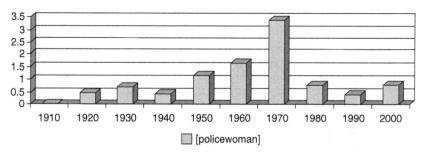

Figure 5.6 The frequency of "policewoman" in COHA by decade (frequency calculated per million words)

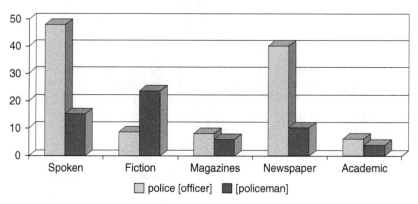

Figure 5.7 The frequency of "police officer" and "policeman" in COCA by register (frequency calculated per million words)

These historical trends reflect changes in written usage, in particular edited written usage, which as mentioned earlier is significantly easier to regulate. But the changes in how American English speakers refer to the police also seem to have successfully infiltrated the spoken language and fundamentally changed the way people talk in addition to how they write. A search of COCA reveals that *police officer* is now the preferred form in all registers except fiction, with spoken language showing the most dramatic preference for the generic term *police officer* (Figure 5.7). There are probably several reasons why fiction consistently proves to be an outlier in terms of trends with nonsexist language usage, including: fiction set in earlier periods understandably employs older, more conservative language; the gender of characters is often known, so it is possible to use gender-specific terms rather than generic ones; the register is not accountable to academic style guidelines; and authors can have specific reasons for having characters use dialogue that does not adhere to nonsexist language.

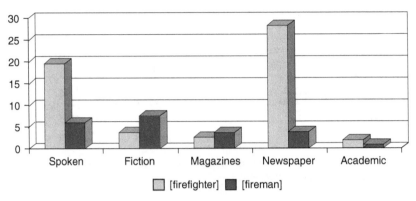

Figure 5.8 The frequency of "firefighter" and "fireman" in COCA by register (frequency calculated per million words)

The use of *firefighter* as compared with *fireman* shows a similar historical shift in usage. The rise in the generic term and the decline in the *-man* form seem to start a bit later, in the 1980s rather than the 1970s, and it is in the 2000s that *firefighter* becomes more frequent than *fireman* in written text. In this case too, the shift to the generic term *firefighter* has successfully infiltrated the spoken language as well as the written to become the more common form – except, again, in fiction (see Figure 5.8).

As the choice of *police officer* and *firefighter* suggests, different generic alternatives have been selected to replace a *-man* word as generic. And the choice is rarely a *-person* word. With *chairman*, the generic term of choice seems to have been *chair* over *chairperson*. An alternative form for *mailman* has taken a bit longer to work out but seems to have settled on *mail carrier* or *letter carrier*. Speakers themselves have sorted out which alternatives seem unsuitable (e.g., *mailperson*, probably due at least in part to homophony with *male-person*, but also in general *-person* forms have not been favored). One seemingly unlikely alternative was *flight attendant*, which in this case was a way to avoid the bias inherent in *stewardess* and the earlier *air hostess*. *Flight attendant*, with its four syllables and incorporation of the not very common noun *attendant*, seemed like a mouthful. But in the end, it has become entrenched both in written and spoken American usage (Figures 5.9–5.11).

The nonsexist alternative *flight attendant* gains momentum in usage in the 1980s, in the wake of second-wave feminist efforts on multiple fronts. The term itself is older than one might expect, first cited in the *OED* in 1947. As the *OED* captures in its citations, in 1957 the *Occupational Outlook Handbook* from the US State Department was already recognizing the term, but it was the parenthetical as opposed to the accepted term: "Stewardesses or stewards

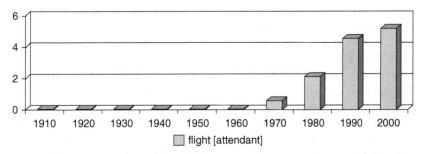

Figure 5.9 The frequency of "flight attendant" in COHA by decade (frequency calculated per million words)

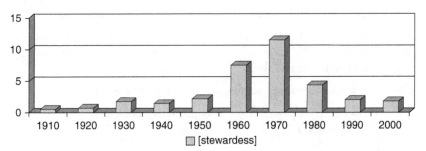

Figure 5.10 The frequency of "stewardess" in COHA by decade (frequency calculated per million words)

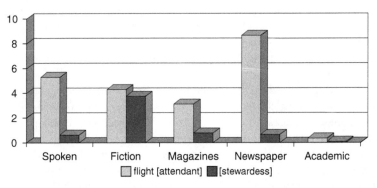

Figure 5.11 The frequency of "flight attendant" and "stewardess" in COCA by register (frequency calculated per million words)

(sometimes called flight attendants) are aboard almost all passenger planes operated by the commercial airlines."

As all of these examples of nonsexist language reform make clear, politically and socially responsive prescriptivism can have dramatic effects on usage, both written and spoken. So dramatic, in fact, that they can become invisible, much like the reappropriation of the term *woman* itself by the feminist movement. In the twenty-first century, we can lose sight of the negative connotations this term carried in the nineteenth and early twentieth century, contrasted with the polite term *lady*.

A woman was female but not necessarily feminine or refined in the socially sanctioned ways. Catharine Sedgwick captures the distinction in *Redwood: A Tale* (1824):

You must know, grandmamma, there is a young woman here – lady I suppose I must call her – for to confess the truth, she has every appearance of being one, that has inspired papa with the most surprising admiration from the first moment that he saw her. (COHA)

Almost fifty years later, the sentiment is echoed in Bartley Theodore Campbell's *Little Sunshine* (1873), making it clear that a lady has acquired the socially valued social and domestic skills:

Lily Davis: No woman is a lady, madam, who is not a good wife. (COHA)

And even in 1922, Margaret Wade Campbell Deland contrasts a woman with a lady in *The Vehement Flame*:

I adored him! How could he care for that common, ignorant woman I saw on the porch? A woman who wasn't a lady. A – a bad woman! (COHA)

In the early 1960s, the journal *American Speech* published two short notes in its Miscellany section about the synonymy of *lady* and *woman* – clearly a notable linguistic development at the time, the result of ongoing semantic shifts (Ackerman 1962; Moe 1963). In 1961, Ann Landers in her column came to the conclusion, "The words are now used interchangeably" (quoted in Ackerman 1962, 284), as *lady* became less associated with high social position and *woman* acquired less negative connotations.

The steady decline of *lady* in the second half of the twentieth century speaks to the success of feminist efforts to liberate the woman, and the word *woman*, from the etiquette strictures restricting the lady to her pedestal. At this point, even the more conservative *Associated Press Stylebook* advises in its 2012 edition: "Do not use [*lady*] as a synonym for *woman*. *Lady* may be used when it is a courtesy title or when a specific reference to fine manners is appropriate without patronizing overtones." Self-censoring of *lady* predates such institutionalized proscription of it, which in turn affirms the successful reappropriation of *woman*. The next chapter takes up the powerful linguistic process of reappropriation as part of the process of socially responsive prescriptivism in Modern English.

6   Reappropriation and challenges
       to institutionalized prescriptivism

The question of whether historically disparaging terms can sometimes be used in non-disparaging ways surfaces in some unexpected places. For example, how should the US Patent and Trademark Office handle applications for self-disparaging trademarks, such as Dykes on Bikes? Decisions about patents and trademarks date back over two hundred years, back to the first patent statute of 1790. Contention over the trademarking of disparaging terms is much newer. The word *dyke* to refer to a lesbian is not cited in the *Oxford English Dictionary* until 1942, and throughout its history, the word has often been used disparagingly. This history became relevant to the Patent and Trademark Office in 2003, when the potential trademark of Dykes on Bikes crossed its desk. Governing trademark law, known as the Lanham Act, bars trademarks that comprise "immoral, deceptive, or scandalous matter" or "may disparage... persons... institutions, beliefs, or national symbols, or bring them into contempt, or disrepute" (quoted in Anten 2006, 399). The language of this law brings to the fore the critical question of who determines what is and is not disparaging, and who has the right to use certain historically loaded identity terms in what contexts – questions central to this chapter.

For more than a century, the United States has witnessed vigorous and often heated debates about the terms used to refer to marginalized social groups, both more neutral identity terms and historically derogatory terms. The twentieth century and the beginning of the twenty-first century have also seen remarkably successful attempts to replace and reclaim identity labels, including terms related to gender and sexuality and terms related to race and ethnicity. These debates reveal an intense focus on the relationship of words to identity (particularly group identity) and raise questions about who gets to use words, who gets to tell people not to use words, and how to harness the social and political power of words. The resulting self-consciousness about how speakers should and shouldn't use the language has the power to affect actual usage – which makes it important to the history of the language.

The debates themselves are also worthy of attention. The meta-discourse about language circulating around its actual use provides a critical context for understanding speakers and their linguistic choices – in this case, their choices about historically disparaging terms. Indeed, these debates about identity labels in the twentieth and twenty-first centuries should be framed as some of the key language debates that characterize this period in the history of English, much as the inkhorn debates are used to characterize the Early Modern period. These debates are challenging traditional linguistic authority and challenging tradition about who gets to call the linguistic shots – with, of course, resistance to that challenge. These public discussions of language usage are also encouraging unusual democratic participation in the debate about language "correctness," far beyond any discussion of more traditional issues of grammatical correctness established through the process of language standardization. Speakers do not necessarily defer to traditional language authorities on the identity labels given to them, and traditional language authorities now sometimes explicitly defer to the speakers themselves. This shift constitutes an important part of the "linguistic history" of English at this historical moment.

In the past, the Patent and Trademark Office (PTO) has not been entirely consistent in its decisions about what counts as disparaging. As Todd Anten (2006) describes in a note for the *Columbia Law Review*, the PTO has generally rejected applications with historically derogatory terms referring to social groups, even when submitted by members of those groups as an act of linguistic reclamation; but the Office has also made exceptions. For example, the PTO registered TECHNODYKE for a lesbian website in 2001, but it has historically rejected all other applications with the word *dyke*. In making these rejections, PTO examiners have sometimes relied on dictionary definitions in defending the decision; for example, in the case of DYKEDOLLS, the examiner concluded from several dictionary definitions that "[t]hese dictionary definitions all show that the term 'DYKE' is a derogatory term used for homosexual women" (Anten 2006, 417).[1] Considering this inconsistency, Anten makes a proposal for how to factor the reappropriation of slurs into the Lanham Act. He argues that if the applicant for a trademark is a member of the group in question, the examiner at the PTO should follow a policy of "pure deference" – in other words, the examiner should not assume that a term is "intrinsically disparaging" if the applicant states that for a substantial composite of the group, the term is no longer disparaging in all contexts. This assertion could then be tested by publishing the proposed trademark in the *Official Gazette*, where it would be open to challenge from any members of the group to whom the term refers, who would have the power to assert that the word in question is intrinsically disparaging.

---

[1] Anten (2006) provides additional examples of inconsistent decision-making by the PTO, such as the following: as early as 1994, examiners approved marks containing "queer" but in 2000 rejected CLEARLY QUEER; in 2003 the PTO registered the mark HEEB for a Jewish culture magazine but in 2005 denied an application to register THE BIG HEEB BREWING COMPANY.

This solution to the PTO's conundrum about how to determine what is and is not intrinsically disparaging is idealistic in several respects, including the relative ease of determining the insider or outsider status of an applicant. But, in the context of this chapter, I am less interested in the pragmatics of the solution than in Anten's underlying argument for a shift in linguistic authority from a more centralized institution (in this case, the PTO, which often relies on standard reference materials such as published standard dictionaries) to a social group. The argument seeks to institutionalize a move that social groups are also sometimes taking on their own at this moment in the history of English. Implied in Anten's proposal is a sense that groups uniquely own their identity terms and are, therefore, uniquely authorized to rule on them. They know better than dictionaries or government-appointed examiners what these specific words mean and how meaning shifts in context. In this way, Anten captures something important about the current cultural zeitgeist. The proposal for handling these trademark applications also encourages public debate about the status of reappropriated negative terms – a public debate that has been happening for decades, both in print and in speech, in public and in private. These debates have fundamentally changed the guidelines for formal written usage as well as for spoken usage.

The third edition of the *Publication Manual of the American Psychological Association* (1983) contains the following admonition about nouns referring to ethnic groups: "You should try to ascertain the most acceptable current terms and use them" (44). The sentence is new to the third edition of the manual, undoubtedly a response to discussions about identity terms in the post-Civil Rights era. In the fourth edition, published in 1994, the advice is worded: "Respect people's preferences; call people what they prefer to be called" (48), and it cites Rosalie Maggio's *The Dictionary of Bias-Free Usage* (1991). The wording suggests a sense that the ground continues to shift under the editors' feet, as well as a recognition that the authority for appropriate usage, with these kinds of identity labels, lies not in their hands.

One public response to this shifting ground has been, at least at times, a sense of frustration, especially from speakers outside the groups asking to be respected linguistically. How, ask some outsiders to the group, can they be sure they are using the preferred term for a social group when it keeps changing? Is it "fair" (and I use the scare quotes here intentionally) to be asked to keep track of people's preferences for names? In its resistance to the politicizing of language, this concern is reminiscent of complaints about politically correct language more generally. The concern resists the burden of responsibility put on speakers, especially in more powerful social groups, to be respectful in the language they use toward and about historically marginalized groups. At some level, the question about "fairness" attempts to shift the burden to the speakers in the historically marginalized social group: they should be consistent and steadfast in their preferences – they should make one choice and stick with it, no matter how the language and social context might change. This discourse of "fairness" becomes more about effort than about judiciousness. It also minimizes the discursive choices that speakers in more marginalized social groups have to make almost every day in order to respect the linguistic codes of the mainstream discourse established by speakers in power. There's nothing "fair" about that. The need to respect linguistic prescriptions comes down to power, and power shifts often involve contention. Edwin Battistella (2005, 97), in the book *Bad Language*, offers this important reminder:

As with objections to slang, objections to social neology may arise less on linguistic merits than from the additional work that adapting to language change creates for some speakers. When naming becomes variable, speakers must decide what form to use. New usage reduces the privilege of one set of speakers to use their norms without fear of embarrassment or discomfort.

Generally, people don't hastily expend effort to cede power.

The public debates about identity labels, as is true of debates about politically correct language in general, can also try to minimize the importance of language and naming: it's "just language," the argument goes, and groups should be more concerned with larger issues of social justice than with names.[2] Changing names will not, critics assert, change social conditions.

But many social groups are concerned about names, as well as about many other social justice issues, exactly because names are part of our social reality. As Galinsky et al. (2003, 230) put it succinctly, "For individuals and groups faced with prejudice, tackling the negative connotations of group labels may be a means of addressing prejudice itself." The old adage "Sticks and stones can break my bones but words can never hurt me" simply does not hold up under much scrutiny. Words are enormously powerful. Words don't just describe the world, they do things in the world – among those, taking action (e.g., making a promise), helping to parse the world into comprehensible categories, and/or creating, maintaining, or damaging social relationships. Naming is fundamentally about respect,[3] and some names have histories that are much more about disrespect than about respect. So some historically marginalized groups have

---

[2] An earlier version of this sentence was worded "try and minimize," as opposed to the current "try to minimize." In response to a reader's questioning the "correctness" of *try and*, I decided to change the wording to *try to*, even though the construction *try and* + [infinitive] goes back at least to the sixteenth century and prescription against it in, for example, Strunk and White (1979) is not well founded. Spoken and written English at this point diverge with respect to this construction: a study by Charlotte Hommerberg from 2003 shows that in British English, *try and* accounts for 71 percent of the spoken instances of the construction but only 24 percent of the written; in American English *try and* accounts for 24 percent of spoken, and 5 percent of written (cited in Tottie 2009, 343–349). My choice to revise just perpetuates the divergence.

[3] See Adams (2009) for a discussion of how social power is negotiated through naming with a specific focus on nicknames.

been engaged in various kinds of politically responsive prescriptivism, in this case sometimes from outside institutionalized venues of language authority, knocking on the door of those institutions and calling on them to change their ways. The revisions to the *Publication Manual of the American Psychological Association* show some of the effects of that knocking.

These prescriptions focus on what linguists now call linguistic reappropriation (also sometimes called linguistic reclamation), or the "taking back" of negative terms, such as *dyke* by lesbian communities. Linguistic reappropriation sometimes gets wrapped up in discussions of other forms of what Battistella calls "social neology," in particular the creation of new identity terms (e.g., *African American*) to replace a stigmatized identity term. All of this socially responsive prescriptivism aims to change how people refer to each other and conceptualize each other.

Defining linguistic reappropriation

To date, there has been relatively little published scholarship on the phenomenon of linguistic reappropriation – and it should be noted that the Microsoft Word spell checker does not yet like the word *reappropriation* as a "real" word (it was underlined in red in this manuscript until I added it to the dictionary in my program). Galinsky et al. (2003, 222), in one of the few substantive studies of the phenomenon, provide a useful starting definition of *reappropriation*: "the phenomenon whereby a stigmatized group revalues an externally imposed negative label by self-consciously referring to itself in terms of that label." In another valuable article-length treatment of the phenomenon, Robin Brontsema (2004, 1) only implies some revaluing: "Linguistic reclamation, also known as linguistic resignification or reappropriation, refers to the appropriation of a pejorative epithet by its target(s)." But the revaluing is critical to the enterprise and needs to be in the definition. Chen (1998, 130), in her definition, usefully specifies that the revaluing may be positive or oppositional: "The term 'reclaiming' refers to an array of theoretical and conventional interpretations of both linguistic and non-linguistic collective acts in which a derogatory sign or signifier is consciously employed by the 'original' target of the derogation, often in a positive or oppositional sense."

Given the additional legal uses of the term *reclamation*, which are also related to the pursuit of social justice, I have chosen to use *(linguistic) reappropriation* as my primary term for the linguistic phenomenon. In the earlier part of the twentieth century, the word *reappropriation* was used in academic articles often in religious contexts, both more anthropological and more textual (the reappropriation of monuments, of biblical stories, etc.), and occasionally in reference to unexpended balances in the Senate and once to an abandoned trademark term. Once the term *reappropriation* appeared in Jacques Derrida's work in the late

1960s, the term took on a new life, referring to the reappropriation of symbols, of the supernatural, and of Derrida himself. The noun *reappropriation* was added to the *OED* in 2009 in revisions for the third edition, and the definition of the verb *reappropriate* was expanded to include 'to reclaim for one's own use' – a meaning broad enough to encompass linguistic efforts along these lines.

By the 1990s, the term *reappropriate* appears in reference to the linguistic process of revaluing pejorative terms. Earlier scholars used terms such as *inversion* (see Sims Holt 1972) or described the process without a specific term (see Bennett 1967).[4] One potentially useful link to the appropriation of the term *reappropriation* by linguistics is its use by feminists in reference to the reappropriation of power. In the following excerpt, Sally McConnell-Ginet (1989, 49) uses the term *reappropriate* in reference to power, but specifically the power to name:

Meanings are produced and reproduced within the political structures that condition discourse: though a sexist politics may have helped some men to 'steal the power of naming,' that power – a real one – can be *reappropriated* by feminist women and men building new language communities. (italics added)

By the mid-1990s, the term became established enough in linguistics as a description for the process that it could appear without further explanation. For example, Rudolf Gaudio (1994, 55) includes the following endnote about the word *queer* in his article "Sounding Gay," which is about the pitch properties of male speech, not about lexical choices: "The term *queer* has been revived and reappropriated in recent years by lesbian, gay, and bisexual activists. It applies to all people who face societal oppression because of their sexual orientation, and its reappropriation signals a refusal by queer people to assimilate or 'pass' into the heterosexual majority." However, the term is often still explained, as Deborah Cameron (1995, 147) does in *Verbal Hygiene* when she uses the verb *reclaim* rather than *reappropriate* and puts the latter in scare quotes: "The other point is that effects of pejoration are not, in fact, total, and there are verbal hygiene strategies that specifically resist those effects by 'reclaiming' – i.e., proposing deliberately to ameliorate – taboo words and insults."[5] Even in 1995, *reappropriate* was not a term or process that could be taken for granted in scholarship.

Around the same time, the word *reappropriation* pops up in the press. For example, in the article "PC Is a Label to Be Worn with Pride" (4/09/94) in the *Sydney Morning Herald* (Australia), Paola Totaro writes: "Minority cultures in Australia have had the guts – and freedom in the wider community – to

---

[4] Stanley's (1970) article about homosexual slang appears to predate widespread reclamation efforts for *queer* or *dyke*. The word *gay* is not discussed in any detail.

[5] For excellent relatively recent treatments of taboo words and other "bad language," see Allan and Burridge (2006), Battistella (2005), and McEnery (2006).

reappropriate words once deemed insulting and inject them with humour." Totaro chooses to name and define the process simultaneously. And she describes the positive revaluing as characterized by humor.

Any definition of reappropriation should also account for its goals. Brontsema (2004) has done pioneering work to show that the debate about reappropriation is more complicated than whether members of a group are supportive of reclaiming a word or opposed to it. As she describes, the process of reappropriating a term can aim for neutralization of a term – that is, bleaching a term of its negative connotations such that it can be used as a neutral name for a group. In this case, success would entail that the term loses at least some of its social power, be that to offend or to unite; it is no longer loaded in positive or negative ways. Reappropriation can also strive for value-reversal, such that a term becomes a positive term of solidarity. Another means for uniting a group through reappropriation exploits the stigma of the term itself to call attention to social attitudes and discrimination, making the term a radical statement, "a *sign* of a stigma, rather than a tool of a stigma" (Chen 1998, 138). As these three goals capture, different approaches to reappropriation make different assumptions about the extent to which the negative connotations or stigma attached to a word can be changed or bleached. Importantly, arguing that a word's stigma cannot be erased does not necessarily negate the importance of reclaiming it or undermine efforts to do so.

Reappropriation efforts can also differ in the intended scope of acceptable use (Brontsema 2004). Some efforts strive to encourage neutral or positive use of a historically disparaging term more broadly in a speech community – that is, both by the "in-group" to whom the label refers and by the "out-group" who often has used the word in derogatory ways in the past (e.g., *woman, queer, gay*). In some instances, a group appropriates a new term that may not have had a negative history to replace a term that has come into disfavor for negative connotations (e.g., the campaign for *African American* and *Black* rather than *Negro*). Or reappropriation may more narrowly advocate use only within the in-group as a kind of in-group language, disempowering the often more powerful and larger "out-group" (which will, of course, encompass many other kinds of "in-groups") from using the term (e.g., the N-word).[6]

---

[6] In this chapter I will use both the euphemism "the N-word" and the word *nigger* (and its phonologically altered form *nigga*, which is the form that has been most often reappropriated within the African American community). The word *nigger* is arguably (and it is an argument I am willing to make) the most volatile, powerful word in American English. While I am a linguist, I am also a speaker living in this particular historical moment, and I am highly aware that I am not in the in-group empowered to use the terms *nigger* or *nigga* in their reappropriated forms and meanings. I have read widely on the debate about whether or not anyone should say this word, even when discussing its power as part of a linguistic discussion. I have read about teachers who have lost their jobs over this word, even as they were trying to talk about its offensiveness. I understand the arguments that the word must be said in order to address its power and that "the N-word" is an

Both of these approaches are powerful linguistic moves. The first approach aims to change general discourse. It takes a term with a history of hateful usage and tries to bleach it of those connotations in all contexts – to take the degradation out of the word for all speakers. The second approach creates new social taboos that heighten awareness about discrimination. It draws lines between those who have been discriminated against by a term and those who have had the power to use the term to discriminate. It empowers those who have been discriminated against to censure unacceptable use of the derogatory term – both as a derogatory term and as a reappropriated term, based on the premise that for those out-group speakers it can never be reappropriated. For them, the term will always be derogatory.

Public debates over stigmatized terms for social groups, like almost all debates that are technically about language, are about more than language. In talking about language, speakers often debate underlying issues of race, immigration, gender equality, and more. The derogatory terms in question in this chapter are particularly loaded as they are about group identity and the power to define one's own social identity, rather than being defined by others. Speakers can feel a sense of ownership with these terms that parallels perhaps only personal names, which has allowed speakers to challenge institutionalized linguistic authority with these terms in unusual ways. With our own names, we may feel personally insulted or hurt if someone gets our name wrong – and we feel authorized to say what is right and wrong in terms of how our name is pronounced and spelled, as well as how it is used (for example, we may police who gets to use a nickname). With most other words in the lexicon, speakers defer to dictionaries or other institutionalized resources for judgments about spelling, pronunciation, meaning, and usage. But identity terms have become an exception, an area of the lexicon where speakers have been asserting their right to question established authority about meaning and usage.

Public debates have focused particularly on terms for highly salient social groups based on race and ethnicity, gender, sexuality, and religion (as opposed to, say, *geek*, which arguably has been reclaimed but with less charged discussion). The twentieth and twenty-first centuries, with successful movements for civil rights for a range of social groups, have been especially concerned with groups' rights to name themselves and, in several cases, reappropriate epithets. In all cases, these discussions are inherently political ("campaigns

---

unhelpful euphemism. I also feel strongly about respecting the history and power of this word. When I give public talks, I heed John Rickford's caution about how using the word in any context can backfire: "Let's say you're trying to have a conversation and meanwhile you're standing on the person's foot. If you don't take your foot off, it's unlikely that you'll achieve the larger goals of your conversation" (quoted in "The N-word" on salon.com, by Chris Colin). In this written context, I use the word when talking about the word itself, and I use the euphemism when describing the public debate, as the debate itself generally employs the euphemism.

for change") and they have raised questions not just about the power of words and group unity but also about censorship, double standards, and language authority more generally. These debates have been passionate and public. Speakers have a clear sense that words are more than just words, even when they try to make exactly that argument. The debates have taken place inside the in-group community about what is appropriate as well as outside the community about the politicization of language.

Scholars have affirmed the important stakes involved in reappropriation, as have participants. Anten (2006, 434) writes: "The reappropriation of slurs is not a mere exercise in linguistic gymnastics; rather, it is a potent strategy of identity creation and maintenance." It is the power to name oneself, whether on the individual or group level, rather than having to accept the names that others, in power, decide upon. It is the power to assert that a word has negative meanings, that it reinforces stigmas, rather than having to accept the arguments of others, in power, that a word is fine because people don't mean it negatively, or it is "just a word," or it's the easiest and most logical way to name the group without resorting to "euphemism." Words are never "just words," and identity terms are part of self-definition. As Anten (2006, 422) asserts, quoting Brontsema on this important point: "The reappropriation of former slurs is an integral part of the fostering of individual and group identity, recapturing 'the right of self-definition, of forging and naming one's own existence.'" John Baugh (1999, 93) notes that a group's introspection can result in terminology changes, which can in turn foster group identity as well as challenge the status quo.

All tied up in reappropriation, as is true of the nonsexist language reforms discussed in the previous chapter, is the issue of respect: respect for the right to name one's own group and one's own self; respect for the right of a group to say what an identity term means to them and, therefore, what it means more broadly; and respect for the lines that may get drawn about who is authorized to use a reappropriated term. Then within historically marginalized social groups, the ability to reappropriate can raise complicated questions about respect. Does a group respect itself by reappropriating a historically derogatory term and defuse its power through self-reference within the community? Or does a group disrespect itself by adopting a derogatory term imposed by others for use within the community, and thereby perhaps legitimize its use outside the community in ways that might remain derogatory? The answers to these questions are far from settled. But the debate itself rests on a critically important premise: that historically marginalized groups have the power to prescribe what is and is not a derogatory label. In that power lies a challenge to the traditional lines laid down by the social groups in control of mainstream public discourse about what constitutes offensive language in public discourse (see McEnery 2006). That challenge explains some of the contestation by socially powerful groups of the changing standards for publicly acceptable language.

Evaluating the importance of reappropriation

Given everyday speakers' awareness of the debates around identity terms, it is surprising that in linguistics textbooks, reappropriation can be hard to find.[7] A survey of the dozen or so introductory texts on the shelf in my office turned up three mentions, one of which is in the textbook *How English Works: A Linguistic Introduction* (2012) that I co-authored with Michael Adams. Given my own interest in reappropriation, this is probably not surprising. But I cannot exempt our co-authored textbook from the critique I am undertaking here, because while we give the phenomenon attention under semantics, we fall short in the credit we give to the debate itself as part of the history of the language, as I will discuss. In *How English Works*, reappropriation receives a paragraph-long discussion in the section on semantic change (227), in which we link the phenomenon to the processes of pejoration and amelioration – the processes through which a word's meaning becomes, respectively, more negative or more positive over time. As we describe, in cases of reappropriation, the pejorated word is positively affected by a social group's conscious effort to "take back" a word, and the reappropriation effort may be contested.

Where and how reappropriation fits in lexical semantics revisits the question of how important conscious change is within a language's history (as I discuss in Chapter 2). Prototypical examples of semantic change involve words that change largely below speakers' conscious awareness. In textbooks about the structure and the history of English, these examples typically make up the entire discussion of a process like amelioration. To provide one stock example, the word *awesome* came to refer to something very good as opposed to something worthy of awe – potentially for a variety of reasons – without a lot of fanfare or conscious effort. The *OED* cites a weakening of the word in the early 1960s such that it could be used to mean 'remarkable, prodigious', and by 1980 it was being used to mean 'great, stunning' in slangy contexts. While readers old enough to remember the 1980s may have been aware that something slangy was happening with the word *awesome*, the shift itself was not the result of a concerted, conscious effort by slang speakers. To take a second example, the amelioration of the word *nice*, which used to have much less nice meanings, has been occluded in the mists of time, but, in all likelihood, speakers did not notice the subtle shifts in the word from 'foolish, simple' to 'lascivious', to 'ostentatious' (in relation to dress), 'particular in matters of conduct or reputation', and 'fussy, fastidious', to 'refined, cultured', and then to 'respectable, virtuous'.

---

[7] Textbooks are a conservative genre and may not always incorporate the most cutting-edge work in a field. But they also help to establish "canonical knowledge" in a field and train future scholars in a field.

These two examples stand in stark contrast to the recent attempts to reappropriate the word *dyke*, which have resulted in the word going to court. The word *dyke* first appears in English (according to the *OED*) in 1942 in reference to a lesbian or 'masculine woman'. The *OED* has yet to update its label, which currently reads "slang." Merriam-Webster more accurately includes the label "often disparaging"; the *American Heritage Dictionary of the English Language* (5th edn.) uses the label "offensive slang" and puts the word *disparaging* in the definition: "Used as a disparaging term for a lesbian." None of the three definitions captures attempts among some lesbians to reappropriate the term and, thereby, make it less disparaging.

The use of the term within the lesbian community as a neutral or positive term – a way to establish solidarity – became more public in the attempt to reclaim the term by groups such as Dykes on Bikes, who gained notoriety in 1976 at the San Francisco Pride parade. The fight about whether or not the word could be successfully ameliorated or reappropriated made its way into the courts when the San Francisco Women's Motorcycle Contingent applied to register a trademark for DYKES ON BIKES in 2003 (see Leonard 2007 for a good summary). When the application was rejected (the examiner determined the name was disparaging to lesbians), the group took it to the Trademark Trial and Appeal Board of the US Patent and Trademark Office, making the argument that the word had undergone linguistic reappropriation. The Appeal Board found the arguments persuasive enough to return the case to the examiner, who granted the trademark in 2006 – at which point it was promptly challenged by Michael J. McDermott as being disparaging to men. Later in 2006, the US Court of Appeals for the Federal Circuit dismissed the challenge.[8] And the reasoning behind the decision is important: the court determined that McDermott, as a man, was not implicated in the mark and, therefore, did not have the standing to claim that he would be damaged by it. The court authorized the lesbian community – not a man, not a dictionary, and not the courts themselves – to determine the meaning of the term used to refer to the community and whether or not it was disparaging to them.

As just this one example suggests, scholars are not doing justice to the complexity or importance of reappropriation by making it a note under semantics (if it gets included at all), and its importance rests both in the nature of the debate itself and its ability to affect usage. Yet, in discussions of prescriptivism and/or the language debates that characterize the modern period, reappropriation almost never appears. For example, in the revision of C. M. Millward's classic *A Biography of the English Language* for the third edition (published in

---

[8] In this same year, 2006, the actor Damon Wayans made newspaper headlines for his prolonged battle to trademark NIGGA for a line of clothing and for a retail store. For such efforts, Wayans appears in the Hall of Shame on the website of the United Voices for a Common Cause (UVCC), discussed later in this chapter.

2012), there is no mention of reappropriation, either in discussions of semantic change or in discussions of the Modern English language context – where, for example, debates about spelling reform receive significant attention. Spelling reform and the "progressive prescriptivism" it embodies as a force to change standard written English certainly merit attention. But, from a bird's eye view of the second half of the twentieth century into the twenty-first, spelling reform would not be as visible as reappropriation as a source of major public concern about language. Laurel Brinton and Leslie Arnovick's recent *The English Language: A Linguistic History* (second edition, 2011) also does not mention modern debates about reappropriation in the chapter on Modern English, where the authors do spend time on public concerns about the effects of the Internet and other electronic technologies on English. The discussion of semantic change in an earlier chapter includes no examples of reappropriated terms under pejoration or amelioration; the example words all underwent semantic change below the radar. Strikingly, in the discussion of semantic change, there is a subsection called "Social Change" which opens with the important statement "Social factors also motivate semantic change" (89). But the subsequent examples do not touch reappropriation, which is clearly a social factor that has had a hand in semantic change; instead, the examples include the infiltration of technical words into the general lexicon (e.g., *extrovert*, *interface*), and the imitation of slang by non-marginalized groups.

I do not provide these examples to criticize these highly admirable textbooks but rather to point out that linguists have largely marginalized these debates when we think about the modern period. I myself am fully culpable. In *How English Works*, Michael Adams and I include almost five pages about social forces that have influenced Modern English (457–461). We discuss: prescriptivism and the standard variety, the media, imperialism and war, and globalization. Nowhere in the discussion of prescriptivism or in any other subsection do we address the heated debates about identity terms or politically correct language that have occurred in the Modern English period. Nor do we cross-reference the section on politically correct language in an earlier chapter. We do not, in other words, frame these language debates as explicitly relevant to understanding the history of the language in the modern period.

Recent editions of some major dictionaries are ahead of textbooks in this arena, as they grapple with the effects of reappropriation on word meaning and the subtleties of usage – e.g., whether or not a word will be taken as offensive and if so, in what contexts. In the Preface to the fourth edition of the *American Heritage Dictionary* (2000), Geoffrey Nunberg addresses the issue of reappropriation directly (although he does not use the term) in terms of its implications for a dictionary. The treatment is worth quoting at length for the prominence that it gives to reappropriation as a sociolinguistic factor and for its explicit abnegation of authority to rule on acceptable or "correct" usage:

Usage and Social Diversity Over the last 30 years, one of the most radical changes in the scope of language criticism has been its extension to a wide range of usages involving questions of social diversity. There have been widespread public discussions, for example, about the names of groups defined along lines of ethnicity, religion, race, physical capacity, and sexual orientation. Some of these discussions are summarized in Usage Notes such as those at *Anglo, Asian, black, Chicano, color, deaf, Eurasian, gay, gender, handicapped, Hispanic, homosexual, Jew, Kanaka, Latina, Native American,* and *queer.* In one sense these questions are not new, but in the past they were not taken up as part of the public discussion of language. It is only in recent times that these issues have emerged as critical questions, as a result both of the rise of official pluralism and of a more general interest in the political and ideological aspects of language.

In matters like these, of course, a dictionary has no authority to dictate "correct" usage (at least not in the linguistic sense of the term). Most of these words are subject to a great deal of variation, even among members of the group they apply to, and their connotations and use can change very rapidly. But dictionaries can help by providing information on the social and linguistic backgrounds of these questions, which can be quite complex – information that may spare some readers from resorting to unnecessary circumlocution and others from giving inadvertent offense. (xxix)[9]

Nunberg alludes to discussions older than the past thirty years – and, in fact, some of the debates before the 1970s were fairly public. But the debates have become especially prominent in the past fifty years. In terms of creating the usage notes for these identity terms, the editors of the *American Heritage Dictionary* do not rely on the Usage Panel as they do for many other contested issues of usage, with good reason: the Usage Panel, as a whole, would not bring the needed insider knowledge about in-group versus out-group meanings and subtleties to provide clear or expert guidance on acceptability.[10]

---

[9] The fifth edition of the dictionary, published in 2011, has a new preface about usage written by Steven Pinker, the new chair of the Usage Panel. He remarks on the proliferation of Usage Notes for "sensitive terms for kinds of people." His tone is a bit less serious: "Careful attention must be paid, because despite the various rationalizations, the choice of an acceptable term for people in a given decade has no semantic rhyme or reason . . . The terms rotate through the polite lexicon as a current one gets tainted by an emotional coloring and calls for a fresh replacement. Woe betide the speaker who does not keep up" (xix). The slightly flip tone of the phrase "no semantic rhyme or reason" and of the final line seems to question the social usefulness and fairness of asking speakers to keep up with this rotation of terms. This prefatory note does not recognize the complex histories of many identity terms.

[10] I have been a member of the American Heritage Usage Panel since 2005, and the questionnaires I have completed in the past eight years have never contained questions about the acceptability of loaded identity terms in specific contexts. The questions typically focus on issues of pronunciation (e.g., whether stress can be placed on the first and/or second syllable of *hegemony,* whether the /t/ in *often* is silent), lexical meaning (e.g., whether *literally* can acceptably mean 'figuratively', whether *lay* now has an intransitive meaning in addition to a transitive one), and grammatical usage (e.g., whether *they* can acceptably be used as a singular generic pronoun, whether *mitigate* can be followed by the preposition *against*).

The *Random House Historical Dictionary of American Slang* also addresses reappropriation, again without actually using that term, in the prefatory material "Comments and Labels about Usage and Status" (vol. I, 1994: lii):

Ethnic and racial epithets are classic examples of the double lives led by some English words. What makes them epithets (or "slurs") is their willful use to demean or degrade. Yet, within the insulted groups, the same words may be used in mere derision or rough humor; in recent use, some terms, such as *dyke, nigger,* and *queer,* have been used self-referentially in an attempt to defuse their effects as epithets of hatred. It is such variation in intent and effect that warrants the use of "usu." [usually] with labels for these terms. [usu. = a label "to indicate that 'mainstream standards' are flexible and are primarily based on situation and speaker-to-speaker relationships."]

While the opening addresses explicitly racial and ethnic epithets, two of the three specific examples are terms referring to a group's sexual orientation. All of these terms capture deplorable histories of bigotry and degradation. The dictionary describes attempts "to defuse their effects as epithets of hatred." So can such word histories be defused? Can the words be redeemed for use by any speakers?

Exactly these questions have characterized the debates surrounding the reappropriation of identity terms in the queer community and in the African American community,[11] the two case studies taken up in the remainder of this chapter. Through these case studies, I cannot do justice to the complexity of the debates about reappropriation; nonetheless, the sheer volume of material published about these issues in a range of public venues speaks to the importance of the debate for understanding this sociolinguistic moment in the history of English.

Reappropriation in the queer community

In the limited scholarly literature available on reappropriation, *queer* often appears as a key case study, and the public negotiation over the word's reappropriation usefully captures some of the positions that characterize the debate about reappropriation more generally. The word *queer* has not yet gained full acceptance as a reappropriated term that could be used neutrally for the queer community in institutionalized media such as mainstream newspapers, although readers will probably have noticed that I have chosen to use the word as a neutral identity label in this chapter. The *American Heritage Dictionary of the English Language* (5th edn., 2011) describes the word as currently undergoing the process of reappropriation, and perhaps this helps explain why the editors

---

[11] Shorthand phrases such as "the queer community" or "the African American community" can misleadingly suggest homogeneity and unity within what is in fact a very diverse set of communities. I have chosen to use the phrases in this chapter as a shorthand, recognizing their ongoing widespread use by members of the diverse communities they represent. But I hope readers will bear this caveat in mind about the communities to which the phrases refer.

use the usage note on *queer* to define the process of reappropriation more generally, captured in the first sentence of the note:

A reclaimed word is a word that was formerly used solely as a slur but that has been semantically overturned by members of the maligned group, who use it as a term of defiant pride. *Queer* is an example of a word undergoing this process. For decades *queer* was used as a derogatory adjective for gays and lesbians, but in the 1980s the term began to be used by gay and lesbian activists as a term of self-identification. Eventually, it came to be used as an umbrella term that included gay men, lesbians, bisexuals, and trans-gender people. Nevertheless, a sizable percentage of people to whom this term might apply still hold *queer* to be a hateful insult, and its use by heterosexuals is often considered offensive. Similarly, other reclaimed words are usually offensive to the in-group when used by outsiders, so caution must be taken with their use when one is not a member of the group. (1443)

Although the earlier history of the word *queer*'s reappropriation is one charac-terized by "defiant pride," it is important to note that at least for some speakers, neutralization of the term is one central goal.

As indicated by current public debates about "gay marriage" (used synony-mously with "same-sex marriage" and "marriage equality") and "gays in the military," the word *gay* has successfully become a fairly neutral term (although it may be marked as male), generally preferred over the word *homosexual* given the medicalized connotations of the latter. In the first few decades of the twentieth century, when the word *gay* started to be used in reference to the homosexual community, the word carried more negative connotations of pro-miscuity and depravity. The word was reappropriated by the gay community by the 1960s, a decade which witnessed key turning points in the movement for gay rights such as the Stonewall riots; and dictionaries like American Heritage defer to the community for the word's neutral meaning: "The word *gay* is now stand-ard in its use to refer to people whose sexual orientation is to the same sex, in large part because it is the term that most gay people prefer in referring to themselves" (*AHD* 2011, 728). The most controversial questions about the word *gay* now revolve around whether it can effectively be a cover term for the homosexual or queer community given that it is often used specifically to refer to homosexual men, and whether the word *gay* remains offensive as a singular noun referring to an individual.

The word *gay* provides a fascinating case study of the effects of pejoration and reappropriation on a word's frequency of usage. As a search of the Corpus of Historical American English suggests, the word starts declining in frequency in the first few decades of the twentieth century, which is when the *OED* indicates it came to refer to the homosexual community, often in negative or loaded ways (Figure 6.1). The 1960s through the 1980s witness a precipitous decline, the moment when the word is the focus of reappropriation efforts and public attention. It is not surprising that speakers and writers are wary of the

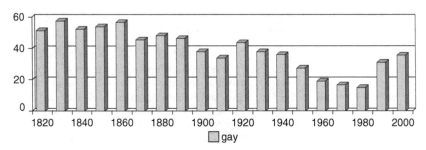

Figure 6.1 The frequency of the word "gay" in the Corpus of Historical American English (per million words)

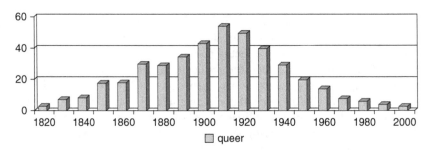

Figure 6.2 The frequency of the word "queer" in the Corpus of Historical American English (per million words)

term as its meaning is negotiated, when the boundary lines of what might cause offense are unclear. The rise in frequency in the 1990s into the 2000s suggests the success of the reappropriation efforts.

The trajectory in frequency for the word *queer* over the twentieth century looks similar to that for *gay* in terms of the decline after the early decades, during which the word took on derogatory or taboo meanings in reference to the gay community (Figure 6.2). But there is not yet the up-tick that successful reappropriation can inspire. That process is still in progress, and speakers and writers remain uncertain in many contexts about whether *queer* is now acceptable as an identity label for use by outsiders to the community.

Academia was one of the early adopters of *queer* as a descriptive, reappropriated term for the area of scholarly inquiry known as queer theory, an approach that theorizes sexuality and critically examines traditional categories of gender and sexuality as well as heteronormativity more generally. The *OED*'s earliest citation appears in 1990 in *Representations* in a reference to a conference on "Queer Theory," and the scare quotes appear in the citation, indicating that the term was relatively new and that the publication might have been distancing itself from taking a position on the term as appropriate or not. But even fifteen years later in academia, discomfort with the connotations of the word *queer* and with the authority to use it can surface – the word's reappropriation remains in process. One personal anecdote is relevant here. When Michael Adams and I wrote the first edition of *How English Works* (2006), we included a section titled "Queer Sociolinguistics," which summarized some of the recent sociolinguistic work on language and sexuality, including research that appeared in a wonderful collection called *Queerly Phrased* (1997). When the chapters were being reviewed before publication, one reviewer (an anonymous faculty member at another institution) called us out for the section title, asserting that it would be offensive to readers. This reader did not accept the term as reappropriated, even in academic contexts. Michael and I decided to use the moment in the text to highlight the word's reappropriation: we retained the title and added a note that "queer sociolinguistics" is one term of choice for scholars who work in this subfield, thereby deferring to the "in group" and authorizing them to determine what is and is not disparaging or successfully reappropriated.

The adjective *queer* is of uncertain etymology, according to the *OED*. It first appears in written English in the early sixteenth century (1513 is the first citation in the *OED*) meaning 'strange, odd, peculiar' as well as 'of dubious character'. By the mid-eighteenth century it had taken on the additional meaning of 'unwell, faint, giddy', and phrases such as "a queer stomach" or "a queer feeling in the stomach" still show up in current medical literature. The late nineteenth century witnessed the word's extension to refer to homosexuals, as a noun, and by the early twentieth century there is also evidence for the adjective *queer* referring to homosexuals and/or homosexuality. Given the ongoing use of the word to mean 'strange' if not also 'dubious', it is not hard to see the disparagement inherent in this semantic extension. But in the second edition of the *OED*, published in 1989, the derogatory connotations are not acknowledged. The noun is labeled as "slang," and the adjective is unlabeled.

In the current revisions to the *OED* for the New Edition, which are being published online as they are completed, the process of reappropriation has become a presence, and *queer* provides a good example of how the public debates have shaped some dictionary editors' decisions about how to handle these words. The second edition (1989) provides the following definition as part (b) under definition 1 of the adjective *queer*, with part (a) describing the word's meaning as 'strange, odd, etc.':

Of a person (usu. a man): homosexual. Also in phr. *as queer as a coot* (cf. coot *n.1* 2b). Hence, of things: pertaining to homosexuals or homosexuality. orig. *U.S.*

The revision, which was published in December 2007, adds the equivalent of a usage note that addresses reappropriation. The meaning is also now categorized as a third, separate meaning of the adjective.

3. *colloq.* (orig. *U.S.*). Of a person: homosexual. Hence: of or relating to homosexuals or homosexuality ...

Although originally chiefly derogatory (and still widely considered offensive, esp. when used by heterosexual people), from the late 1980s it began to be used as a neutral or positive term (originally of self-reference, by some homosexuals; cf. QUEER NATION *n* ...) in place of *gay* or *homosexual*, without regard to, or in implicit denial of, its negative connotations. In some academic contexts it is the preferred adjective in the study of issues relating to homosexuality (cf. *queer theory n* ...); it is also sometimes used of sexual lifestyles that do not conform to conventional heterosexual behaviour, such as bisexuality or transgenderism.

The editors now acknowledge the derogatory history and use of the word with this meaning and address some of the complicated dynamics of in-group versus out-group use with reappropriated terms. The entry for the noun has also been significantly revised:

2. *colloq.* (freq. *derogatory*). A homosexual; *esp.* a male homosexual.

Although originally chiefly derogatory, since the late 1980s it has been used as a neutral or positive term, originally by some homosexuals (see QUEER *adj.*[1] 3).

It would not have been possible for the second edition to recognize the reappropriation of the term *queer*, given the timing of its publication in 1989, but it certainly could have recognized the derogatory meanings that drove that reappropriation.

The word *queer* was reappropriated in the late 1980s, specifically by the magazine *OutWeek* to refer to the activist LGBT community. The word was seen as simultaneously inclusive and radical. Gabriel Rotello, the former editor of *OutWeek* (the magazine was published in New York from 1989 to 1991), describes his motivations and regrets about the reappropriation of the word in the piece "Last Word: The Word that Failed," which appeared in *The Advocate* on August 15, 2000. He begins by explaining his decision to use *queer* as a cover term for the gay, lesbian, bisexual, and transgender community in *OutWeek*:

As one of the people responsible for promoting the word queer, I have a confession to make: I'm beginning to think it was a mistake, and I wouldn't mind if it just quietly faded away. Obviously I didn't always feel that way. Back in the late '80s, I was the editor of an in-your-face magazine called OutWeek, and I was desperate for a new word that would reflect the radical new gay world we were building. Queer was my number 1 choice ...

As a journalist with limited word space, I needed a simple word that could encompass everybody's crowding under the rainbow flag. That's when we noticed queer. People bandied it about at activist gatherings, a Boston-based publication called Gay Community News used it in print, and I, for one, liked the ring. There were other contenders: rainbow community, Uranians, even fags. But queer fit the radical zeitgeist, so we began using it in OutWeek and encouraged others to do so. When a new activist group dubbed itself Queer Nation, the die was cast. Queer was definitely here.

It is unusual in the history of any word to be able to pinpoint this specifically the source of a semantic shift, and a small group's conscious efforts to change a word's meaning rarely succeed. But as Rotello describes, *OutWeek* proved to be a powerful platform from which to promote this new use of *queer*, and the word with its reappropriated meaning took on momentum and changed usage more broadly. But not, as Rotello explains, without resistance:

> The trouble was that lots of older activists hated it. They argued that queer was a term of oppression and that to use it was to implicitly endorse the dictionary's verdict that there was something 'odd and suspicious' about homosexuals. They had spent their lives fighting that idea, they argued, and this represented a huge step backward ... I figured this debate would quickly peter out and people would just get used to the idea of 'reclaiming' queer as a positive word. But many never did. Instead, a term I had hoped would bring everyone together did the opposite – it divided the hip, cool, younger activists from their unhip, uncool elders.

As Rotello captures, the word's reappropriation was a defiant act, not only in relation to the out-group but also in many ways in relation to older members of the in-group:

> To be brutally honest, maybe part of queer's allure was the fact that it outraged the older generation ... Queer was – in part, anyway – a way of sticking it to them, kind of like getting a tattoo to freak out your parents. But while a tattoo is a personal decision, imposing a word on an entire community is not. When that word outrages a huge portion of that community, it is an act of division.

Rotello ends the piece with what he frames as a comforting prediction: the word *queer*, he opines, does not have much of a future beyond the 1990s. Over a decade after Rotello published this piece, his prediction has proven inaccurate: *queer* seems to fill a gap as a cover term for the LGBT community that *gay* cannot or does not.[12]

But *queer* remains contested, even though it is often cited as an example of successful reappropriation. In 1997, the National Lesbian, Gay, Bisexual, Transgender Student Association changed its name to the National Queer Student Coalition. It was then not invited to a White House Summit on Youth due to concerns that the organization might be too radical, according to W. Brandon Lacy Campos (2003), who served as co-chair of the organization. A few years later, Campos defends the umbrella term *queer* in the blog entry "Queer?" in *Brown Tones: A Progressive Voice in Regressive Times* (January 3, 2003). Responding to an email from a reader who felt the word *queer* was still derogatory, Campos writes:

---

[12] The word *queer* can also provide a way to recognize the fluidity of sexual identity and broaden the scope of the community name to LGBTQ.

The word queer has done what most negative word reclamation has been unable to do: it has become a word of unification for LGBTI [Lesbian, Gay, Bisexual, Transgender, and Intersex] communities.

These differing perspectives on the success of the word *queer*'s reappropriation led to a lawsuit in 2003, after the New York State Department of State turned down an application for non-profit status for the organization Queer Awareness, making the argument that the word *queer* is degrading and the name violates, therefore, Section 301 of the Not-for-Profit Corporation Law. Christopher Benecke, who helped start the organization, retorted that the word's meaning had changed through reappropriation, a meaning now recognized by dictionaries such as American Heritage. Benecke added:

Ironically in prohibiting the use of the word 'queer' to protect New York's citizens from being offended by it, the State only prolongs and promotes the negative implications that the State finds so offensive. (quoted in Schindler 2003)

The Department of State initially countered with Merriam-Webster's description of the word as usually derogatory, but it did finally reconsider its ruling. (Notable again here is the deployment of dictionary editors' decisions as prescriptively authoritative and relevant to legal determinations.)

In 2003, the Bravo television series *Queer Eye for the Straight Guy* was a runaway success and brought the word *queer* with its reappropriated meaning even more into the mainstream (although within the show, it referred exclusively to gay men). But concern was far from over. To take just one example, the magazine *Out* published a letter to the editor from reader Mark McNease in July 2007 in which he expressed his sense that reappropriation, rather than constituting an act of respect, perpetuates disrespect:

We cannot be outraged when others call us what we call ourselves. Until we say we are as offended by the use of words like *fag* and *queer* by our own as we are by the likes of Coulter we have nothing to be offended by. The black community is finally confronting the consequences of embracing a word steeped in pain and humiliation. It is time we followed suit.

The year 2007 was a controversial year indeed for the word referred to throughout most of the controversy as the N-word, as I discuss in the next section.

The debates about the reappropriation of the word *queer* reveal important perspectives in debates about reappropriation more generally, which surface in debates about the N-word as well. The power being negotiated in these debates is important for understanding the process of institutionalizing socially responsive prescriptivism. As early adopters of *queer* for the LGBT community asserted, reappropriation can be a form of political defiance and/or subversion. To take the word back and use it with pride is one of the best ways to negate or reverse negative meanings. It also challenges assumptions about who has the power to say what is and is not acceptable language, as Randall Kennedy (1999–2000, 90–91) argues with respect to the word *nigger*: "[Some politically progressive African Americans] maintain that they use *nigger* not in subjection to racial subordination but in triumphant defiance to it, a defiance that includes saying what one pleases regardless of how it strikes the sensibilities of E. R. Shipp, Bill Cosby, Tipper Gore, L. Delores Tucker, William Bennett, or any other would-be arbiters of taste and respectability." In a single word can reside a much bigger power struggle about who gets to set the ground rules for publicly acceptable discourse and about the possibility of different rules for different speakers. McNease, in the letter to *Out*, captures one pervasive counterargument: out of self-respect, a group should not reappropriate pejorative terms, based on the assumption that they will always remain pejorative; in this way, by not reappropriating the word, the group can model appropriate language use both within and outside the community. One concern is that reappropriation, if unsuccessful, can authorize ongoing use of the word with derogatory meanings by speakers outside the community. In response, some supporters of reappropriation argue that not to reclaim is to be silenced by majority use, to let the derogatory meanings "win." But, others counter, not to use the term is to help ease it, and its inherently pejorative meanings, out of usage. The desire to erase a derogatory term from the lexicon, however, often meets with serious resistance from those who think that a word's history carries important lessons and who believe that words can be used in radical ways that ask listeners to reconsider their prejudices.

A more global objection overarches all these specific arguments and counterarguments: the assertion that by talking about words, speakers are ignoring "real" issues, such as discrimination and structural inequities. A frivolous focus on words distracts and deflects. It creates "euphemisms" which then may need to be replaced because they take on the negative connotations of the words they themselves replaced.[13] Words are not the issue, the argument goes; they point us to the "underlying" issue, and changes to words may obscure what underlies them.

In some ways, the debate about reappropriation itself provides the counter to this global objection: people care about words because words do matter. Prejudice and discrimination happen through language as well as in many other ways. Arguing about words does not preclude fighting for equality in other arenas; this is not a zero-sum game. And the words we use actually affect the debates about the social and political issues we use the words to talk about.

In 2010, a New York Times/CBS News poll about gays in the military revealed two things: most Americans support members of the gay community serving in the military, and the wording of the poll question affects the results

---

[13] See Cameron's (1995, 143–148) excellent discussion of the implications of calling politically correct language euphemistic, as well as Allan and Burridge (2006, 96–100).

(Hechtkopf 2010). For example, when the question to respondents was whether they favored or opposed "homosexuals" serving in the military, 59 percent were in favor, and 29 percent were opposed. When the question to respondents was whether they favored or opposed "gay men and lesbians" serving in the military: 70 percent were in favor, and 19 percent were opposed. That is over a 10 percent gain in approval, well beyond the margin of error (3 percent).

Language has the power to shape how speakers respond to an issue, and specifically in this case the language of naming. There is a reason why these issues make headlines, and as the following section illustrates, the headlines were abuzz in 2007 about the N-word(s). To understand twenty-first century English usage, histories of English must account for these debates.

Reappropriation and naming in the African American community

The word *niggardly* is falling out of use in American English (see Figure 6.3), and there is nothing happenstance about the decline. The word's first two syllables are homophonous with one of the most, if not the most, explosive words in the American English lexicon (as well as several other varieties of English). In 1999, David Howard, the head of the Office of Public Advocate for the Washington, DC, mayor Anthony Williams, was forced to resign after a furor erupted over his use of *niggardly* in a meeting where he was describing his budgeting. Within hours of the meeting, word was circulating that Howard had used a racial epithet, and the incident soon made a splash in the headlines of the *Washington Post* and beyond.

The word *niggardly* is etymologically unrelated to the word *nigger*. But etymology is irrelevant to the word's fate. The speaker who hears *niggardly* can easily and logically reparse the word as *nigger* + *-ed* + *-ly* (or *nigger* + *-ly*), in which case the word becomes a highly offensive racial epithet (see Pinker

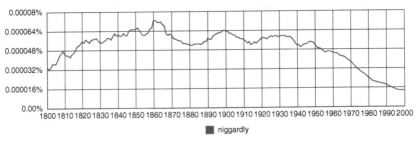

Figure 6.3 The frequency of "niggardly" in English books, 1800–2000, in Google Books Ngram Viewer

1999 for a good discussion).[14] The mayor eventually asked Howard to rescind his resignation, so he did not in fact lose his job over the word. But the incident speaks to the incendiary power of this racial epithet specifically and to the tension surrounding identity terms for and within the African American community more generally, which has influenced speakers' sense of appropriate public language. It also reflects the fact that conversations about these words are news – they make headlines in the public discourse.

Throughout the twentieth century and into the twenty-first, the name for the African American community has been a source of public discussions, largely within but also outside the community. Tom Smith (1992) argues that the process has been more contentious for African Americans than other groups, given the ways that a long history of racial discrimination has affected the meaning of most if not all historical racial labels. And, he notes, names matter: "While symbolic, these changes [in preferred labels] have not been inconsequential. For symbols are part and parcel of reality itself" (513). The debates over names were raging during the Civil Rights era, and in 1967, Lerone Bennett, Jr. published a lengthy piece in *Ebony* called "What's In A Name?: National Controversy Rages over Proper Name for Americans of African Descent." The article focuses on whether the label *Negro* remains acceptable or should be replaced by *black/Black* or *Afro-American*. And *Ebony*, in fact, started to use *Black/black* rather than *Negro* fairly shortly thereafter.

The aim of naming and renaming efforts has consistently been to find a group label that instills group pride and self-esteem and often, in addition, captures activist, progressive sentiments. As both Bennett and Smith capture in their valuable overviews, the word *colored* was the dominant term in the mid- to late nineteenth century, although not without some resistance.[15] The term *Negro* began to gain greater acceptance in the late nineteenth century, a movement led by influential Black leaders such as Booker T. Washington and W. E. B. DuBois. Bennett (1967, 50) summarizes that "for a short spell," the word *Negro* was adopted as a radical or at least progressive term: "a term of militancy, self-consciously used by black men defiantly asserting their pride of race." The term was rejected, however, by those who saw it as a term of reproach or degradation used by Whites – a position that continues to echo through debates about reappropriation today, although often about different words. The word *Negro* has today fallen into disfavor, but a century ago its reappropriation seemed a possibility. The *Negro Year Book* asserted in 1919: "There is an increasing use

---

[14] The suffix *-ed* regularly attaches to nouns to create adjectives such as *cultured, moneyed*, and *bigoted*.

[15] The fifth annual convention of the colored people of America, convened in 1835, passed a resolution recommending the abandonment of the word *colored* in speech and writing (quoted in Bennett 1967, 48).

of the word 'Negro'. . . to designate us as a people. The result is that the word 'Negro' is, more and more, acquiring a dignity that it did not have in the past" (quoted in Bennett 1967, 50).

The capitalization of the word *Negro* in that quote may seem unremarkable to modern eyes, but it would have been noted at the time. A not well-publicized fact in the history of American English is that the 1920s witnessed a prolonged and finally successful struggle over the spelling of the word *Negro*, specifically its capitalization. In *The Crisis* (May 1930), DuBois credits letter-writing campaigns by Roscoe Conklin Bruce and the National Association for the Advancement of Colored People (NAACP); DuBois quotes Bruce as saying, "the colored people of the United States desire to have the word Negro capitalized, and their wishes ought to be respected" (172). And while it took the Government Printing Office longer, by 1930 the *Atlantic Monthly* and the *New York Times* had heeded the call. The *New York Times* made the following announcement in an editorial in 1930: "In our 'style book' 'Negro' is now added to the list of words to be capitalized. It is not merely a typographical change; it is an act of recognition of racial self-respect for those who have been for generations in the 'lower case'" (quoted in DuBois 1930, 172). As this editorial makes clear, a capital letter is not just a capital letter. Names and their spelling have the power to signify respect – and in this case, in the face of a history of disrespect.

The stakes of this spelling reform are higher than the spelling reforms more typically included in history of English textbooks, such as the loss or maintenance of final silent *-e*'s (e.g., *have* versus *hav*) or the shift from an initial *ph-* to *f-* in *fantasy*. And while debates over correct use of apostrophes are impassioned and merit attention, this attention should never be at the expense of the impassioned debates over identity terms.

In the mid-twentieth century the term *Black* (usually capitalized) came more into favor, at first as a more radical or militant term, bolstered by Stokely Carmichael's book *Black Power: The Politics of Liberation in America* (1967) and supporters of the Black Power Movement. The term jostled with *Afro-American* and later *African American* (both terms are still debated, but the former has largely fallen out of favor, except in some academic contexts). By 1974, a *Newsweek* poll indicated that *Black* had gained majority acceptance and lost its more radical connotations (see Smith 1992, 502–503). Most newspapers and magazines shifted their usage over the next decade. Then, in 1988, Jesse Jackson and other leaders in the African American community began to advocate *African American*. An opinion piece in the *New York Times* in 1988 quotes Jackson as follows: "Just as we were called colored, but were not that, and then Negro, but not that, to be called black is just as baseless." The editorial notes the relatively quick shift from Black but concludes in support of a community's right to name itself:

If the new name catches on, it will challenge headline writers and disconcert citizens only recently accustomed to black. But people ought to be able to call themselves whatever they wish. The desire to choose one's label is as American as apple pie, and as political as other recent progressions. ("Negro, Black and African-American")

As this brief summary makes clear, the ground has been shifting in terms of preferred names for and within the African American community. And the shifting preferences have influenced usage, from newspaper style guides to everyday speech. Those shifts are an important part of the history of the language, and so is the debate itself.

Debates have been even more heated about the use of the N-word, and interestingly, the participants in the debate have sometimes reflected on the importance of the conversation itself. For example, in 2007, *Ebony* published a special issue called "Who Are You Calling A. . . .?" to put the debate about words on the front page, so to speak. The editor, Sylvester Monroe, recognized that the debate was as important as any outcome in terms of language use: "You will be part of an uncomfortable, frank, sometimes contradictory yet necessary conversation . . . In the end, it is the conversation itself that matters." In 2006, an episode in the third season of the television show *All of Us* had the adults debating the appropriate use of the N-word. A review praised: "this installment of *All of Us* addresses an emotionally charged topic with humor and insight, entertaining viewers while also, one would hope, prompting a conversation or two across the land" (mediavillage.com by Ed Martin). And 2006–2007 saw these conversations happening across the country.

One complication of public debates about the N-word is that the word itself is so explosive in American English that many speakers and writers generally avoid it. In this way, the debate navigates whether and which speakers have the right to speak the unspeakable, both in terms of content and rhetoric. The debate in 2006–2007 was not new; the N-word(s), including both the variant *nigger* and the reanalyzed *nigga*, has long been a volatile term. But the debate was unusual in its public intensity and in its revolutionary campaign to bury the word.

The debate about the N-word has been, in fact, a critical meta-discourse about reappropriation, the power of words, and the power to prescribe in socially responsive ways. I outline here some key moments leading up to the heated discussions of 2006–2007 and then a summary of those discussions to capture this historically important meta-discourse – to make the case for its importance to understanding this moment in the linguistic history of American English.

In 1995, the N-word made headlines as part of the case against Mark Fuhrman in the criminal trial of O. J. Simpson; the word was presented as potential evidence that Fuhrman held racist attitudes. In 1997, the *Seattle Times* banned the word *nigger* in news stories. In the pilot episode of the television show *Scrubs* in 2001, J. D., who is White, asks his best friend Turk, who is Black, "If we're both singing along, and knowing that otherwise I would never use the word, am

I allowed to say – ," and Turk cuts him off, "No." In 2002, law professor Randall Kennedy published the powerful book *Nigger: The Strange Career of a Troublesome Word*, which set off debate about whether the title alone was allowing non-African Americans to use the word in illegitimate ways. In February 2006, a teacher at Valley Traditional High School was suspended for using the N-word toward a student; the article about the case itself includes a disclaimer at the beginning about the need to spell out the word and its variants.[16]

The Ban the N-Word campaign (www.banthenword.org) began in May 2004, and it describes its goals on the website as follows:

Ban The N-Word is a campaign to put an end to the widespread acceptance and use of this insulting, derogatory, degrading, demeaning, malicious, venomous, debilitating, and self-defeating word. And for the record, a term of "endearment" it is not.

Linguist Geneva Smitherman, one of the most prominent scholars of African American English, disagrees in her chapter "The N-words" in *Word from the Mother* (2006). She distinguishes the subversive word *nigga* ("rebellious, defiant, do-what-the-fuck-I-wannuh attitude") from the derogatory term *nigger* ("compliant, conformist, eager-to-please-the-White-folk") within the African American community (49), and she provides eight different meanings of the N-word, including very positive ones, when used by Blacks to address other Blacks (she stresses the word is *address*, not *call*).[17] Smitherman (2006, 52–53) sees little use in debating the merits of reappropriation or in banning the word; she writes, "Linguistic technicalities aside, all the hysteria about and dissin of Black comedians, Hip Hop artists, and young people for their frequent public use of the term ain gon stop the flow of nigga. Truth be told, Blacks done been usin nigga in they everyday conversations since enslavement."

But the efforts to ban the word continued. In April 2006, the non-profit corporation United Voices for a Common Cause (UVCC) was founded, and one of its primary purposes is to eradicate the use of the N-word by African Americans. The description of the group on its website states:

Recognizing that negative lyrics, scripts, dialog and scenes which enter the human ears and sight has a negative effect on the human mind and in of itself lends to a debilitating, self-defeating image hereby declares censorship on the use of the n-word by African Americans.

The group pledges in its mission statement not to use the word, and in so doing, in 2006, it captured a cultural zeitgeist. UVCC's website features a Hall of

---

[16] Multiple cases of teachers being dismissed for use of the N-word have received newspaper coverage. To provide just one example, in July 1998, Professor Ken Hardy used the N-word in a communications class at Jefferson Community College in Louisville, Kentucky and was fired for the term (his intention in using the word in class was determined not to matter).

[17] See also Rahman (2012) for a useful discussion of the N-word by Black comedians.

Shame in which actors, comedians, writers, and others are inducted for disrespecting the African American community by using the word.

In May 2006, attorney Roy Miller from Atlanta challenged Blacks in the US and beyond to mark out the N-word in their dictionaries on August 1 of that year. His efforts gained the support of the London-based organization Ligali, which describes itself as a Pan-African Human Rights Organization that "challeng[es] the misrepresentation of African people, culture and history in the British media" (www.ligali.org). In October 2006, the Black Music Congress held a packed debate in England about the "n word and insidious racism."

Then, in November 2006, the N-word made headlines not for proactive efforts to censor it but for its uncensored and highly offensive use by comedian Michael Richards at the Laugh Factory comedy club in West Hollywood. Richards, famous for his portrayal of Cosmo Kramer on the television program *Seinfeld*, went on a tirade in response to an African American audience member who (he seems to have felt) interrupted the act, in which he called him "nigger" multiple times and referred to the lynching of African Americans for offenses. The anger and hatred in the outburst were shocking, and Richards was chastised in the media. Notably, what made headlines was the use of the N-word, not the appalling reference to lynching. That word itself, at this point, proves as hateful as any other speech act.

In the weeks that followed, Black comedians found themselves talking about the use of the word and its role in comedy and beyond. Paul Mooney, a comedian who has long used the word in his stand-up comedy and a recurring guest on "Chappelle's Show," told CNN: "The tape shocked me. I finally got the gist of the word." He pledged: "We're gonna stop using the 'N word.' I'm gonna stop using it. I'm not gonna use it again and I'm not gonna use the 'B word' [*bitch*]. And we're gonna put an end to the 'N word.' Just say no to the 'N word.' We want all human beings throughout the world to stop using the 'N word.'" He referenced Richard Pryor, who swore off using the N-word in 1979 after a trip to Africa. The Laugh Factory subsequently banned the word.

Efforts to ban the word spread from there. On November 25, 2006, for example, the *Journal Sentinel* published an editorial by Eugene Kane titled "The N-word has no place in schools." Kane recognizes the difference between White and Black speakers using the word but comes to a fairly sweeping conclusion for policy: "Ban the N-word in all MPS schools [Milwaukee Public Schools], but first explain why. If you are heard saying it anywhere on school property, you will be suspended or expelled. (This is about conversation, not 'Huck Finn' or journalism class.)"

In January 2007, the magazines *Ebony* and *Jet* stated they would no longer print the word *nigger*. On February 28, 2007 the New York City Council adopted a moratorium on the N-word; the resolution was introduced by City Councilman Leroy Comrie and was recognized to be a "symbolic gesture" as there was no penalty involved for infractions. Comrie also asked the television network BET to stop using the word in its shows. Comedian Chris Rock, whose comedy routines are replete with the word, rejected the rationale of the request: "Enough real bad things happen in this city to worry about how I am going to use the word." The mayor of Brazoria, Texas, Ken Corley sought to outlaw the N-word with a fine of $500, but he dropped the effort due to First Amendment issues. A subsequent news article praised: "it certainly did generate an important, and exceptionally civil, discussion" in the town (Wiehl 2007). Discussion of the N-word took place on the *Daily Show*, the *Colbert Report*, and National Public Radio.

The spring of 2007 also saw the publication of syndicated columnist Jabari Asim's book *The N Word: Who Can Say It, Who Shouldn't, and Why*. In the book, Asim provides an invaluable history of the word and then tries to navigate its different uses in the African American community at the end of the twentieth century, from its use to powerfully critique ongoing racism to its casual, friendly use among friends. Asim finds the latter more troubling and a "failure of the imagination." He finds reappropriation unpersuasively ahistorical: if young people knew the history, he argues, they would not use the word – the history would not convince them to reappropriate it. It is "a shorthand for subhuman."

Then on April 4, 2007 (a day when Asim was being interviewed about his book by Diane Rehm on NPR), Don Imus sparked a national debate on free speech and the use of demeaning language when he called the women on the Rutgers University women's basketball team "nappy-headed hos" on his radio show "Imus in the Morning." Imus lost his job (although the show was back on the air within a year), and the airwaves were abuzz about the question of how to curtail racist and misogynistic language without imposing censorship. The focus shifted or broadened to encompass decency, misogynistic references, and the N-word in popular culture, with hip-hop taking center stage. Suddenly, the words *bitch*, *ho*, and *nigger* got wrapped up together as indicative of language and cultural attitudes that needed to be changed (see Awkward 2009 for an excellent discussion of the broader cultural implications of the event and its aftermath).

Later in April, Russell Simmons, co-founder of Def Jam records and one of the industry's most successful names, called for voluntary restrictions on all three words in public versions of songs and proposed setting up an industry watchdog to recommend guidelines for lyrical and visual standards. Simmons and Benjamin Chavis, who co-founded with Simmons the Hip-Hop Summit Action Network, put out a statement with the following recommendation:

We recommend that the recording and broadcast industries voluntarily remove/bleep/delete the misogynistic words 'bitch' and 'ho' and the racially offensive word 'nigger' . . . Our internal discussions with industry leaders are not about censorship. Our discussions are about the corporate social responsibility of the industry to voluntarily show respect to

African Americans and other people of color, African American women and to all women in lyrics and images.[18]

This recommendation represented a reversal in position from a statement by Simmons and Chavis from April 13: "[offensive references in hip hop] may be uncomfortable for some to hear, but our job is not to silence or censor that expression."

In an interview with *Time Magazine*, Simmons stated, "The dialogue is more important than Imus. The fact that we are discussing race is inspiring." In terms of his changing his position: "I think it is some self-analysis. The outrage [over the Imus situation] made me think about it. I am allowed to have a different opinion." This comment alone captures the power of public dialogue about words and why these meta-discussions must be considered part of the history of the language.

The National Action Network, a prominent civil rights organization founded by Al Sharpton, launched the Decency Initiative that spring. Its website explains:

The Decency Initiative was created in order to reduce the dialogue of indecency that has become pervasive in our community as a form of entertainment. We are calling for the removal of "nigga", "bitch", and "ho" from the lexicon of the music and entertainment industry. The Decency Initiative has already caught hold across the nation and continues to inspire people to become active participants through its positive message.

In July, the Decency Initiative went after the celebrity website TMZ for calling an outfit worn by Beyoncé Knowles a "roboho performance outfit." Gender and race became entangled. Al Sharpton stated in an interview on Fox News:

Calling any woman a 'ho' is demeaning and abusive and it should not be tolerated on any level ... [TMZ] should be denounced by the entire community for glorifying the continued oppression of women with this derogatory term. Racism in America is perpetuated by ignorance and hate and using one's airwaves or media entity to promote it is a blatant setback to civil rights and the advancement of equality.

Ebony published its special issue called "Who Are You Calling A....?," and when senior editor Sylvester Monroe was interviewed on NPR's "Day to Day" (June 21, 2007), he explained:

I don't know where to put the blame, really. I think there's enough blame to really go around ... what I hope we're beginning to do is to start to facilitate the conversation ... It's where we get the hip-hop generation to understand how the civil rights generation really sees no way to anesthetize the N-word. What we have is two groups of people who I think want to be in the same space, but they can't get there because they don't – they're not hearing each other.

---

[18] These were much quoted by the media. For a useful summary, consult www.nydailynews.com/ entertainment/gossip/statements-russell-simmons-article-1.209348 (April 25, 2007).

Monroe said that he uses the word in private conversations and noted that "membership has its privileges." He continued:

It is simply part of the multicultural kind of society I live in. And I would daresay that there are words like that in many cultures and ethnicities that are used just like that. I reserve the right to use that word in private. But I also understand the negative connotations of that word and the hurt [unintelligible] and therefore I wouldn't ever use it in public.

The interviewer linked the issue of who can say the word and who cannot with the broader question of labels for the community: "I think it leaves many people who are outside of that community really struggling, not even knowing whether to use the word black or African-American. You know, what are those of us who are not blacks supposed to make of all of this?" The interviewer, who is White, gives voice to the discomfort of being on the outside of power when it comes to naming and creating the rules of acceptable public discourse. Geneva Smitherman (2006, 60) acknowledges the challenge that use of the N-word within the African American community presents to long-standing power structures: "Some Whites view this as the operation of a linguistic double standard, representing a kind of Black privilege. Well, yeah, that's what it is, make no bones about it. It's a symbolic challenge to White hegemony, one of the precious few to which Brothas and Sistas can lay claim in this society."

The NAACP asked all Americans to consider the question of what it would mean to bury a word when it conducted a formal burial of the N-word at its annual convention in Detroit on July 9, 2007. They orchestrated a formal procession with a casket from Cobo Arena to Hart Plaza, which was described as the "centerpiece of the convention." There were similar burials in cities around the country, with national media coverage and debate (almost entirely about the "N-word" referred to euphemistically). Philadelphia mayor John Street asserted: "This word has been used to denigrate and dehumanize African Americans. If you can kill this word, then people can begin to be free in a different kind of way. There is no question that ... this message will be far-reaching. It is a simple message that has great appeal." Professor Michael Eric Dyson of Georgetown, in a published interview, countered: "I don't think you can bury words. I think the more you try to dismiss them, the more power you give to them, the more circulation they have" (Hinton 2007).

On August 7, 2007, Al Sharpton's National Action Network sponsored a national "Day of Outrage," with rallies in over twenty cities, to protest the use of *nigga*, *bitch*, and *ho* in the music recording industry. NAN asked hip-hop artists to stop recording degrading lyrics or lyrics that offend racial groups and establish a standard of decency that music executives could apply to censor lyrics (similar to the censoring of words offensive to police officers, Jews, and other ethnic groups).

Over that summer, platinum-seller hip-hop artist Chamillionaire announced that his new album "Ultimate Victory" would be cuss- and N-word free. He asserted it was a moral issue, not a monetary one. Master P also announced he would make clean music. Twista, in contrast, stated: "It would have to pay something real strong to make me change the way I do my music."

The complexity of this conversation about language far surpasses this brief summary, but here's the point: this is one of the most important conversations happening about language at the turn of the millennium. It's all about the power of words – to harm, to critique, to unite. It's about power. It's about racism and discrimination. It's socially responsive prescriptivism at work and in the works, as individuals and organizations seek to establish institutionalized regulations about acceptable or unacceptable use of powerful words.

Challenging lexicographical authority

The conversations about identity terms have also involved speakers challenging lexicographical authority in unusual ways. In general, dictionaries carry a striking amount of authority, both in the everyday lives of speakers ("go look it up in the dictionary") and in places like the courts, as captured in some of the examples in this chapter (for a longer discussion; see Landau 2001; Curzan 2000). The dictionary is the place to find answers about "what words mean," and speakers often defer to dictionary definitions. But not with these identity terms.

In 1997, Merriam-Webster was challenged by two Michigan women, Delphine Abraham and Kathryn Williams, who proposed a boycott of the Merriam-Webster dictionary if it did not revise or delete its definition of *nigger* as "a black person – usu. taken to be offensive." While the definition in the ninth and tenth editions states that this use is usually offensive and subsequently provides a usage note emphasizing that the term is a racial slur, the concern was that the definition puts "a black person" first, potentially suggesting synonymy. The NAACP took up the cause and called for a revision (see Kennedy 2002, 135; Smitherman 2006, 93–94). NAACP President Kweisi Mfume explained, "The NAACP finds it objectionable that the Merriam-Webster would use black people as a definition for a racist term" (AP, 10/17/97). In 1998, Merriam-Webster assigned a task force and consulted with various language experts to consider how it defines offensive words and whether to change its practice of listing definitions historically.[19] The revised definition of *nigger* foregrounds

---

[19] Dictionary editors have been left trying to navigate difficult territory around the success or lack thereof of reappropriation efforts, as well as the incendiary nature of the word in general. The *Random House Historical Dictionary of American Slang* (1994/1997) describes the word as "surviving among black speakers as an affectionate, ironic, jocular, or occasionally complimentary epithet."

the offensive nature of the word and cross-references the usage note before any attempt at a definition.

These efforts did not keep Merriam-Webster out of trouble or out of the headlines over identity terms. In 1999, a listener in Seattle called GAYBC Radio Network about the synonyms for *homosexual* in the AOL thesaurus (powered by Merriam-Webster), which included *pedophile*. Not synonymous and highly offensive. The news hit the Internet, and within twenty-four hours, the thesaurus had been taken down from AOL and the Merriam-Webster site. Within three days, Merriam-Webster had removed *homosexual* from the thesaurus and issued a public apology. This incident highlights one way the Internet is changing the history of English: opening a space for these public debates and allowing challenges and change in institutionalized linguistic authority in new ways.

With the identity term *gay*, a national educational organization in the United States has taken a socially responsive prescriptive role beyond what any standard dictionary usage note or label could or would undertake. In 2008, the Gay, Lesbian, and Straight Education Network co-sponsored the "Think Before You Speak" campaign to promote awareness of bias against the LGBTQ community and curtail derogatory, anti-LGBTQ language. Spotlighted is the phrase "that's so gay," which younger speakers have been using at the beginning of the twenty-first century to refer to things they regard as stupid, uninteresting, or otherwise unworthy. The campaign has involved public service announcements on the radio and television (also available on the website www.thinkb4you speak.com). These announcements feature some speakers using "that's so gay" as a derogatory term and then being chastised and corrected by another speaker, in some cases a celebrity like Wanda Sykes or Hilary Duff. In one announcement, two teenage girls stand behind the register in a drugstore:

JULIA: So are you going out tonight?
EMMA: I can't. My parents say I have to be home right after work.
JULIA: That's so gay.
EMMA: It's totally gay.
At this point, the two are interrupted by a more middle-aged woman with her basket of items, who says, "Ucchhh, that's so Emma and Julia."
JULIA: Why are you saying that's so Emma and Julia?
CUSTOMER: Well, you know, when something is dumb or stupid, you say, 'That's so Emma and Julia.'
EMMA: Who says that?
CUSTOMER [*shrugging her shoulders*]: Everyone.

There is then a voice-over: "Imagine if who you are were used as an insult." All announcements end with the imperative "Knock It Off." The NBA sponsored one "Think Before You Speak" ad after multiple incidents with players saying homophobic things during games.

Will these ads change usage and mean that speakers stop using *gay* in offensive ways to mean 'stupid'? It's hard to know. Many conscious language reform efforts fail, but this chapter and the previous one have highlighted efforts that have met with notable success in changing usage. And, when the efforts involve widespread, heated, and well-publicized debate about what is and isn't acceptable usage, their presence alone is noteworthy for our understanding of the language and its sociolinguistic context at the turn of the millennium.

In the conversations described in this chapter, speakers are negotiating among themselves where to look for linguistic authority. They are highlighting their right to work out the meaning and social power of words in their communities and are turning to or being guided by nontraditional linguistic authorities (e.g., magazines, the NAACP). Those outside the community are expressing discomfort with the awareness that traditional language authorities do not necessarily hold or remain unchallenged – that they, as speakers, must figure out the linguistic terrain in real time. In the process, speakers are negotiating censorship and self-censorship on local and institutional levels. These discussions involve a remarkable level of participation, fostered at least in part by the Internet. These movements are not always successful (e.g., burying the N-word), but they have fundamentally changed aspects of modern usage – and people's attitudes about and awareness of a set of identity terms as contested linguistic ground.

7   Finding shared ground: public conversations about prescriptivism

In May 2012, Joan Acocella published a review in the *New Yorker* of Henry Hitchings' new book *The Language Wars: A History of Proper English* that frustrated many a linguist and lexicographer due to its oversimplification of the prescriptive–descriptive "war" and some of its misinformation about descriptive approaches to language. Mark Liberman (2012) responded on the blog Language Log: "either the topic was not felt to be important enough to merit elementary editorial supervision, or there is no one at the magazine with any competence in the area involved." His frustration with the lack of linguistic knowledge among even the highly educated is palpable. And then came the end of the review, where Acocella tries to undercut Hitchings' critique of prescriptive approaches to language by pointing out that Hitchings went to Oxford, wrote a dissertation about Samuel Johnson, and follows the formal conventions of edited standard English in his academic English. He talks the talk, she argues, but does not walk the walk.

This attack, which reproduces many similar ones on "descriptive linguists" over the years, fundamentally misunderstands the argument that the vast majority of linguists – who by training take a descriptive approach to language – are making about prescriptive rules of all sorts, be they about standard English, formal style, restoration of older forms, or politically responsive language reform. The misunderstanding is captured starkly by Ryan Bloom (2012) in his New Yorker Page-Turner blog post written a little over two weeks after Acocella's review, in which he sets up "straw descriptivists," asserting the following:

People who say otherwise, who say that in all situations we should speak and write however we'd like, are ignoring the current reality. This group, known as descriptivists, may be fighting for noble *ideas*, for things like the levelling of élitism and the smoothing of social class, but they are neglecting the real-world costs of those ideas, neglecting the flesh-and-blood humans who are denied a job or education because, as wrong as it is, they are being harshly judged for how they speak and write *today*.

This depiction of descriptivists misses the fact that part of what descriptivists describe is the standard variety of the language, along with nonstandard varieties, as well as the ideologies that surround both standard and nonstandard varieties. Linguists are well aware of the standard variety's social power and importance. Being a descriptivist is not synonymous with saying that everyone should talk and write however they want to all the time.[1] Being a descriptivist is understanding the social conventions of language – and standardization is a big part of that. It is, in fact, possible, as a descriptive linguist, to say in the same breath that nonstandard varieties are fully legitimate and rule-governed and that there are good reasons for speakers and writers to master the conventions of standard English and deploy them in situations where that is expected. Steven Pinker (2012) wrote an eloquent response to the Acocella review in *Slate*, in which he made this point with the following example: "[T]he valid observation that there is nothing inherently wrong with *ain't* should not be confused with the invalid inference that *ain't* is one of the conventions of standard English."

In this brief concluding chapter, rather than rehashing the argument about what descriptivists are actually saying (see Curzan 2009 for more of my thoughts on that issue), I focus on what the argument itself represents in terms of the ongoing struggles of linguists to talk with non-linguists about prescriptivism in ways that seem to make sense or stick in any lasting way. Linguists lament that people of all education levels often seem more inclined to listen to self-proclaimed prescriptive language experts like Lynne Truss, Ellie Grossman, and William Strunk and E. B. White, than to linguists. When it comes to physics, people turn to physicists as the experts to consult on the topic; when it comes to language, people often turn to experts without training in linguistics. For the public conversation about prescriptivism to be a productive one, we need to highlight the common ground on which we stand, clarify the terms we use, and offer pragmatic paths to realistic goals.

The project is a timely one. Prescriptivism continues to be a powerful force in the day-to-day experiences of many speakers and writers, both linguists and non-linguists. The past few decades have witnessed an array of important efforts by linguists invested in bringing linguistic knowledge and understandings to the teaching of language at many levels, and some have met with notable success. But much work remains to be done. Unfortunately, I must differ with David Crystal, who optimistically closes *The Stories of English* (2004, 525) with this assertion: "We are coming towards the close of a linguistically intolerant era." Living in the UK may give Crystal more reason for optimism (the UK has witnessed some key curricular reforms, among many other factors), but even there Lynne Truss's *Eats, Shoots & Leaves* outsold *The Stories of English* and any other descriptive approach to language by, well, a lot. Crystal does admit

---

[1] Being a descriptivist may make one more prone to using singular 'they' to refer back to the antecedent *everyone* in published writing, as the majority of us would do in speech.

that the repercussions of over two centuries of powerful institutionalized prescriptivism present a challenge:

And we seem to be approaching an era when nonstandard usages and varieties, previously denigrated or ignored, are achieving a new presence and respectability within society, reminiscent of that found in Middle English, when dialect variation in literature was widespread. But we are not there yet. The rise of Standard English has resulted in a confrontation between the standard and nonstandard dimensions of the language which has lasted for over 200 years, and this has had traumatic consequences which will take some years to eliminate. Once people have been given an inferiority complex about the way they speak or write, they find it difficult to shake off. However, it is only a matter of time. (523)

The phrasing "a matter of time" could suggest that the resolution of the standard-nonstandard "confrontation" will happen by itself, but I am not so sanguine. Nonstandard varieties continue to be misunderstood and denigrated. Standard varieties continue to be referred to as "good English" or just plain "English." Linguists have the opportunity and the responsibility to foster a conversation about language that could help us reach something like the "modified prescriptivism" advocated by Edwards (2012). We should aim for what I will call a "linguistically informed prescriptivism" that recognizes the value of a standard variety and helps people master it without denigrating nonstandard varieties, that teaches formal registers without dismissing the legitimacy of informal ones.

For this conversation to work, at this moment in history, everyone has to find ways to listen: to each other within the context of this specific discussion as well as to how speakers and writers are actually using the language and talking about the language. Those of us who are linguists are probably best positioned to take primary responsibility for ensuring that listening can and does happen. As I have argued throughout this book, a key starting point is taking prescriptivism seriously as a sociolinguistic phenomenon, disentangling its various strands and understanding its effects on speakers and writers.

Words matter

All participants in the public conversation about prescriptivism, linguists and non-linguists alike, come from a place of deep caring about language. But we don't always share the same language, or at least the same meanings of key words. As discussed in Chapter 1, linguists and non-linguists typically do not share the same meaning for the word *grammar*, which is how many native speakers of English can say "I don't know grammar," or "my grammar isn't very good," or "I am linguistically (or grammatically) challenged." They are talking not about their systematic knowledge of how to use English to communicate meaningfully with other English speakers but rather about their control of a restricted set of rules for "good" or "proper" English, an English that they feel will be judged harshly by experts. And judged harshly it is by critics like Grossman, who in the first two pages of her book criticizes "mistakes" by an unnamed Pulitzer Prize-winning journalist as well as Jim Lehrer and infantilizes those who do not use what she calls "good English," stating that she does not make mistakes because she is "old enough to know better" (1997, 2).

The insecurities these criticisms instill in speakers and writers can make it difficult for non-linguists to listen to linguists who sound like they are saying that "grammar rules" don't matter/ are silly/ are arbitrary/ aren't well founded. I want to pause here to look closely at this list, because it captures one source of miscommunication between linguists and non-linguists. We as linguists need to be very careful about the wording of critiques of prescriptive rules. If we take this list as an example, two of these descriptions are not true, and two of them can easily be misconstrued.

Let me begin with the two items in the list that are not true: prescriptive rules don't matter, and prescriptive rules are silly. Prescriptive grammar rules do matter. As detailed throughout this book, prescriptive ideas are now well entrenched in the United States, the UK, and many other English-speaking nations. Mastery of many of these rules or conventions for standard or "good" English can be important for speakers' social, educational, and professional advancement. For this reason, prescriptive rules are also not silly – and certainly do not feel that way – for the speakers and writers who need to learn them in order to achieve specific educational, social, or professional goals. The stakes are very real. These rules also do not seem silly to all the writers, teachers, editors, and others who have spent years being told that these rules represent language used "correctly" and "well." For all of us to engage in a productive conversation about the legitimacy of language that does not follow those rules, it is important to start by recognizing that all of us are right in thinking our language will be judged by these standards of language correctness at least some of the time, at least at this historical moment.

The two other descriptions of prescriptive rules – that they are arbitrary and that they aren't well founded – are largely true but can be misleading. When linguists assert that prescriptive rules are arbitrary, they are acknowledging that many rules, like the ones detailed in this book, stem from one or more prescriptive language commentators' beliefs about what makes good English (perhaps especially those about style and restoration of older forms). The statement about arbitrariness is less accurate in reference to rules about standardization. For better or worse, the selection of a standard variety of the English language has never been completely arbitrary: it has reflected which variety of English is spoken and written by the speakers with social, economic, and political power and control over the institutions that promote the standard language and serve gatekeeping functions. One could say it is "arbitrary" linguistically in that there is nothing structurally or linguistically superior about the form that is selected as standard; but it is not arbitrary socially or sociolinguistically. The adjective *arbitrary* may also conjure up for readers or listeners a sense that the prescriptive rules are enforced inconsistently. It is certainly true that different prescriptive language authorities vary in exactly which set of prescriptive rules they enforce – although there is less variation in the category of standard-enforcing prescriptive rules. But the notion of prescriptive inconsistency may not ring entirely true for folks who have had many of the same or what seem like very similar prescriptive rules enforced in many a classroom or workplace. When linguists use the word "arbitrary" in sweeping reference to prescriptivism, it can undermine our credibility given speakers' experience with language standards and the enforcement of prescriptive grammatical rules.

In terms of the well-foundedness of prescriptive rules, linguists may once again be talking at cross-purposes with the people they want to reach. Prescriptive rules about style or restoration of older forms may rely solely or at least originally on the personal judgment of one or a handful of mavens who have a microphone – that is, a publisher or published forum – to disseminate the judgment, and these are often not especially linguistically well founded. But some prescriptive rules about effective style do usefully attempt to minimize ambiguity, create aesthetically pleasing parallelism, avoid wordy constructions, or eliminate discriminatory language or the like – all goals that have a solid foundation. The principle of following the rules in high-stakes settings is also well founded, as speakers and writers may be judged severely for not following them. So, once again, the wording of the critique can muddy the waters.

To engage rather than dismiss the prescriptive voices in public discourse about language, it helps to emphasize the shared ground: all of us share a deep concern about language. From there, disentangling the different strands of prescriptivism can build more productive interventions in the educational sphere and beyond.

Prescriptivism redefined

Chapter 1 proposes four strands of prescriptivism: standardizing, stylistic, restorative, and politically responsive. Linguists and non-linguists agree about the value of a standard variety of a language. It provides a valuable shared medium of communication. One important goal of schooling is helping students master the standard variety, so that they can use it when it will benefit them. The acquisition of standard English does not have to come, however, at the expense of nonstandard varieties that students may bring with them to school. The curriculum could usefully shift to an additive model of language/dialect acquisition as opposed to a replacive one, where instruction relies on the words *standard* and *nonstandard* (or versions like *school* and *non-school*), not *right* and *wrong*, *good* and *bad*; instruction should help students expand their linguistic repertoires, not "improve their grammar." Toward those ends, linguists could help teachers and students understand which parts of prescriptive grammar promote standard language use, as opposed to the parts that focus on style.

Politically responsive prescriptivism could be linked into such conversations in terms of changing standards. For example, what singular generic pronoun would be considered standard today? And who decides? Students and teachers can discuss what individual and collective actions may or may not change published guidelines for usage. The prescriptivism of standardization also could and should involve critical examination of how lexicographers apply labels such as *slang* and *nonstandard* and how they try to handle an ever-changing language.

With stylistic prescriptivism, it will benefit everyone involved to recognize that the rules focus primarily on written language and the rules are most applicable in formal registers. With this caveat, students and teachers can have thoughtful discussions about which rules usefully improve formal written prose, by making it aesthetically pleasing or less ambiguous or the like, and which rules make the prose feel stilted. Again, the conversation moves away from "correctness" and toward rhetorical choices, which is a more empowering place from which to speak or write. It also allows writers to talk about how nonstandard language choices can be clarifying, aesthetically pleasing, and rhetorically effective too. Socially responsive prescriptivism involves many of the same issues, in terms of audience considerations and rhetorical choices, but the choices can be more loaded in terms of the social values and agendas driving the language prescriptions. For this reason, it is all the more important to have a well-informed and well-reasoned discussion of the prescriptions and their underlying rationales rather than imposing them as the "correct way to do things." As long as the Microsoft grammar checker continues to use the language of error, educators need to encourage a more critical view of the suggested corrections, using the pop-up boxes as a prompt for discussion of the applicability of various rules. In the long run, I hope that we can exploit the potential of the grammar checker's pop-up boxes as powerful mechanisms for delivering a more linguistically informed perspective on prescriptive rules of various types, as well as other aspects of writing.

Restorative prescriptivism has been a favorite target for criticism of the prescriptive project as a whole. Instead, the prescriptive recommendations involved could spark a conversation about whether the prescribed forms will actually be the ones that are judged, as well as the appeal of older forms in some cases but not others. That conversation need not undermine the value of all prescriptive advice in other contexts, if the different strands are disentangled.

If language education can move away from the language of error and correctness, perhaps the teaching of "grammar" can become exploratory, interesting, and rewarding for teachers and students alike. Rather than rote exercises about "correctness" that often undermine students' confidence in their language abilities, a grammar curriculum can cover the same ground and make students feel more fully equipped as speakers and writers: with a richer linguistic repertoire and some key meta-understandings for when to deploy different kinds of English.

In presenting this hopeful vision about a mutually respectful and productive public conversation about language that crosses the lines of formal academic training in linguistics, I am returning to an argument that Geoffrey Nunberg made thirty years ago in his piece "The Decline of Grammar" in the *Atlantic Monthly* (1983). He writes:

What we need now is not more invective – we have had plenty of that – but a return to civil discussion of the problems of grammar and their social importance. If the eighteenth century was the great age of English grammar, it was because problems of usage were considered worthy of serious consideration by the best minds of the day, from Pope and Johnson to Lord Chesterfield and Joseph Priestley ... Only three ground rules are needed for such a discussion: it should be well informed, it should be nonpartisan, and it should be backed by a measure of courage and tolerance.

The last point about tolerance is especially important. For non-linguists, this may entail open-mindedness and tolerance for variation and change in language. For linguists, it may involve open-mindedness and tolerance for the strongly held beliefs people bring to language. In this space, we may find a starting point for genuine and fruitful conversation.

When prescriptive types ridicule speakers who do not follow any of a variety of prescriptive rules, linguists get their backs up. When linguists ridicule prescriptivists and/or prescriptive rules, language sticklers get their backs up. As a result, any productive conversation about prescriptivism and language/ grammar instruction gets stymied, to the detriment of school curricula and young people. There is more common ground for both "sides" than is usually portrayed. Prescriptivists and descriptivists, to hold onto this oversimplified binary for a bit longer, both believe in the value of the standard language, and both have their personal likes and dislikes about language usage. It comes with caring deeply about language. With respect to these strongly held language preferences, Nunberg provides this important reminder, usefully distinguishing between shared convention and personal pet likes and peeves:

Of course, it is not only out of cowardice that we may want to adhere to rules that seem unjustified. Civility must be kept in mind when considering usage; that is what gave "polite prose" its name. Once there is a wide consensus that a certain usage is preferable, it behooves us to conform to it out of deference to public opinion, particularly if our private objections are only grammatical, with no basis in principle. Furthermore, there is a clear risk of irresponsibility in counseling others to disregard rules that they may be judged by. Finally, we don't want to underestimate the importance of nostalgia as a conservative force. I myself do not use *disinterested* to mean "uninterested," not because

I think it is a sin to do so but because I am fond of the older sense of the word. We all have our "bower-birds' treasures," as Fowler called them, which are no more harmful than any other antiquated mannerisms it may please us to affect. But we would do best to reserve these for our personal usage manuals, recognizing a distinction between the private decisions that we come to about usage and the public course we counsel. Where we cannot be bold, we can at least be tolerant.

We are not yet at the end of the era of prescriptivism, a fact with at least two key implications for linguists. First, as has been discussed throughout this book, language history must account for prescriptivism. James Milroy and others have written extensively about how standardization has shaped the telling of histories of English. As Milroy (1992, 1999) points out, histories of English tend to be histories of Standard English, but the history of English is the history of the many varieties of English included in the label "English." It is also the history of the spoken, the written, and the relationship of the two. Language history must account for speakers' encounters with a range of linguistic factors, including contact with speakers of other languages and with prescriptivism. It must also take seriously the development of language ideologies and attitudes as part of understanding a language's history.

Second, linguists need to account for the power and nature of prescriptivism in formulating talking points that can effectively open and foster conversation with non-linguists about how language works and how prescriptivism fits into that picture. Given prescriptivism's entrenchment in powerful institutions, including the educational system for over two hundred years, linguists should not be surprised that the conversation will be a prolonged one. It will help to establish firmly shared ground about standard English and educational goals, as a place to talk about what linguistic tolerance and well-informed discussion of language can and should involve. As importantly, prescriptive beliefs about language should not be dismissed as "ill-founded." They may not have a solid grounding in modern linguistic principles, but prescriptive beliefs about language have a strong foundation in the history of Modern English and in the lived experience of English speakers and writers. The history of English is happening all around us, and the conversations we're having about prescriptivism are part of that history.

References

Ackerman, Louise M. 1962. "Lady" as a Synonym for "Woman." *American Speech* 37: 284–285.

Acocella, Joan. 2012. The English wars. *New Yorker* (May 14): 115–120.

Adams, Michael. 2008. Nicknames, Interpellation, and Dubya's Theory of the State. *Names* 56: 206–220.

2009. Power, Politeness, and the Pragmatics of Nicknames. *Names* 57 (2): 81–91.

2012a. Lexicographical Description in a Culture of Correctness. Paper presented at Norma e uso nella lessicographia bilingue: XVI–XXI secolo, Universitá degli Studi di Catania, October 18–20.

2012b. Resources: Teaching Perspectives. In *Historical Linguistics of English: An International Handbook*, vol. II, edited by Alex Bergs and Laurel Brinton, 1163–1178. Berlin; New York: de Gruyter.

Alford, Henry. 1875 [1864]. *The Queen's English*. 5th edn. London: Daldy, Isbister.

Alford, Henry. 2005. Not a word. *New Yorker* (August 29): 32.

Allan, Keith and Kate Burridge. 2006. *Forbidden Words: Taboo and the Censoring of Language*. Cambridge: Cambridge University Press.

Alston, R. C. 1965. *A Bibliography of the English Language from the Invention of Printing to the Year 1800. Vol. I. English Grammars Written in English*. Leeds: E. J. Arnold.

American Heritage Dictionary of the English Language, 4th edn. 2000. Boston; New York: Houghton Mifflin.

American Heritage Dictionary of the English Language, 5th edn. 2011. Boston; New York: Houghton Mifflin.

Anderwald, Lieselotte. 2012. Variable Past-Tense Forms in Nineteenth-Century American English: Linking Normative Grammars and Language Change. *American Speech* 87 (3): 257–293.

Anten, Todd. 2006. Self-Disparaging Trademarks and Social Change: Factoring the Reappropriation of Slurs into Section 2(a) of the Lanham Act. *Columbia Law Review* 106: 388–434.

Ascham, Roger. 1570 [1863]. *The Scholemaster*. Ed. John E. B. Mayor. London: Bell and Daldy.

Asim, Jabari. 2007. *The N Word: Who Can Say It, Who Shouldn't, and Why*. Boston; New York: Houghton Mifflin.

Atkinson, Dwight. 1999. *Scientific Discourse in Sociohistorical Context: The Philosophical Transactions of the Royal Society of London, 1675–1975*. Mahwah, NJ; London: Lawrence Erlbaum.

Auer, Anita and Victorina González-Díaz. 2005. Eighteenth-century Prescriptivism in English: A Re-Evaluation of Its Effects on Actual Language Usage. *Multilingua* 24: 317–341.

Awkward, Michael. 2009. *Burying Don Imus: Anatomy of a Scapegoat.* Minneapolis: University of Minnesota Press.

Bailey, Richard W. 1991. *Images of English.* Ann Arbor: University of Michigan Press.

2006. Talking about Split Infinitives. *Michigan Today News-E* (June). www.umich.edu/NewsE/06_06/words.html

Baldwin, Sandy. 2002. Purple Dotted Underlines: Microsoft Word and the End of Writing. *Afterimage* 30.1 (Jul/Aug): 6.

Balhorn, Mark. 2009. The Epicene Pronoun in Contemporary Newspaper Prose. *American Speech* 84(4): 391–413.

Barber, Charles. 1997. *Early Modern English.* Revised edn. Edinburgh: Edinburgh University Press.

Barnbrook, Geoff. 2005. Johnson the Prescriptivist? The Case for the Prosecution. In *Anniversary Essays on Johnson's Dictionary*, edited by Jack Lynch and Anne McDermott, 92–112. Cambridge: Cambridge University Press.

Baron, Dennis. 1982. *Grammar and Good Taste: Reforming the American Language.* New Haven: Yale University Press.

1986. *Grammar and Gender.* New Haven: Yale University Press.

Battistella, Edwin L. 2005. *Bad Language: Are Some Words Better than Others?* New York: Oxford University Press.

Baugh, Albert C. and Thomas Cable. 2002. *A History of the English Language.* 5th edn. Englewood Cliffs, NJ: Prentice Hall.

Baugh, John. 1999. *Out of the Mouths of Slaves: African American Language and Educational Malpractice.* Austin: University of Texas Press.

Beal, Joan C. 2009. Three Hundred Years of Prescriptivism (and Counting). In *Current Issues in Late Modern English*, edited by Ingrid Tieken-Boon van Ostade and William van der Wurff, 35–54. Bern: Peter Lang.

Beal, Joan C., Carmela Nocera, and Massimo Sturiale, eds. 2008. *Perspectives on Prescriptivism.* Bern: Peter Lang.

Beal, Joan C. and Massimo Sturiale. 2008. Introduction. In *Perspectives on Prescriptivism*, edited by Joan C. Beal, Carmela Nocera, and Massimo Sturiale, 9–19. Bern: Peter Lang.

Beam, Christopher. 2008. Epic Win: Goodbye, schadenfreude; hello, fail. *Slate* (October 15). www.slate.com/id/2202262.

Béjoint, Henri. 2010. *The Lexicography of English: From Origins to Present.* Oxford: Oxford University Press.

Bennett, Lerone, Jr. 1967. What's in a Name? Negro vs. Afro-American vs. Black. *Ebony* (November): 46–54.

Biber, Douglas, Stig Johansson, Geoffrey Leech, Susan Conrad, and Edward Finegan. 1999. *The Longman Grammar of Spoken and Written English.* Harlow, Essex: Pearson Education.

Bloom, Ryan. 2012. Inescapably, You're Judged by Your Language. *New Yorker Page-Turner* (May 29). www.newyorker.com/online/blogs/books/2012/05/language-wars-descriptivists.html

Blount, Roy. 2008. *Alphabet Juice.* New York: Farrar, Strauss, and Giroux.

Bourdieu, Pierre. 1991. *Language and Symbolic Power.* Malden, MA: Polity Press.

Bradley, Mary O. 2008. Country rife with sloppy English. *Ann Arbor News* (March 12).

Brinton, Laurel J. and Leslie K. Arnovick. 2011. *The English Language: A Linguistic History.* 2nd edn. Don Mills, Ontario: Oxford University Press.

Brontsema, Robin. 2004. A Queer Revolution: Reconceptualizing the Debate over Linguistic Reclamation. *Colorado Research in Linguistics* 17 (1): 1–17.

Cable, Thomas. 2008. History of the History of the English Language: How Has the Subject Been Studied? In *A Companion to the History of the English Language,* edited by Haruko Momma and Michael Matto, 11–17. London: Blackwell.

Cameron, Deborah. 1995. *Verbal Hygiene.* London; New York: Routledge.

Campos, W. Brandon Lacy. 2003. Queer? *Brown Tones: A Progressive Voice in Regressive Times* (January 3).

Chapman, Don. 2008. The Eighteenth-century Grammarians as Language Experts. In *Grammars, Grammarians and Grammar-Writing in Eighteenth-century England,* edited by Ingrid Tieken-Boon van Ostade, 21–36. Berlin; New York: Mouton de Gruyter.

Chen, Melinda Yuen-Ching. 1998. "I Am an Animal!": Lexical Reappropriation, Performativity, and *Queer.* In *Engendering Communication: Proceedings from the Fifth Berkeley Women and Language Conference,* edited by Suzanne Wertheim, Ashlee Bailey, and Monica Corston-Oliver, 128–140. Berkeley, CA: Berkeley Women and Language Group.

Cheshire, Jenny. 1999. Spoken Standard English. In *Standard English: The Widening Debate,* edited by Tony Bex and Richard J. Watts, 129–148. London; New York: Routledge.

Christian, Darrell, Sally Jacobsen, and David Minthorn, eds. 2012. *Associated Press Stylebook 2012.* New York: Associated Press. http:www.apstylebook.com

Colin, Chris. 1999. The N-Word. *Salon.com* (November 8). www.salon.com/1999/11/08/nword.

Coote, Edmund. 1596. *The English Schoole-maister.* London: Printed by the Widow Orwin, for Ralph Jackson and Robert Dextar.

Crowley, Tony. 2008. Class, Ethnicity, and the Formation of Standard English. In *A Companion to the History of the English Language,* edited by Haruko Momma and Michael Matto, 303–312. London: Blackwell.

Crystal, David. 1997. *The Cambridge Encyclopedia of Language.* 2nd edn. Cambridge: Cambridge University Press.

2004. *The Stories of English.* London: Lane.

2006. *The Fight for English: How Language Pundits Ate, Shot, and Left.* Oxford: Oxford University Press.

Curzan, Anne. 2000. Lexicography and Questions of Authority in the College Classroom. *Dictionaries* 21: 90–99.

2003. *Gender Shifts in the History of English.* Cambridge: Cambridge University Press.

2009. Historical Corpus Linguistics and Evidence of Language Change. In *Corpus Linguistics: An International Handbook,* edited by Merja Kytö and Anke Lüdeling. Berlin; New York: Walter de Gruyter. 1091–1109.

Curzan, Anne and Michael Adams. 2012. *How English Works: A Linguistic Introduction.* 3rd edn. (1st edn., 2006). New York: Pearson Longman

Davies, Mark. 2007–. *Time Magazine Corpus: 100 Million Words, 1920s–2000s.* Available online at http://corpus.byu.edu/time

2008–. *The Corpus of Contemporary American English: 450 million Words, 1990–Present.* Available online at http://corpus.byu.edu/coca

2010–. *The Corpus of Historical American English: 400 Million Words, 1810–2009.* Available online at http://corpus.byu.edu/coha

Defoe, Daniel. 1697. *An Essay upon Projects. London. The Stoke Newington Daniel Defoe Edition,* edited by Joyce D. Kennedy et al. New York: AMS, 1999.

Derrida, Jacques, 1969. The Ends of Man. Trans. Edouard Morot-Sir et al. *Philosophy and Phenomenological Research* 31 (1): 31–57.

Dobrin, David N. 1990. A New Grammar Checker. *Computers and the Humanities* 24: 67–80.

DuBois, W. E. B. 1930. The Capital N. *The Crisis* (May): 172.

Ebony Magazine. 2007. Special Report: Who You Callin' a. . . ? 62 (9) (July).

Edwards, John. 2012. Foreword: Language, Prescriptivism, Nationalism – and Identity. In *The Languages of Nation: Attitudes and Norms*, edited by Carol Percy and Mary Catherine Davidson, 11–36. Bristol: Multilingual Matters.

Finegan, Edward. 1980. *Attitudes Toward English Usage: A History of the War of Words.* New York: Teachers College Press.

1992. Style and Standardization in England: 1700–1900. In *English in Its Social Contexts*, edited by Tim W. Machan and Charles T. Scott, 103–130. New York: Oxford University Press.

2001. Usage. In *The Cambridge History of the English Language, Volume VI: English in North America*, edited by John Algeo, 358–421. Cambridge: Cambridge University Press.

Fisher, John H. 1996. *The Emergence of Standard English.* Lexington, KY: University Press of Kentucky.

Fitzmaurice, Susan 1998. The Commerce of Language in the Pursuit of Politeness in Eighteenth-century England. *English Studies* 79: 309–328.

Fowler, H. W. 1965 (reissued in 1996). *A Dictionary of Modern English Usage.* 2nd edn., revised by Sir Ernest Gowers. New York; Oxford: Oxford University Press.

Fowler, H. W. and F. G. Fowler. 1908. *The King's English.* 2nd edn. Oxford: Clarendon Press.

Galinsky, Adam D., Kurt Hugenberg, Carla Groom, and Galen Bodenhausen. 2003. The Reappropriation of Stigmatizing Labels: Implications for Social Identity. *Research on Managing Groups and Teams* 5: 221–256.

Garner, Bryan. 1998. *A Dictionary of Modern American Usage.* New York; Oxford: Oxford University Press.

2005. Book Review: Don't Know Much about Punctuation: Notes on a Stickler Wannabe: *Eats, Shoots & Leaves: The Zero Tolerance Approach to Punctuation.* By Lynne Truss. *Texas Law Review* 83(5): 1443.

Gaudio, Rudolf P. 1994. Sounding Gay: Pitch Properties in the Speech of Gay and Straight Men. *American Speech* 69(1): 30–57.

Gilman, E. Ward, ed. 1994. *Merriam-Webster's Dictionary of English Usage.* Springfield, MA: Merriam-Webster.

González-Díaz, Victorina. 2008. On Normative Grammarians and the Double Marking of Degree. In *Grammars, Grammarians and Grammar-Writing in Eighteenth-century England*, edited by Ingrid Tieken-Boon van Ostade, 289–310. Berlin; New York: Mouton de Gruyter.

Gordon, Matthew J. 2001. *Small-Town Values and Big-City Vowels: A Study of the Northern Cities Shift in Michigan*. Publication of the American Dialect Society 84. Durham, NC: Duke University Press.

Görlach, Manfred. 1989. Fifteenth-century English – Middle English or Early Modern English? In *In Other Words: Transcultural Studies in Philology, Translation, and Lexicology Presented to Hans Heirich Meier on the Occasion of His Sixty-Fifth Birthday*, edited by J. Lachlan Mackenize and Richard Todd, 97–106. Dordrecht, Holland; Providence, RI: Fortis.

1999. Regional and Social Variation. In *The Cambridge History of the English Language, Vol. III: 1476–1776*, edited by Roger Lass, 459–538. Cambridge: Cambridge University Press.

Gorrell, Robert M. and Charlton G. Laird. 1972. *Modern English Handbook*. 5th edn. Englewood Cliffs, NJ: Prentice Hall.

Green, Jonathon. 1996. *Chasing the Sun: Dictionary Makers and the Dictionaries They Made*. New York: Henry Holt.

1998. *Cassell's Dictionary of Slang*. London: Orion.

Grossman, Ellie. 1997. *The Grammatically Correct Handbook*. New York: Hyperion.

Haist, Caroline. 2000. An Evaluation of Microsoft Word 97's Grammar Checker. Report: ED438538. Retrieved June 22, 2010 from ERIC, Resources in Education (RIE).

Halliday, Michael and J. R. Martin. 1993. *Writing Science: Literacy and Discursive Power*. London: Falmer Press.

Hartwell, Patrick. 1985. Grammar, Grammars, and the Teaching of Grammar. *College English* 47(2): 105–127.

Hechtkopf, Kevin. 2010. Support for gays in the military depends on the question. CBS News (February 11). www.cbsnews.com/8301-503544_162-6198284-503544.html

Heidorn, George E. 2000. Intelligent Writing Assistance. In *Handbook of Natural Language Processing*, edited by Robert Dale, Hermann Moisl, and Harold Somers, 181–207. New York: Marcel Dekker.

Hewitson, Michelle. 2004. Likeable defender of the commas. *New Zealand Herald* (September 4).

Hickey, Raymond. 2012. Standard English and the Standards of English. In *Standards of English: Codified Varieties around the World*, edited by Raymond Hickey, 2–32. Cambridge: Cambridge University Press.

Hinton, Eric. 2007. Cornel West vs. Eric Michael Dyson: N-Word Debate Resurfaces. DiversityInc.

Hockett, Charles F. 1957. The Terminology of Historical Linguistics. *Studies in Linguistics* 12 (3–4): 57–73.

Hodson, Jane. 2006. The Problem of Joseph Priestley's (1733–1804) Descriptivism. *Historiographia Linguistica* 33(2): 57–84.

Hommerberg, Charlotte and Gunnel Tottie. 2007. Try to or Try and? Verb Complementation in British and American English. *ICAME Journal* 31: 45–64.

Honnegger, Mark. 2005. *English Grammar for Writing*. New York; Boston: Houghton Mifflin.

Huddleston, Rodney and Geoffrey K. Pullum. 2002. *The Cambridge Grammar of the English Language*. Cambridge: Cambridge University Press.

Huddleston, Rodney and Geoffrey K. Pullum. 2005. *A Student Introduction to English Grammar*. Cambridge: Cambridge University Press.

Janda, Richard D. and Brian D. Joseph. 2003. On Language, Change, and Language Change: Or, of History, Linguistics, and Historical Linguistics. In *The Handbook of Historical Linguistics*, edited by Brian D. Joseph and Richard D. Janda, 3–180. Malden, MA; Oxford, UK: Blackwell.

Jespersen, Otto. 1933. *Essentials of English Grammar*. London: Allen & Unwin.

Johnson, Eric. 1992. The Ideal Grammar and Style Checker. *Text Technology* 2 (4) (July): 3–4.

1997. The Current State of Grammar and Style Checkers. *Text Technology* 7 (1): 18–21.

Johnson, Samuel. 1755. *Dictionary of the English Language*. London: Dodsley, Hitch, Mellar, Longman, and Knapton.

Johnstone, Barbara, Jennifer Andrus, and Andrew E. Danielson. 2006. Mobility, Indexicality, and the Enregisterment of "Pittsburghese." *Journal of English Linguistics* 34 (2): 77–104.

Jones, Richard Foster. 1953. *Triumph of the English Language*. Palo Alto, CA: Stanford University Press.

Jonson, Ben. 1640 [1892]. *Discoveries Made upon Men and Matter*. Edited, with introduction and notes, by Felix E. Schelling. Boston: Ginn & Company.

Kane, Eugene. 2006. The N-Word Has No Place in Schools. *Journal Sentinel* (November 25).

Kennedy, Arthur G. 1927. Hothouse Words versus Slang. *American Speech* 2(10): 417–424.

Kennedy, Janice. 2004. The inner nitpicker lashes' out: just when you thought punctuation was a mute (moot) point, along comes Lynne Truss to champion it's (its) return. *Ottawa Citizen* (May 2).

Kennedy, Randall. 1999–2000. Who Can Say "Nigger"? And Other Considerations. *Journal of Blacks in Higher Education* 26: 86–96.

2002. *Nigger: The Strange Career of a Troublesome Word*. New York: Vintage.

Lakoff, Robin. 2004 [1975]. *Language and Woman's Place: Texts and Commentaries*. Edited by Mary Bucholtz. Oxford: Oxford University Press.

Landau, Sidney I. 2001. *Dictionaries: The Art and Craft of Lexicography*. 2nd edn. Cambridge: Cambridge University Press.

Leech, Geoffrey, Marianne Hundt, Christian Mair, and Nicholas Smith. 2009. *Change in Contemporary English: A Grammatical Study*. Cambridge: Cambridge University Press.

Lerner, Harriet E. 1976. Girls, Ladies, or Women? The Unconscious Dynamics of Language Choice. *Comprehensive Psychiatry* 17(2): 295–299.

Leonard, Arthur S. 2007. DYKES ON BIKES Triumph on Trademark Appeal. courhttp:// newyorklawschool.typepad.com/leonardlink/2007/07/dykes-on-bikes-.html

Liberman, Mark. 2012. Rules and "Rules." *Language Log* (May 11). http://languagelog. ldc.upenn.edu/nll/?p=3951

Lippi-Green, Rosina. 2012. *English with an Accent: Language, Ideology, and Discrimination in the United States*. (1st edn., 1997.) London; New York: Routledge.

Livia, Anna and Kira Hall, eds. 2007. *Queerly Phrased: Language, Gender, and Sexuality*. Oxford; New York: Oxford University Press.

Lowth, Robert. 1762. *A Short Introduction to English Grammar*. London.

Lynch, Jack. 2009. *The Lexicographer's Dilemma*. New York: Walker & Company.

McArthur, Tom. 1986. *Worlds of Reference; Lexicography, Learning and Language from the Clay Tablet to the Computer*. Cambridge: Cambridge University Press.

ed. 1992. *The Oxford Companion to the English Language*. Oxford; New York: Oxford University Press.

McConnell-Ginet, Sally. 1989. The Sexual (Re)Production of Meaning. In *Language, Gender, and Professional Writing*, edited by Francine W. Frank and Paula A. Treichler, 35–50. New York: MLA.

McDermott, Anne. 2005. Johnson the Prescriptivist? The Case for the Defense. In *Anniversary Essays on Johnson's Dictionary*, edited by Jack Lynch and Anne McDermott, 113–128. Cambridge: Cambridge University Press.

McEnery, Tony. 2006. *Swearing in English: Bad Language, Purity and Power from 1586 to the Present*. London; New York: Routledge.

McGee, Tim and Patricia Ericsson. 2002. The Politics of the Program: MS Word as the Invisible Grammarian. *Computers and Composition* 19: 453–470.

Machan, Tim. 2009. *Language Anxiety: Conflict and Change in the History of English*. Oxford: Oxford University Press.

McMahon, April. 1994. *Understanding Language Change*. Cambridge: Cambridge University Press.

McWhorter, John. 1998. *Word on the Street: Debunking the Myth of a "Pure" Standard English*. Cambridge, MA: Perseus.

2008. *Our Magnificent Bastard Tongue: The Untold History of English*. New York: Gotham Books.

2012. A Matter of Fashion. *New York Times Opinionator* (July 9). http://opinionator.blogs.nytimes.com/2012/07/09/a-matter-of-fashion

Maggio, Rosalie. 1991. *The Dictionary of Bias-Free Usage: A Guide to Nondiscriminatory Language*. Phoenix, AZ: Oryx Press.

Mair, G. H., ed. 1909. *Wilson's Arte of Rhetorique, 1560*. Oxford: Clarendon.

Marsh, George P. 1863. *Lectures on the English Language*. 4th edn. New York: Charles Scribner.

Martin, Ed. Review: All of Us. mediavillage.com.

Menand, Louis. 2004. Bad comma: Lynne Truss's strange grammar. *New Yorker* (June 28): 102–104.

Metcalf, Allan A. 2002. *Predicting New Words: The Secrets of Their Success*. Boston: Houghton Mifflin.

2004. *Presidential Voices: Speaking Styles from George Washington to George W. Bush*. Boston: Houghton Mifflin Harcourt.

Michael, Ian. 1970. *English Grammatical Categories and the Tradition to 1800*. Cambridge: Cambridge University Press.

Millar, Sharon. 1998. Language Prescription: A Success in Failure's Clothing? In *Historical Linguistics 1995: Selected Papers from the 12th International Conference on Historical Linguistics, Manchester, August 1995*, vol. II, edited by Richard M. Hogg and Linda Van Bergen, 177–188. Amsterdam: John Benjamins.

Millward, C. M and Mary Hayes. 2012. *A Biography of the English Language*. 3rd edn. (1st edn., 1989; 2nd edn., 1996.) Boston: Wadsworth, Cengage Learning.

Milroy, James 1992. *Linguistic Variation and Change: On the Historical Sociolinguistics of English*. Oxford; Cambridge, MA: Blackwell.

1999. The Consequences of Standardisation in Descriptive Linguistics. In *Standard English: The Widening Debate*, edited by Tony Bex and Richard J. Watts, 16–39. New York: Routledge.

Milroy, James and Lesley Milroy. 1991. *Authority in Language: Investigating Language Prescription and Standardisation*. 2nd edn. London; New York: Routledge.

Milton, John. 1644. *Areopagitica*, at http://files.libertyfund.org/files/103/1224_Bk.pdf

Minkova, Donka. 2004. Philology, Linguistics, and the History of [hw] ~ [w]. In *Studies in the History of the English Language II: Unfolding Conversations*, edited by Anne Curzan and Kimberly Emmons, 7–46. Berlin; New York: Mouton de Gruyter.

MLA Handbook for Writers of Research Papers, Theses, and Dissertations. 1st edn., 1977. 2nd edn., 1984. 3rd edn., 1988. 4th edn., 1995. 5th edn., 1999. 6th edn., 2003. 7th edn., 2009. New York: Modern Language Association of America.

Moe, Albert F. 1963. "Lady" and "Woman": The Terms' Use in the 1880s. *American Speech* 38: 295.

Momma, Haruko and Michael Matto. 2008. History, English, Language: Studying HEL Today. In *A Companion to the History of the English Language*, edited by Haruko Momma and Michael Matto, 3–10. London: Blackwell.

Morton, Herbert C. 1994. *The Story of Webster's Third: Philip Gove's Controversial Dictionary and Its Critics*. Cambridge: Cambridge University Press.

Mugglestone, Lynda, ed. 2006. *The Oxford History of English*. Oxford: Oxford University Press.

Mullan, John. 2004. [features page] *Guardian* (London) (July 2): 4.

Murray, Lindley. 1795. *English Grammar*. York: Wilson, Spence and Mawman.

Negro, Black, and African American. Opinion. 1988. *New York Times* (December 22).

Nevalainen, Terttu and Helena Raumolin-Brunberg, eds. 1996. *Sociolinguistics and Language History: Studies Based on the Corpus of Early English Correspondence*. Amsterdam; Atlanta: Rodopi.

2003. *Historical Sociolinguistics: Language Change in Tudor and Stewart England*. London: Longman.

Newman, Michael. 1997. *Epicene Pronouns: The Linguistics of Prescriptive Problem*. New York; London: Garland.

Nunberg, Geoffrey. 1983. The Decline of Grammar. *Atlantic Monthly* (December): 31–46. Available at www.theatlantic.com/past/docs/issues/97mar/halpern/nunberg.htm.

2000. Usage in *The American Heritage Dictionary. The American Heritage Dictionary of the English Language*, 4th edn., xxvi–xxix. Boston; New York: Houghton Mifflin.

O'Conner, Patricia and Stewart Kellerman. 2009a. *Origins of the Specious: Myths and Misconceptions of the English Language*. New York: Random House.

2009b. The I's have it. *New York Times* (February 23).

Oxford English Dictionary, online. 1989 (2nd edn.), 2007 (new edn.). Oxford University Press. http://dictionary.oed.com.proxy.lib.umich.edu

Osselton, N. E. 1958. *Branded Words in English Dictionaries before Johnson*. Groningen: J. B. Wolters.

Pauwels, Anne. 1998. *Women Changing Language*. London; New York: Longman.

Perales-Escudero, Moisés D. 2011. To Split or to Not Split: The Split Infinitive Past and Present. *Journal of English Linguistics* 39 (4): 313–334.

Percy, Carol. 2008. Mid-century Grammars and Their Reception in the Monthly Review and the Critical Review. In *Grammars, Grammarians and Grammar-Writing in*

Eighteenth-century England, edited by Ingrid Tieken-Boon van Ostade, 125–142. Berlin; New York: Mouton de Gruyter.

Percy, Carol and Mary Catherine Davidson, eds. 2012. *The Language of Nation: Attitudes and Norms*. Bristol: Multilingual Matters.

Phillips, Edward. 1658. *The New World of Words*. London: Printed by E. Tyler, for Nath. Brooke.

Pinker, Steven. 1994. *The Language Instinct*. New York: W. Morrow.

1999. Racist language, real and imagined. *New York Times* (February 2).

2012. False Fronts in the Language Wars: Why New Yorker Writers and Others Keep Pushing Bogus Controversies. *Slate* (May 31). www.slate.com/articles/arts/the_good_word/2012/05/steven_pinker_on_the_false_fronts_in_the_language_wars_.html

Potter, Reva and Dorothy Fuller. 2008. My New Teaching Partner? Using the Grammar Checker in Writing Instruction. *English Journal* 98: 36–41.

Publication Manual of the American Psychological Association (APA). 1st edn. (revised), 1967. 2nd edn., 1974. 3rd edn., 1983. 4th edn., 1994. 5th edn., 2001. 6th edn., 2010. Washington, DC: American Psychological Association.

Pullum, Geoffrey K. 2009. 50 Years of Stupid Grammar Advice. *Chronicle of Higher Education* (April 17). http://chronicle.com/article/50-Years-of-Stupid-Grammar/25497

Rahman, Jacquelyn. 2012. The N Word: Its History and Use in the African American Community. *Journal of English Linguistics* 40(2): 137–171.

Random House Historical Dictionary of American Slang. 1994 (vol. I), 1997 (vol. II). Edited by J. E. Lighter. New York: Random House.

Raumolin-Brunberg, Helena. 1996. Historical Sociolinguistics. In *Sociolinguistics and Language History: Studies based on the Corpus of Early English Correspondence*, edited by Terttu Nevalainen and Helena Raumolin-Brunberg, 11–37. Amsterdam; Atlanta: Rodopi.

Read, Allen Walker. 2003. The Beginnings of English Lexicography. *Dictionaries: Journal of the Dictionary Society of America* 24: 187–226.

2002 [1986]. The Allegiance to Dictionaries in American Linguistic Attitudes. In *Milestones in the History of English in America*, edited by Richard W. Bailey, 110–120. Durham, NC: Duke University Press.

Romaine, Suzanne. 1982. *Socio-historical Linguistics: Its Status and Methodology*. Cambridge: Cambridge University Press.

Rotello, Gabriel. 2000. Last Word: The Word that Failed. *The Advocate* (August 15).

Rothstein, Edward. 2000. Is a word's definition in the mind of the user? *New York Times* (November 25).

Saussure, Ferdinand de. 1983. *Course in General Linguistics*. Ed. Charles Bally and Albert Sechehaye, with the collaboration of Albert Riedlinger. Translated and annotated by Roy Harris. London: Duckworth.

Schindler, Paul. 2003. Just How Queer Are We? *Gay City News* 2 (46) (November 13–19). http://204.2.109.187/gcn_246/justhowqueer.html

Shaughnessy, Mina P. 1977. *Errors and Expectations: A Guide for the Teaching of Basic Writing*. New York: Oxford University Press.

Shellenbarger, Sue. 2012. This embarrasses you and I. *Wall Street Journal* (June 20).

Sims Holt, Grace. 1972. "Inversion" in Black Communication. In *Rappin' and Stylin' Out: Communication in Urban Black America*, edited by Thomas Kochman, 152–159. Urbana, University of Illinois Press.

Skapinker, Michael. 2004. [no title] *Financial Times* (July 7): 10.

Skinner, David. 2012. *The Story of Ain't: America, Its Language, and the Most Controversial Dictionary Ever Published*. New York: HarperCollins.

Sledd, James and Wilma R. Ebbitt. 1962. *Dictionaries and That Dictionary: A Casebook on the Aims of Lexicographers and the Targets of Reviewers*. Chicago: Scott, Foresman.

Smith, Jeremy J. 1996. *An Historical Study of English: Function, Form, and Change*. London; New York: Routledge.

Smith, Tom W. 1992. Changing Racial Labels: From "Colored" to "Negro" to "Black" to "African American." *Public Opinion Quarterly* 56 (4): 496–514.

Smitherman, Geneva. 1991. "What Is Africa to Me?": Language, Ideology, and *African American*. *American Speech* 66 (2): 115–132.

2006. *Word from the Mother: Language and African Americans*. London; New York: Routledge.

Stanley, Julia P. 1970. Homosexual Slang. *American Speech* 45 (1/2): 45–59.

Strunk, William and E. B. White. 1979. *The Elements of Style*. 3rd edn. New York: Macmillan.

Swift, Jonathan. 1969. *A Proposal for Correcting, Improving and Ascertaining the English Tongue*. London, 1712, edited by R. C. Alston. Menston, England: Scolar Press.

Szmrecsanyi, Benedikt. 2012. *That, which*, zero: prescriptivist influences on English relativizer usage. Paper presented at the Freiburg Institute for Advanced Studies, Albert-Ludwigs-Universität Freiburg, May 9.

Thomas, George. 1991. *Linguistic Purism*. London; New York: Longman.

Thomason, Sarah G. 2007. Language Contact and Deliberate Change. *Journal of Language Contact* 1 (Thema): 41–62.

Thomason, Sarah Grey and Terrence Kaufman. 1988. *Language Contact, Creolization, and Genetic Linguistics*. Berkeley: University of California Press.

Tieken-Boon van Ostade, Ingrid. 1982. Double Negation and Eighteenth-century English Grammars. *Neophilologus* 66 (2): 278–285.

2000. Female Grammarians of the Eighteenth Century. *Historical Sociolinguistics and Sociohistorical Linguistics*. www.let.leidenuniv.nl/hsl_shl/femgram.htm

2002. Robert Lowth and the Strong Verb System. *Language Sciences* 24 (3–4): 459–469.

2006. Eighteenth-century Prescriptivism and the Norm of Correctness. In *The Handbook of the History of English*, edited by Ans van Kemenade and Bettelou Los, 539–557. Malden, MA: Blackwell.

2008a. The 1760s: Grammars, Grammarians and the Booksellers. In *Grammars, Grammarians and Grammar-Writing in Eighteenth-century England*, edited by Ingrid Tieken-Boon van Ostade, 101–124. Berlin; New York: Mouton de Gruyter.

2008b. The Codifiers and the History of Multiple Negation in English, or Why Were 18th-century Grammarians So Obsessed with Double Negation? In *Perspectives on Prescriptivism*, edited by Joan C. Beal, Carmela Nocera, and Massimo Sturiale, 197–214. Bern: Peter Lang.

2008c. Grammars, Grammarians and Grammar Writing: An Introduction. In *Grammars, Grammarians and Grammar-Writing in Eighteenth-century England*, edited by Ingrid Tieken-Boon van Ostade, 1–14. Berlin; New York: Mouton de Gruyter.

ed. 2008d. *Grammars, Grammarians, and Grammar-Writing in Eighteenth-century England*. Berlin: Mouton de Gruyter.

2011. *The Bishop's Grammar: Robert Lowth and the Rise of Prescriptivism*. Oxford: Oxford University Press.

2012. The Codification of English in England. In *Standards of English: Codified Varieties around the World*, edited by Raymond Hickey, 33–51. Cambridge: Cambridge University Press.

Totaro. Paola. 1994. PC is a label to be worn with pride. *Sydney Morning Herald* (April 9).

Tottie, Gunnel. 2009. How Different Are American and British English Grammars? In *One Language, Two Grammars?*, edited by Günter Rohdenburg and Julia Schlüter, 341–353. Cambridge: Cambridge University Press.

Trudgill, Peter. 1999. Standard English: What It Isn't. In *Standard English: The Widening Debate*, edited by Tony Bex and Richard J. Watts, 117–128. London; New York: Routledge.

Truss, Lynne. 2003. *Eats, Shoots & Leaves: The Zero Tolerance Approach to Punctuation*. New York: Gotham Books.

Urban Dictionary. www.urbandictionary.com

van Gelderen, Elly. 2006. *A History of the English Language*. Amsterdam/Philadelphia: John Benjamins.

Vernon, Alex. 2000. Computerized Grammar Checkers 2000: Capabilities, Limitations, and Pedagogical Possibilities. *Computers and Composition* 17: 329–349.

Vorlat, Emma. 1975. *The Development of English Grammatical Theory, 1586–1737, with Special Reference to the Theory of Parts of Speech*. Leuven: Leuven University Press.

Waldren, Murray. 2004. That's language. *Weekend Australian* (January 24): B09.

Webster's Third New International Dictionary of the English Language. 1961. Ed. Philip Gove and others. Springfield, MA: G. and C. Merriam.

Weingarten, Gene. 2001. Below the beltway. *Washington Post* (April 22).

Weinreich, Uriel, William Labov, and Martin Herzog. 1968. Empirical Foundations for a Theory of Language Change. In *Directions for Historical Linguistics*, edited by W. Lehmann and Y. Malkiel, 97–195. Austin: University of Texas Press.

Wiehl, Lisa. 2007. Stick and stones and the N-word. FoxNews.com (January 29). www.foxnews.com/story/0,2933,248184,00.html

Wild, Kate. 2009. Johnson's Prescriptive Labels – A Reassessment. *Dictionaries* 30: 108–118.

Williams, Joseph M. 2005. *Style: Ten Lessons in Clarity and Grace*. 8th edn. New York: Pearson Longman.

Wolfram, Walt. 1991. *Dialects and American English*. Englewood Cliffs, NJ: Prentice Hall.

Wolfram, Walt and Natalie Schilling-Estes. 2006. *American English: Dialects and Variation*. 2nd edn. Malden, MA: Blackwell.

Wood, Frederick T. 1962. *Current English Usage: A Concise Dictionary*. New York: Macmillan.

Yagoda, Ben. 2007. *When You Catch an Adjective, Kill It: The Parts of Speech, for Better and/or Worse*. New York: Broadway Books.

Yáñez-Bouza, Nuria. 2006. Prescriptivism and Preposition Stranding in Eighteenth-century Prose. *Historical Sociolinguistics and Sociohistorical Linguistics*. www.let.leidenuniv.nl/hsl_shl (> contents > articles).

2008a. Preposition Stranding in the Eighteenth Century: Something to Talk about. In *Grammars, Grammarians and Grammar-Writing in Eighteenth-century England*, edited by Ingrid Tieken-Boon van Ostade, 251–277. Berlin; New York: Mouton de Gruyter.

2008b. To End or Not to End a Sentence with a Preposition: An 18th-century Debate. In *Perspectives on Prescriptivism*, edited by Joan C. Beal, Carmela Nocera, and Massimo Sturiale, 237–264. Bern: Peter Lang.

Zimmer, Ben. 2010. In Defense of Harding the Bloviator. *Visual Thesaurus* (July 29). www.visualthesaurus.com/cm/wordroutes/in-defense-of-harding-the-bloviator/

2012. How baseball gave us 'jazz': the surprising origins of a 100-year old word. *Boston Globe* (March 25).

2013. All the president's words: whatever happened to our neologizers-in-chief? *Boston Globe* (January 20). http://bostonglobe.com/ideas/2013/01/20/all-president-words/hmyLFIS4TfHx7ctH67bMEI/story.html?camp

Index

CPSIA information can be obtained
at www.ICGtesting.com
Printed in the USA
LVHW051527090123
736779LV00004B/602